THE QUICKENING

"There are three things I noticed about Gregg. This man has a great passion for God, he truly is in love with the Divine . . . The second thing I noticed about Gregg is he loves human beings. He is a person I would trust with anything that was going on in my life. The third thing I noticed about Gregg is he is *one smart dude*: a deeply wise man, a humble man and a brilliant man." **Andrew Harvey, Global Mystic, Author of *The Hope*, Founder and Director of the Institute for Sacred Activism**

" . . . a well written, funny, brilliant book!" **Jon Mundy, PhD, author of *Living A Course in Miracles*, Executive Director of All Faith's Seminary International**

"As a retreat program director, I have experienced the lessons of . . . the gurus of our spiritual celebrity circle today. But Gregg was one of a handful that shook me to the core of my very being in an absurdly short time -something like two to three hours! His work is literally life changing, the most powerful in which I have ever participated!— **Darlene Wilson, Former Program Director, Omega Institute at the Crossings**

"In his down to earth way, Gregg presents the most important science-based spiritual and therapeutic breakthroughs of our time."—**Dr. Allan L. Botkin, author of *Induced After Death Communication*, Director, the Center for Grief and Traumatic Loss**

"This book is a true gem. We all have our own emotional challenges in life. With wit, wisdom and insight Gregg reveals to us the cutting edge ways we can meet these challenges swiftly and thoroughly, once and for all."—**David H. Ehl, author of *You Are Gods***

"From its' very first page, The Quickening will engage you with its descriptive prose and an examination of personal growth and development that . . . we are each destined to encounter in life. It is both an engaging page-turner and a thought-provoking analysis." **Kevin J. Todeschi, Executive Director and CEO, the Edgar Cayce Work**

"Those of us involved in alternative ways of working with folks, know the concept of quickening . . . Gregg does a beautiful job of explaining this process. His expertise, sense of humor and non new-agey way of writing is refreshing. Just open your mind, open your heart, and dive in. You won't regret it."—**Karen Finley Breeding, Psychotherapist and Executive Director of Eupsychia Institute**

"I have done a lot of workshops and seminars in my time, but Gregg is among the best . . . [W]orking with him using some of the techniques in this book comprise the most moving experiences I have had in the last forty years in the Cayce work and metaphysics." **Jeanette Welch, Former Program Director, Association for Research and Enlightenment, Houston Center**

"The Quickening is a compelling read –lighthearted, down-to-earth, profound, *funny,* and rich with mesmerizing stories of transformation. [Unterberger] is the George Carlin of healing. The Quickening is the most entertaining and informative introduction to the modern psycho-spiritual healing tool shop."—**Miradrienne Carol, Author of *Choose Love Now***

THE QUICKENING

Leaping Ahead on
Your Spiritual Journey

Gregg Unterberger, M.Ed., LPC

4th Dimension Press ■ Virginia Beach ■ Virginia

4th Dimension Press
215 67th Street
Virginia Beach, VA 23451-2061

ISBN 13: 978-0-87604-734-7

Cover design by Christine Fulcher

To Jane,
For a man of many words, this time words fail me.
It's simple really.
Your love, your unflinching belief in me, makes it all possible.

Author's Note

Like many counselors who write about their work, I have chosen to share some stories from workshop participants and individual clients from across the country. I have also included some personal information from my own life. Specific names and details have been altered to protect certain individual's identities. I am, first and foremost, a licensed professional counselor; confidentiality and honoring the trust of my clients is critical to my work. However, the reader can rest assured that as incredible as these naratives may seem, I have not inflated the content of these events. The central focus and heart of all the stories told herein are true.

Who Was Edgar Cayce?

Throughout this book, you will occasionally see quotes that are attributed to Edgar Cayce. Each quote is followed by a series of numbers, which indicate the "reading" that the quote was pulled from. I wanted to take a moment to explain who Edgar Cayce is and how the reading numbers work.

Edgar Cayce (1877–1945) has been called "the sleeping prophet," "the father of holistic medicine," "the miracle man of Virginia Beach," and "the most-documented psychic of all time." For forty-three years of his adult life, he had the ability to put himself into some kind of self-induced sleep state by lying down on a couch, closing his eyes, and folding his hands over his stomach. This state of relaxation and meditation enabled him to place his mind in contact with all time and space and gave him the ability to respond to any question he was asked. His responses came to be called "readings" and contained insights so valuable that even to this day Edgar Cayce's work is known throughout the world. Hundreds of books have explored his amazing psychic gift, and the entire range of Cayce material is accessed by tens of thousands of people each and every day.

During Cayce's life, the Edgar Cayce readings were all numbered to provide confidentiality. So in the case of 294-1, for example, the first set of numbers ("294") refers to the individual or group for whom the reading was given. The second set of numbers ("1") refers to the number in the series from which the reading is taken. Therefore, 294-1 identifies the reading as the first one given to the individual assigned #294.

Although the vast majority of the Cayce material deals with health and every manner of illness, countless topics were explored by Cayce's psychic talent: dreams, philosophy, intuition, business advice, the Bible, education, childrearing, ancient civilizations, reincarnation, personal spirituality, improving human relationships, finding your mission in life, and much more.

Contents

Acknowledgments

Traditionally, this is the part of the book where authors drone on about everyone who has contributed to bringing their book into fruition. Readers may be inclined to skip over this section. This is entirely understandable, given that most authors feel the need to acknowledge not only the seminal figures in their lives but everyone else, including, apparently, green grocers, taxi drivers, the company that manufactures their inkjet printer, their dog sitter, and their Aunt Agatha—*ad nauseam*, boring you, dear reader, to tears.

I will be no exception. After all, can one be too grateful? You have my sympathies.

Julie Andrews reminds us (with enough sugar to rot our molars) to "start at the very beginning, a very good place to start." My parents, Drs. Robert and Betty Unterberger, were my first spiritual teachers. I was blessed to grow up in a home where meditation was taught and metaphysics were discussed over meatloaf and peas as far back as I can remember. By extension, I want to acknowledge their teachers as well: the Jungian psychologist Dr. Sara Robbins and physicist and mystic Dr. Raynor Johnson. They are my spiritual lineage. Long before he was on the board of the Institute of Noetic Sciences (IONS), the late Walter Starcke took time to answer a teenage Gregg's pesky spiritual questions and modeled that you could be into metaphysics without surrendering your critical thinking skills or a keen ability to use colorful language at select moments. (See below.)

Dr. Frank Allen literally turned my life upside down one weekend in 1988, and I still have not recovered. I awakened from the blissful slumber of ignorance and have been facing off with my demons ever since. I may yet forgive him. Through literally thousands of hours of therapy, Frank has been a supervisor, mentor, co-leader, giant pain-in-the-ass, and a friend. Although we have grown to differ in our therapeutic approaches in many ways, I am eternally grateful to him, even though (as he has so often pointed out), I am *one sick lizard*.

My friends Kathy Nevils and Angeline Eckholm enthusiastically believed in me from the start and offered important reality checks along the way. John Lee and Marvin Allen were early mentors and demonstrated for me a fierce masculinity that was heart-centered and not abusive. Dr. John Garcia at Texas State University was instrumental in my training as a therapist and as a human being. I am constantly building on my Integrative and Holotropic Breathwork training with Jacquelyn Small, Tav Sparks, and Dr. Stanislav Grof. Long live the Great Bear Shaman!

Dr. Elizabeth Neeld, a dear family friend, helped me to sift through the legal end of this work, and also her audiobook *Yes, You Can Write* has long been an inspiration. She would vouch that this book, for better or worse, is my "authentic voice." Mike Tomelleson, my legal counsel, offered not only sage advice on intellectual properties but his enthusiasm and understanding of Edgar Cayce and metaphysics was a Godsend. One typically acknowledges their editor, lest they secretly hack out the author's favorite chapter. But I offer Jennie Taylor Martin my thanks, because she has been such a staunch supporter and really understood the tone of this tome—and that was vital. Jennie, my gratitude for being honest, constructive, and gentle with the red Marks–A-Lot.

Dr. Allan Botkin, the developer of Induced After-Death Communication (IADC), has been generous with his time and wisdom. I hope, when I grow up someday, to be as courageous as he is. Dr. Brian Weiss has revolutionized psychology in the Western world by demonstrating and popularizing the credibility of past-life regression therapy. I continue to be honored that he and his daughter Amy Weiss chose to feature my work in his book *Miracles Happen*, and I am grateful for the many hours I have spent training under him.

I am heartened by the friendship and support of Andrew Harvey, a global mystic and genuine inspiration. As Churchill observed of FDR, meeting Andrew was "like opening your first bottle of champagne; knowing him was like drinking it." Dr. Elfie Hinterkopf's writings have been influential in my work and her presence a gentle support.

Dr. David Grand, the developer of *Brainspotting*, transformed the way I practice psychotherapy and may yet change the way the world does this work. Thank you, David.

Some people look back on a marriage that ended as a failure. I am fortunate in that I was married to a woman whom for many years was not only my friend and lover, but a spiritual partner. Many thanks to you, Vicki, for all I learned with you and from you. I will see you again

next lifetime, and we can complete whatever went unfinished.
Psychics Tammy Potok and Cindy Myska are also to be thanked for their personal and professional support. Keep me posted on what's next, wouldja?

I am thankful I found a colleague, friend, and true brother in Jack Morrison, LMSW. It was Jack who dragged me to Brainspotting training in return for my favor of dragging *him* into my Transpersonal Breathwork workshops. Apparently, no good deed goes unpunished. So, to Jack, as well as to Chelsea DeKruyff, LPC, Satu Korby, LPC, and Alecia Masood, CMT, thank you for your sincere efforts in Transpersonal Breathwork Experiences. Your compassion and open hearts always made a difference. The love and understanding of my niece and nephew, Ben and Maureen, has always been an inspiration, and they are to thank *me* for fulfilling a key role in their lives: Every child needs a weird uncle.

Norman and Angela Tucker have been an ongoing support and the love and acceptance of their adult grandchildren, Caitlin, Chris, and Matthew made completing this endeavor much easier.

Both the work of Edgar Cayce and *A Course in Miracles* has shaped my spiritual journey and metaphysical worldview. As such, an enormous debt of gratitude is owed to a number of individuals I have never met, including Dr. Helen Shucman, Dr. William Thetford, Dr. Kenneth Wapnick, and Edgar Cayce himself. I am fortunate to call counselor Tom Baker—a former priest and a student of both Cayce and the *Course*—a friend and supporter. We both continue to find ways to "straddle the teachings," exploring wisdom where it blossoms in each.

The administration and staff—past and present—of Edgar Cayce's Association for Research and Enlightenment (A.R.E.) in Virginia Beach, Va., can be credited for taking my work to the national level with special kudos to Kevin Todeschi, Charles Thomas Cayce, Jim Dixon, Darrin Owens, Allison Parker Hedrick, Peter Woodbury, John Van Auken, Renee Branch, Kristie Holmes, Cassie McQuagge, Jeanette Welch, Martha Loveland, and Darlene Wilson. Nadean Phillips of the A.R.E's Southwest Region was a strong supporter early on in my career. Carl Bohannon and Ed Jamail of the A.R.E. Houston Center continue to put me to work and demonstrate what Cayce really meant by the word "cooperation." And space does not permit the mention of dozens of regional A.R.E. volunteers, like Marlene Duet, who have welcomed me to their cities like I was family. Thanks guys, for believing in me.

Finally, there are no words to begin to thank the hundreds of people who have been my individual clients or the thousands who have participated in my workshops across the nation. I sat at your feet and learned from your triumphs and failures. We laughed and wept together. You have informed and transformed my life. That you would risk sharing your hearts with me in the most painful of times and trust me to help you, often overwhelms me. That you have allowed me to stay by your side in my workshops as you stood before the Throne of God Himself astonishes me. What an honor you have bestowed upon me by sharing your journey.

Whether we sat together one-to-one in my office or a hotel suite, in a church or an auditorium with hundreds of participants, or as a handful of people at *The Heart of Forgiveness* in Zion Canyon matters little: Where we have worked together, loved each other, and honored the Divine in ourselves is Holy Ground. I am eternally grateful.

Gregg Unterberger, M.Ed., LPC
College Station, Texas

Have you ever looked at another person's eyes and suddenly found yourself moving through endless corridors of space ad time, merged with another human being? Later, you may have called that either love or madness, but ether way, the "outer you" ceased to be the focus of your consciousness.

Time and space became one and you were focused in an eternal now. For many of us this happens in less intense moments—although just as beautiful—in experiences of attunement with nature. Every person between birth and death is caught now and then by the sudden union with nature—a starry sky on a clear cold night, a shaft of sunlight on a bubbling brook, the moon over a restless ocean, the high notes of the mockingbird who seems to be singing just for the listener, a flash of vivid lightning followed by the roll of distant thunder, or the strange sounds of a tree that is suddenly alive beyond one's wildest imagination.

The mystical literature of the world is filled with descriptions of such experiences. These are the movements of consciousness towards God, the creative energy of this Universe. And you and I need to seek these out.

For one such experience can change the whole course of your life and make this utterly confusing melee here meaningful.

Hugh Lynn Cayce
Venturing Inward

1
Over the Edge

"The spirit will quicken, if the soul will but acknowledge His power, His divine right with thee."

Edgar Cayce reading 262-62

My head violently slammed against the Prius' passenger front seat window as the driver rocketed around the curve. "For God's sake, slow down!" I blurted. But the driver, steely-eyed and deaf to my cries, glared resolutely straight ahead, wraith-like hands clutching the wheel. I was seeing stars and was somewhat in shock. After all, I had known the person behind the wheel for years and had trusted her. I had never seen her drive this way.

My new Prius had been a dream car for me. I had purchased the hybrid, brand new, just a few months ago. It was better for the planet, saved me money on gas, and admittedly, while not a Lexus, was comfortable. I had bought it with all the bells and whistles I had wanted. I regretted allowing her to take the wheel.

The car swerved again to the left, this time not as dramatically, narrowly avoiding some large metals bowls in the road. My head was still muddled, but out of the corner of my eye, in the side mirror, I caught a vision of some kind of scraps in the bowls. Isn't that bizarre? It's as though someone put out some food for some stray dogs, but not on the sidewalk. They put them almost halfway out in the road. If the dogs come out to eat, surely they will get hit by traffic, I thought. Silently, I cursed the unknown perpetrators.

But those thoughts spent only microseconds in my mind as we rapidly approached a bridge that I knew was under construction. One of the lanes of the bridge was complete, while the other was only half finished. "Turn right, turn right, turn right!" I screamed at the top of my lungs, reaching towards the wheel, while the driver yanked it to the left, rumbling over discarded construction lumber, taking a dangerous fork. She shifted gears and stomped on the gas, the car rocketing forward, my neck snapping backwards, my skull banging on the upholstered headrest. Why was she doing this?

In the dim light, I could see we were hurtling towards a black-and-white stripped barricade dead ahead, supported precariously by two sawhorses. The bridge was incomplete; the only thing standing between 2,000 pounds of rolling steel and a 200-foot drop were paltry two-by-fours and flashing yellow lights. "Please," I begged, our speed increasing, "please stop! You're going to kill us!"

But she was hell-bent, the car racing towards a destiny that I didn't choose, didn't want, and couldn't stop. The sound of the nose of the car breaking the barricade was sharp and deafening; the wood retching as it splintered, the headlights shattering, tinkling: ghastly chimes in a symphony of destruction. In an instant, time slowed down beyond slow motion, like something out of a Hollywood action film. I was both in the car and out of the car, observing omnisciently. Outside the car, I could see it arching upward, wheels turning slowly, releasing their grip on the pavement, splintered planks and dust suspended in mid-air. The automobile hung briefly in the sky, all but motionless, reaching its apogee. For a moment, I thought it might take flight, soaring off towards the full moon. But a second later, gravity kicked in, and as the black-and-white lumber pirouetted and spiraled below the wheels, plunging downward, the front of the car began following the debris obligingly, nosing towards the water, hundreds of feet below.

Simultaneously, I was inside the doomed vehicle, gripping the dash, preparing myself for the inevitable impact that would take forever and come too soon. I could hear the metal groan and the low roar of the wind as my field of vision through the windshield tilted from a star–lit night sky, to the cityscape on the horizon before me, and then finally to the waters below as gravity's unrelenting grasp took hold. It was too late: too late to decide not to get in the car, too late to get out of the car, too late to stop the driver. My fate was sealed, certain death was seconds away.

Two very strange thoughts crossed my mind.

First: *Maybe, just maybe, if I keep breathing and relax into the present moment, I could live though this. Second: If I live through this, I will have to get a whole new car.*

And then below me, water, crystal clear, illuminated by some unseen subterranean luminescence, glowed and rushed to meet the windshield of the car.

* * *

I awoke from the dream with a start. My eyes did not open. Mother Nature, in her wisdom, protects the body from acting out dreams physically during sleep as the base of the brain shuts down the neurons in the spinal cord. The formal term is sleep paralysis. But my experience was sheer terror. My heart was pounding, I was breathing heavily, but my body was frozen for several minutes. Gradually, my appendages stirred as I realized I had been dreaming and that I was safe in a hotel bed cocooned in Egyptian cotton, surrounded by fluffy pillows. But that momentary relief transformed into panic as I spontaneously began interpreting the dream. I have learned that with my eyes still closed and my mind close to the sleep state, profusely cycling theta and alpha waves, I can often intuitively understand my dreams. The dream symbols were familiar ones and the meaning was clear, horrifyingly clear.

My new car was the reflection of my new affluent life: my private practice as a therapist was increasingly successful, and I was lecturing all over the country. But the woman behind the wheel had taken control of our very lives: she was "in the driver's seat," not me. I could protest all I wanted, but it was too late. There were scraps to be had; enough to live on, but to stay like a starving dog and eat them might kill me. The bridge, a symbol of transition from one arena of life to another was ahead of us, but she did not take the "right" path, which could take us safely across the water, but instead chose to take the left fork. I would be left. She was literally "driving us over the edge."

The meaning of the dream was plainly evident. The relationship would end. I would have to start my life all over. The water that I was plunging into was all but transparent, indicating clarity was coming, even in what appeared to be destruction. I grimly chuckled to myself: At least the destination is clarity; all I have to do is *die* to get there. A line from St. Francis' prayer surfaced into my awareness, "It is in dying that one awakens to Eternal Life." In the dream, I was all but dead meat. In reality, my physical body wasn't at risk, but my egoic identity was most certainly on the block. There was another bit of promise in the dream, echoing a client's real life experience in a car wreck that I had unconsciously absorbed into my personal dream iconography: If I could just keep breathing and stay in the moment, I might just live through it.

But minutes later, I was weeping in agony in the shower, the steaming hot water mixing with the warmth of my tears. There was no escaping it. I could see what the dream meant, that the relationship was destined to end. Edgar Cayce said that nightmares were often warnings; if so, this was a big-time cosmic heads up. I didn't want this. I begged God to take this all away from me. Ending it would be the antithesis of who I thought I was. I liked being in relationship. I wanted this one to go the distance. I felt like my skin was being ripped from my body. I kept thinking that there must be something I could say or do, only to be haunted by pictures of me begging her to slow down to no avail. I had thoughts of staying, even if it was bad, only to flash back on the starving, stray dogs coming for scraps and being hit by the cars. How many times had I told my clients in therapy that they didn't have to settle for scraps in their relationships, that they were worthy of so much more?

Physician, heal thyself. I couldn't stop her from driving us over the edge, and I couldn't even stay for the scraps without being killed. It felt like the ultimate double bind. My interpersonal skills? My psychological awareness? My compassionate heart? All worthless.

I was powerless. I was seeing my future. I was being warned.

Suddenly, as these thoughts collided in my head in the shower, I was given a vision of a railroad track ending directly in front of me. Another track began to the right about twenty feet away. They were totally disconnected. I immediately understood the vision. I would not be following a gentle curve into a new direction in life. I would not be subtly evolving into a more awakened spiritual being. The transition I was about to make would be the life equivalent of getting a locomotive to jump tracks. I would be literally jumping from one karmic track to another.

I was experiencing a *quickening*.

The next day, I would see my beloved niece get married. Three days later, my father would have a break with reality, not knowing his name, the date, or even the year. Seven days later, one of my best friends would schedule their surgery in an attempt to survive a life-threatening cancer. Ten days later, the woman I had been dating for five years, the woman I thought I was destined to marry, would send me an email telling me the relationship was over.

The barricade was broken; the car was plunging.

2
What Is a Quickening?

"The Spirit will quicken if the soul will but acknowledge his power, his Divine right within thee."
Edgar Cayce reading 262-62

One way in which the Merriam-Webster's Dictionary defines the word "quickening" is as an entering "into a phase of active growth and development." It is a fourteenth-century word that shows up in the King James Version of the Bible in Psalms as a prayer in a moment of desperation: "quicken thou me according to thy word." (Psalms 119:25) Basically, "Hey God, hellooo! I'm dying here. Throw me a bone. I need some help, and it better be soon: I'm talking pedal to the metal." Curiously, I was doing some research into the readings of the American psychic Edgar Cayce who also talked about a quickening of the spirit, a sudden acceleration or growth spurt.

You may have heard of what is referred to by psychotherapists as a "breakthrough session." A quickening may be but another name for this term, which is used by therapists to describe when their clients suddenly take a giant step forward on their healing journey. The inference being that after a certain amount of volition is built up, unconscious resistance to an uncomfortable truth or clarity is "broken through." A little "death" takes place of an old subjective reality that makes room for a new way of thinking or being.

After the dream of my Prius plunging over the edge, I was propelled into another stage of my spiritual growth. My relationship was at an end; I was powerless to stop it. I had to die a little . . . no, I had to die *a lot* that day. I died to the idea of becoming that woman's husband. I died to the idea of a future with her. I died to the idea that since I was a therapist or spiritually awake that I could save the relationship. Not that I wanted it, or welcomed it at the time; to the contrary, initially I fought it. Eventually, the dream led to a return to therapy, a willingness to reach out to others for help in a way heretofore unknown to me and a re-thinking of what I wanted in a partner at this stage in my life. In the therapy business, there's an old saying that, yes, the truth will set you free, but not before it sends you to hell first.

It was a pretty toasty time for me for a number of months.

Sadly, most of us go along the spiritual path slowly, if with any speed at all. More often, we stay largely asleep until the next catastrophe slaps the hell out of us and–if we are lucky–we awaken to the next level. No doubt you could point toward moments of your own where life dealt you a violent change in circumstances that knocked you off your feet, only to find yourself suddenly propelled forward (a life-threatening illness, the sudden loss of a loved one, a crisis of faith in your belief system). This is Saint John of the Cross' "dark night of the soul." Neurosurgeon and mystic, author of the best-selling *Proof of Heaven*, Dr. Eben Alexander, has called these moments, "the gift of desperation." These catastrophic awakenings might be called *spontaneous quickenings*. We didn't choose them, at least not at a conscious level. They happened *to* us.

Happily, some quickenings may be ultimately exceedingly positive, while at the same time, life-changing. The American psychologist Dr. Abraham Maslow wrote at length about *peak experiences*, which he defined as euphoric, ecstatic experiences filled with a deep sense of unity and interconnectedness. Maslow believed that, if integrated, these experiences have life-changing, long-term effects. However, it seems to me that these transformative experiences are seen largely as either a result of painful life circumstances or the grace of God—either of which is seemingly beyond the control of the individual.

Now, you may be saying, not so, there are spiritual disciplines that with practice can lead to these quickenings. To be sure, yoga, meditation, tai chi, among many other forms, may gradually take us toward these kinds of awakenings.

But when I was fourteen years old, I studied transcendental meditation. I was the youngest in my class, surrounded by hippies and intellectuals in a college classroom. I think everyone was touched by my dedication. The dudes with the long hair and the love beads told me that if I learned to meditate I would see heavenly lights and hear the angels sing. Frankly, that is why I took the class. I wanted to hear God speak. I wanted colors and lights and spiritual revelation. But here was a typical meditation session from inside of fourteen-year-old Gregg's head:

"(Repeating the mantra himself) Om, Om, Om, Om, Om, Om, Home, Home on the range, where the deer and the antelope play . . . Range . . . a range is an oven . . . I wonder what Mom is going to cook for dinner?"

I kept going to my TM® class anyway and dutifully received my sacred word, my mantra. But the angels weren't singing and the lights weren't lighting and apparently God was taking a meeting with the Holy Ghost or something, because I sure didn't see Him.

Now, I know that meditation is a spiritual discipline and that it takes time and effort to catalyze those peaceful moments, the "gap between the thoughts" as Deepak Chopra likes to call them. I also know that learning to watch thoughts is essential to developing mindfulness—being fully present in the moment—which I value very highly. I also know that for me, breakthrough experiences came only after years of meditative practice, and even then only sporadically. I can hardly endorse these more typical approaches if you want to move forward rapidly.

Now, before you send me hate mail, I am not suggesting that you give up meditation or yoga or tree hugging or whatever spiritual discipline you ascribe to. I won't give them up either; if you must know, I am especially fond of Sequoias. And by the way, Ponderosas, though scratchy, are quite nice, and you needn't worry, their bark is worse than their bite.

But I am inviting you to consider that in this day and age, technological advances and psychological research are leading us to more than just a better Xbox, brain scan, smartphone, or anti-depressant. What if there were new approaches that could greatly enhance your spiritual awareness? What if there were breakthrough techniques that could save you years of meditative practice? What if I suggested that the traumas of your childhood that block you from your full potential might be resolved in months, not years of therapy? What if I told you that you could consciously recognize your karmic issues from other lifetimes? What if you could resolve issues directly with loved ones that have passed on, without the aid of a medium? What if you could meet Jesus or the Buddha directly? What if you could experience the oneness of the Universe? What if I told you that you could touch the Face of God? What if I told you that the kinds of experiences that saints, poets, and geniuses have had are yours for the asking? What if I told you that you could leap ahead on your spiritual journey into an entirely new way of being in the world?

It boggles the mind.

But I have seen it. I have lived it, and I have watched countless clients and workshop participants have these kinds of experiences. They are the result of specific techniques, deliberately applied in specific settings resulting in real, demonstrable life changes. These quickenings are not wishful thinking. They are reality.

By far, the three biggest impediments to utilizing these techniques are as follows:

1. People are ignorant of these techniques.
2. People believe they are too good to be true.
3. People believe that profound spiritual experiences can only be catalyzed through years of hard work.

Let's address these one at a time. First, the answer to ignorance is education. The book you hold in your hands can be the doorway to opening your mind to these accelerated techniques. And, I urge you to go beyond the cursory explanations I will offer and go directly to the source materials, which I list in the back of this book, to get a deeper understanding of these breakthrough modalities. Or get on Google (or get your grandkids to get you on Google), and let your cursor go wild. You will be amazed at what you find.

Second, these techniques offer such radically profound results in relatively short periods of time that they certainly appear, at first glance . . . okay, even at second glance, to be "too good to be true." I understand. Can you imagine what a breakthrough the typewriter was after pen and ink? Are you old enough to remember your first word processor? Maybe you recall the first time you heard about a voice-recognition system that could convert speech into words on a page.

I remember being a very young boy and sitting in a restaurant with my mother and one of her friends and hearing about a microwave oven for the first time. My eyes went wide! Hamburgers cooked in three minutes? Plates don't get hot in them, but the food inside does? Impossible. It sounded like a magic trick; too good to be true! But, of course, it wasn't. It was simply new technology. These modalities are, too.

Arguably, Edgar Cayce offered in one reading, "there are no shortcuts, [spiritual progress is made] line upon line, precept upon precept." But surely, we can agree that some paths are faster than others. You can get to Los Angeles from New York faster if you don't go by way of Tampa, Fla. One way to account for how a quickening can be accomplished is to look toward a concept called *gauge symmetry*.

Imagine for a moment, that you are at the foot of a very steep incline. There are two paths before you: one is a very steep ladder that goes straight up the side of the mountain; the other is a series of gently sloping switchbacks that zig-zag back and forth, first left and then right, with mild inclines, all the way to the top of the mountain. Which path should you take?

You say to yourself, on the one hand, the switchbacks look a little easier; they won't take as much energy and effort. On the other hand, don't they say that a straight line is the closest connection between two points? Doesn't that mean that the ladder is the faster path?

It is, but there is more to the story than that. As any physicist will tell you, setting aside minor calculations like extraneous friction, either path takes the same amount of energy. Fill in the variables in the equation, and you will see that you can exert yourself more on the ladder for a shorter period of time or take the switchbacks and exert yourself less . . . but over a longer period of time! So, it may be that engaging in a conscious quickening takes every bit as much energy—expressed as faith, commitment, and emotional vulnerability—as more traditional approaches, but like the ladder, it gets you there faster!

So, for those of you who are looking for a "magic bullet," a pill you can take to make you a Tibetan monk overnight, may I remind you that these are accelerated techniques, not presto-chango David Copperfield tricks. But they can save you time. A lot of time.

Finally, people believe that hard work is required to "earn" revelatory experiences. This is very much a Western mindset—the Puritan work

ethic applied to spiritual growth. As children, our good behavior got us
rewards from our parents and teachers. Our dedication and loyalty at
work (theoretically, at least) earn us a raise. At first blush, it doesn't
seem fair that God, Our Father, would grant us a free pass to the front of
the line, since Dad, Our Parent, told us if we didn't behave he would yell
at us or ground us until we reached adulthood.

There is no free vegan lunch and the like.

I understand. Let me be clear, without question, spiritual discipline
has its rewards. But millions of people have had spontaneous spiritual
experiences that have changed their lives apropos of nothing. How do
we account for these breakthroughs? Most of us have had the bootstrap
ideology hammered into us, even when it comes to revelation. But one
doesn't have to look any farther than the New Testament and the story
of Saul "seeing the light" and becoming Paul on the road to Damascus
to discover that transformative experiences can happen unbidden to
the so-called "undeserving."

I think some people associate this with God's grace–a special gift.
Who is to say? Once I saw a painting of a beautiful woman, gazing
toward heaven, flanked by angels–cherubs, actually, floating by each of
her ears. They seemed to me to be ready to whisper the secrets of the
Universe, to sing the song of all of heaven. There was only one problem.

This chick had her fingers in her ears.

Perhaps we are no different. Perhaps angels are whispering to us
constantly, but we are too distracted by the temporal world and our
noisy egos. I want to believe that if we go seeking God that She will
only be too happy to respond! *A Course in Miracles*, a powerful spiritual
pathway lauded by teachers such as Eckhart Tolle, Marianne Williamson,
and Dr. Wayne Dyer, reminds us that "there are many answers you have
already received but have not yet heard."[1] "Knock and the door shall be
opened," Jesus tells us. Maybe we just have to take our fingers out of our
ears and find the right way to knock.

This book is a result of researching, training in, and practicing these
new breakthrough methods–what might be called spiritual technologies–all over the country for the last fifteen years. I have seen them
work for thousands of people both in individual sessions and in workshops. While some techniques have been around for decades and are
rooted in years of research, others are relatively new. Many are well

established and have extensive track records. All have been developed by leaders in the fields of psychology and spirituality. Each has tens of thousands of hours of clinical observations by trained professionals who would testify to their potential. And, yes, some of these modalities have their share of critics. In my estimation, many of these criticisms are simply uninformed naysayers, a bit quick to dismiss something out of hand. And yes, some critics have valid points. But all of the modalities in this book have been demonstrated to be effective–over and over and to my satisfaction–as having the potential to help you leap ahead on your spiritual journey. For my clients and workshop participants, the proof is in the pudding. They would tell you, almost to the number, that they are very different, happier, more spiritually awakened people for having tried these approaches. More than a few would tell you their very lives have been saved.

So obviously, spiritual sweat and tears are not, part and parcel, a prerequisite for spiritual awakenings. According to a 1997 poll commissioned by *U.S. News and World Report*, an estimated fifteen million people have had near death experiences.[2] (We have no figures for how many did downward dog daily as a way to "earn" these experiences.) An estimated forty percent of Americans[3] believe they have had direct contact with loved ones who have passed. But even these transformative moments can be seen simply as "the grace of God," a gift. Perhaps they are. But the danger in this thinking is that we simply have to wait around, a–hopin' and a–wishin' that the Divine will make a little time for us. It seems to resign us to a God who is somewhat fickle and who sometimes bestows grace and sometimes doesn't.

Could it be that the convergence of these techniques are, in fact, a reflection of God's grace? Dr. Helen Shucman, the "scribe" of *A Course in Miracles*, was given information by her own Inner Teacher, a voice that she described as Jesus. The Voice suggested that the world situation was devolving at a dizzying pace (imagine that!) and that a kind of "celestial speed-up," an acceleration in global consciousness, was called for. In fact, according to the Course, "the miracle is a learning device that lessens the need for time. It establishes an out-of-pattern time interval not under the usual laws of time." These same miracles, sudden shifts of personal clarity from fearful thoughts and bodily identification to loving ones, filled with the recognition of our Unity with the Divine, had the ability to abolish the need for certain intervals of time "within the larger temporal sequence." In other words, one way to think about these miraculous quickenings is that we can literally leap ahead in time, thanks to an intense, but relatively brief instant in which we download an entire piece of cosmic jigsaw puzzle and understand the bigger spiritual picture. Interestingly, the work of Edgar Cayce and the Course, among other "special agents" were seen as a part of this speed-up.

"Though the way may seem long," Cayce observed, "a moment in the presence of thine Savior is worth years in the tents of the wicked," (Edgar Cayce reading 705-1) an important concept to remember, not only as you engage your spiritual journey, but also the next time you go camping.

I am asking you to consider with an open mind that there might be specific pathways, modalities, and technologies that allow us to move toward these quickenings more directly, without years of spiritual practice. And yes, maybe a sincere willingness to engage in these new approaches is the faith as big as a mustard seed, that yields these beatific, life-changing experiences. I have seen countless clients and workshop participants without backgrounds in metaphysics or spiritual practice have transformative spiritual experiences using these modalities. These gifts from God are yours for the opening. We might call them *intentional quickenings*.

And for Christ's sake, keep doing your yoga or Om Sweet Om, if that works for you. Let's get beyond an "either/or" dichotomy and embrace an "also/and" approach.

Imagine for a moment, that the next step on your spiritual journey is an old dead tree you have to cut down. If you want to take on the task with a nail file, you can do that. It will take a lot of time, perspiration and, if you are like me, maybe a bit of profanity. When you are done with all the angst, you can be very proud of yourself—your sweaty shirt, bloody knuckles, and all the effort you put into it. But, if that's not fast enough for you, get an ax and a good pair of leather gloves, and you can fell that sucker in a matter of minutes and save money on Band-Aids. Or, if you like, get a crosscut saw and a friend, and you can take it down even faster.

But I'm from Texas, y'all.

I'm gonna give you a chainsaw.

3

Binaural Beat Frequencies: Enlightenment on Demand

"Tones and sounds will be the channel through which the coordinating of forces for the body may make for the first of the perfect reactions . . . "   Edgar Cayce reading 758-38

Eckhart Tolle likes to tell the story of J. Krishnamurti, the Hindu philosopher who was instrumental, among others, in bringing metaphysical concepts to the Western world in the twentieth century. Reportedly, after an extensive tour of America, at one of his lectures, the enlightened teacher leaned forward conspiratorially towards the microphone and said, "Do you really want to know my secret?" A hush fell over the audience members. Here was the ultimate spiritual truth. Were they ready? Could they grasp it?

Krishnamurti said, "I don't mind what happens."

At first blush, that hardly sounds like a revelation, from the man who had a reputation as a "world teacher" and hobnobbed with physicist David Bohm and author Auldous Huxley. In fact, it sounds like someone who is apathetic. But Krishnamurti was hardly that. He was often truly at peace with whatever was happening around him.

Can you imagine what that would be like in your life? Your partner is angry with you, and you can keep your peace. You lose your job, and you can keep your peace. You win the lottery . . . and yes, you can keep your peace. You can even keep only about half the lottery money after taxes, and after hearing that you can *still* keep your peace. Sound like some kind of esoteric Eastern skill? What about the Serenity Prayer that asks God for "the serenity to accept the things that we cannot change," as prayed by millions in the Western tradition known as the Twelve Steps?

But usually, we are anything but serene in the face of things we cannot change. We furiously demand that life and world affairs be different. Our friends and families are expected to become what we "need" them to be. We even attack ourselves: We are not skinny enough, not smart enough, not responsible enough, not spiritual enough, and then we condemn ourselves for being too hard on ourselves!

Our righteous judgments not only interfere with our peace, they often separate us from the people we would want to love most. We are angry that our children or grandchildren have purple hair, got a tattoo, or worse, listen to Justin Bieber. We are angry that our spouses dare to notice someone of the opposite sex. We are angry that our friends did not remember our birthdays. So, we proceed to shut them out of our lives and then wonder why we feel so hurt and alone.

So much of the time, we see peace as something that is dictated by circumstances beyond ourselves. I will feel peaceful when I get out of high school; when I finish college; when I get married; when I get divorced; when I get remarried; when I have children of my own . . . no, wait a minute, make that when the kids move out, oops, they're already gone; I mean, when I see the grandkids again . . . and on and on it goes.

The Bible talks about "the peace that passeth all understanding." To me that speaks of two aspects of the quality of this peace. First, that peace is so intense or so deep that it transcends our normal sense of peace. It is beyond the everyday two-margaritas-and-it's-all-good experience. Second, that particular sense of peace is apparently *beyond rationality*. By definition, it doesn't make sense. What do I mean by that? Well, given that we believe that outer circumstances must dictate our moods, then, we believe if circumstances are perfect, *then* we experience peace. But this kind of peace occurs outside of that domain, when life hands us bologna sandwiches, not surf and turf. Or, for my readers who are vegan, tofu and kale.

Imagine you are sitting on your favorite Caribbean Island with a frosty adult beverage in your hand and your favorite romantic partner by your side. Your retirement is set, you have millions in the bank, you are healthy and vital, your children are successful in school or at work, you have the best friends in the world, and you feel . . . well, pretty freakin' good! Satisfied, maybe even peaceful! And most everyone would say, "That's understandable." That is the peace that is understood by all.

But what about a peace that is beyond understanding, when things are bad? How could we possibly have peace? Wouldn't we just be repressing our feelings? Isn't that denial? Or just plain Pollyanna?

My dear friend Kathy, I often joke, is the most spiritual atheist I have ever met. She was diagnosed with a life-threatening cancer and, understandably, her feelings leading up to her surgery and chemotherapy were a mix of terror, anxiety, depression, and confusion. Simultaneously, her mother was on hospice, death lurking around the corner. There was no guarantee her surgery could save Kathy's life. Like most of us, she had some difficult family relationships. Financial stability was an issue; her inability to work due to illness and the medical costs were a one-two punch in the purse. Her life was a perfect storm of bad news and tough circumstances. We would talk at length about how life would still continue, even while the crisis would move toward some resolution and her life was still right there in front of her. While I encouraged her not to avoid her painful emotions, I also reminded her that even in the worst of times, there were things to be grateful for.

One day, she called me excitedly. "I was at Whole Foods Market today," she told me. "And I was looking at all the beautiful fresh fruits and vegetables and enjoying all the people around me shopping, and the music they were playing was just incredible, some of my favorites from the eighties. I was literally dancing down the aisles. And suddenly it dawned on me that I was happy, genuinely happy. I was amazed. How is that possible? For probably fifteen minutes, I "forgot" that my Mom had just died a month ago and that I was about to have major surgery and one of my best friends is getting a divorce. How is this possible? And even when those things came back to me, I still felt good!"

Kathy "did not mind" her life circumstances in that moment. *It was the peace that was beyond all understanding.* Yet here it was. "My peace I give to you . . . not as the world knows it." And it was happening to a "godless atheist!"

By the way, Kathy *did* live through her surgery and continues trying to be grateful for her every moment. She has good days and she has bad days, but without question, learning to think this way has made all of her days *better* days.

These experiences should throw a steel wrench into the gears of our typical thinking. It does not mean that we *should* feel peaceful or can *always* feel peaceful in the midst of a crisis. Nor does it mean that if we do not feel peaceful or calm when things are difficult then we are a failure. It does mean that *peace really might be possible even in our most painful moments.*

That is good news, because life is going to hand us a lot of crap.

Oh, I am sorry, what I meant to say was "opportunities for growth." Yeah, right.

But it means something even more powerful than that. If peace is possible during times of trial, then we can train the mind, with practice and effort, to catalyze that state. And, by extension, this means we can live in the world in such a way that, increasingly, *we are not the emotional victims of our circumstances.* Instead of all the frenetic, anxious, exhausting, and crazy things we do to control the uncontrollable in our world so that we can feel okay, we could give that up. We could begin to really "accept the things we cannot change" and experience that peace that we all aspire to. Right now.

It is a revolutionary, radical way to think that is as ancient as Buddhism and as fresh as the latest Eckhart Tolle bestseller. Now, this does not mean we don't have goals and preferences, sitting listlessly about. It does mean that, en route to those goals, we are not relegating our experience of peace or happiness to something that will happen someday in the future "when I [fill in the blank]" but instead bring more enjoyment to the moment right now. As the T-shirts say, "The journey *is* the destination."

Strangely, I remember one incredibly successful individual saying to the media, "Getting here was a lot more fun than being here." If that is true, aren't we missing a great ride on the way to the top?

I think traditionally when we talk about cultivating a quiet mind, we think in terms of endless meditation or centering prayer. In the Cayce tradition, we think of the readings that advise us to "watch self go by," meaning we step back and create a conscious awareness of the flow of our crazy thinking. The notion of "mindfulness" has become integrated with newer forms of cognitive behavioral therapies and is changing the way people think, literally. But still . . . it takes time.

To be sure, it would be nice to have the *peace that passeth understanding* twenty-four hours a day, seven days a week. But, if you are like most people, that seems to be something that would take years of meditative practice. Maybe, at present, you can barely sit still and say, "There's no place like OM" for five minutes. It would be nice to have it right now. Too bad there is not some mental switch we can flip that would kick us over into Guru Consciousness.

As it turns out, there *is* a switch, and we can learn to flip it. And relatively quickly, too.

First, we would have to know—qualitatively and quantitatively—what was going on at a neurological level for someone who was experiencing a deep peace, so we could figure out how to reproduce it in others. It would be wonderful if we could look into the head of a Tibetan monk, who has been meditating hooked up to a Peace-O-Meter, and find out how blissed out he is . . . and then figure out how the heck he got there. I wonder what that would look like. Cue the harp music as Gregg strokes his bearded chinny-chin-chin, his eyes looking heavenward . . .

Futuristic computers flash and beep nosily in a control room that overlooks—through a plate-glass window—an experimental station straight out of the Jetsons. A slender monk in ochre robes is seated in a single futuristic tubular chrome and leather chair illuminated by a solitary down light and hooked up to electronic dealie-bobbers, while other monks solemnly chant long "Ooooms" in a semi-circle behind them with one of those big-ass horns blowing a long low note, filling the room with harmonic resonance. Our experimental monk, deep in meditation, smiles ever so subtly and as we gaze at him . . . is that a soft light gently emanating from him? *Meanwhile, behind the plate glass, uber-geeks with pasty complexions in starched white short-sleeved shirts and skinny black ties intently monitor scores of screens and winky-blinky lights. They gaze dumbstruck at the read-outs until one head honcho, sporting a burr haircut, a pocket protector, and black horn-rimmed glasses (sounding amazingly like the pilot on your last trip to Atlanta with his mouth too close to the microphone) ominously breaks the silence.*

"Uhhhhh, Mission Control . . . I've got Thupten Rinpoche here hitting an 8.9 on the Dalai Lama Scale. Uhhhh, yeah, he's red-lining right now. Roger that, we'll keep monitoring him, but at this rate, we anticipate an ETE [Estimated Time of Enlightenment] of about ten minutes. He's gonna start bending the needle and may well vibrate out of his body. Affirmative, we are talking about a total Celestine wave dispersion here. He's throwin' an awful lot of low Theta waves here and kicking up some Hypergamma besides. Let's move to Yellow Alert and have chanting monks and the horns stand down and the Reiki Masters on deck to attune him so he doesn't Nirvana outta here. Uhhhh, Stand-by RMs to energetically ground the subject on my mark: In three . . . two . . . one . . . "

Okay, okay, you're right. I've seen too many *Star Trek* reruns as a child. Okay, I've seen too many *Star Trek* reruns as a child *and* as an adult. But the truth is these kinds of experiments have been done extensively, just without the Ken Adam movie sets. Through an EEG, we can measure the electrical activity of the brain, and we can recognize various states of focus as they correlate to certain kinds of brainwave activity. Our brains actually generate enough electricity to light a ten watt light bulb, which, I guess means we are all pretty dim, if you take that at face value. But, as it turns out, it's the *kind* of electrical activity that counts. After decades of research, studies have demonstrated that different brainwave patterns directly correlate to different states of being. According to sound researcher Dr. Jeffrey Thompson at the Center for Neuroacoustic Research, although there are no *universally* accepted standards for where one state breaks into another, science on our planet has traditionally divided brainwave activity into four major states:

- Beta (13–30 Hz) Concentrated mental ability, concrete problem solving, speaking
- Alpha (8–13 Hz) Calm and relaxed
- Theta (4–7 Hz) Deep meditation, dreaming, creative states, access to the unconscious
- Delta (½–4 Hz) Sleep state, access to intuition and psychic phenomena

Now, if you are not a sound engineer, don't let the "Hz" throw you. Hz simply stands for "hertz" which means cycles per second or how "energetic" the electrical activity is. Once again, imagine that you are at the beach. Déjà vu, huh? When you watch a wave, you identify it by seeing the trough immediately before it, which then rises to a peak and then goes back down again. From trough to peak to trough again is one cycle. Simply put, a higher Hz level just means choppier waves, going by faster: more waves per second. And a low number of cycles per second would be like those subtle slow swells in the waves that you see farther from shore. It really just reflects faster or slower electrical brainwave activity, which makes sense when you think about it. When we are anxious or excited, we are thinking "lots of thoughts" and when we relax, our brains "slow down" and our thinking feels more spacious.

Of course, at any moment, you have lots of different kinds of waves in your head, but one range of wavelength is typically more dominant than others, so if you have a lot of activity in the 13–30 Hz wavelength (i.e., a lot of waves going by), we would say you were in a Beta state with your mind and body alert and engaged with life. You are probably talking or shopping or thinking analytically about that loser you went out with last night and how you are beginning to wonder whether you should have spent all that money on online dating after all.

Now, close your eyes, take a deep breath, and exhale, saying the Universal Mantra of Relaxation: "Ahhhhhhh." You are now beginning to generate slower alpha waves.

Did you do it? Feels nice, huh? See, you are more like the Dalai Lama already. Look at you, leaping ahead on your spiritual journey, even before you finish reading this book, you rascal, you.

If we had you hooked up to the electrical spaghetti swim cap wired to the Univac that they call an electroencephalograph or EEG, we would see more activity in the 8–13 Hz alpha range. Enough alpha waves that you will find yourself feeling relaxed, but focused. This can be useful for light meditation, internal mental reflection (i.e., "pondering," if you will), and, if the alpha state is not too deep, maybe doing some really effective studying.

Legend has it that Thomas Edison so valued this creative twilight arena just before deep sleep that he would nap in an armchair with metal ball-bearings in each hand, positioned over steel bowls. As he dozed, his hands would relax slowly until, eventually, he dropped the ball bearings into the bowls. Their clatter awakened him in the middle of what was very likely an Alpha state or light Theta state. Judging by the, oh, one or two productive ideas that came out of his head, I would say it worked for him.

Edgar Cayce had a name for this zone between wakefulness and slumber; he called it "pre-sleep." He said that the mind was very amenable to instructions in this state, and he helped a young mother successfully cure her child of bed-wetting by having her make audible suggestions as he drifted off to slumber land.

The next level "down," Theta states (4–7 Hz), involving long, slow brainwaves, are associated with deeper, visionary states of meditation, spontaneous problem solving, and psychic experiences, including out-of-body experiences.

Delta states (.5 to 4 Hz) are associated with sleep, but also shamanic or mystical experiences—important to know if you want to do some shape-shifting or soul retrieval. (Where the hell is that thing? I *swear* I put it my jacket pocket when I left the house. God, I hope nobody stole it! Talk about identity theft! Jeez.)

So now that we know where we "need to be," (neurologically speaking) to access mystical experiences, greater intuition, and deep meditation, how do we flip the switch?

Well, first we have to climb into our time machine, fire up the flux capacitor, and go back a few years. Relax and get in. The leather bucket seats have bun warmers so you won't get cold. I bought it used with all the options. As you can see, there is a lot more legroom in here than in the *Back to the Future* car. Bear with me while we leap backward on our spiritual journey.

The year is 1839, and the handsome Prussian gentleman before you with the moustache and graying temples is one Heinrich Wilhelm Dove, known as Hiney to his friends, I am sure. If he were from Texas, like me, where everybody has two names, they would probably just call him Richey Bill.

But I digress.

Perhaps you noticed.

Richey Bill, er, Heinrich was quite the man of letters, now regarded by some as a pioneer in the field of meteorology, early experimental physics, and natural sciences. There is even a crater on the moon named for him, the Richey Bill Crater.

Just kidding, it's called the Hiney Hole.

Okay, so it's called the Dove Crater; it's just north of the crater Pitiscus. Inquiring minds want to know.

For those of you not laughing, I am aghast, aghast, I tell you, at this brief detour into scatological humor. How this escaped my editor is completely beyond me. Spirituality is *very* serious business. Shame, shame on me.

For those of you smiling, thank you for remembering that we take all this enlightenment stuff too seriously sometimes. Come and see me at my next workshop. We will laugh our butts off *and* leap forward.

So, before you are gone too long from the present and your jerkwagon of a boss thinks you are on an extended Red Bull break, here is what is important about Heinrich. He noted that if you sent a musical tone to one ear of, say, 200 Hz, and then another slightly higher tone of, say, 210Hz, to the other ear that this confused the brain, which then manufactured an experience of a "phantom tone" which was the difference between two frequencies, 10 Hz. You might remember from high school biology that the nerve endings in the right ear connect up with the left part of the brain and the nerve endings in the left ear go to the right part of your brain. Apparently, Mother Nature, in her infinite wisdom, decided it was a good idea for us to be born with our wires crossed. In any case, since both hemispheres of the brain were involved in the experience, your entire meat computer begins to attune or *entrain* to this frequency and starts buzzing along at 10 Hz. Hiney called the phenomena *binaural beat frequencies*, now often abbreviated BBF. It sounds like something nightclub disc jockeys with too many pierced body parts generate on weekends. But, stay with me. Binaural simply means "two ears hearing," like you ladies always wish your husband would do.

But, what Richey Bill did not and could not grasp at that point is the application of this technology. Class, do you remember what state you are in when you have lots of 10 Hz activity crackling in your noggin? (You can check the chart. It's okay; I only give open-book tests.) That's right, alpha state. Send two detuned tones to two ears and in a matter of minutes, whaddya got? Instant meditation!

Now, hang on while the g-force pulls the corners of your mouth towards your ears as we leap ahead on our spiritual journey to 1973. "Tie a Yellow Ribbon 'Round the Old Oak Tree" by Tony Orlando and Dawn is at the top of the pop charts and it's a dark, dark day for rock 'n' roll. But on balance, this year marks the publication of "Auditory Beats and the Brain" in *Scientific American* by Dr. Gerald Oster of the Mt. Sinai Medical Center. The article puts together current research and historical findings about BBFs. Suddenly, BBFs become more than just an interesting anomaly and transform into something more credible and useful in the eyes of the academic community.

Around the same time, sound pioneer Robert Monroe was researching BBF. Monroe, an engineer who spontaneously began having out-of-body experiences in the 1950s, believed that BBF technology might be able to help people relax, accelerate learning, and even facilitate astral projection. He manufactured the technology under the brand name, *Hemi-Sync*®, short for hemispheric synchronization, since he noted that when using BBF, there was a more balanced, coherent neural firing of both the creative/artistic right hemisphere of the brain and the linear/rational left hemisphere. *Voila!* "Whole-brain thinking" on demand!

Zip!

And now we are back in the twenty-first century . . . and my fly is closed. You are saying, the little BBF history lesson was fascinating, Gregg, and thank you for closing the barn door, I was beginning to worry about you. But what's in it for me?

Let's say you wake up in the morning at eight o'clock, only to discover that the coffee pot's broken. *Damn,* you say to yourself, *how will I find my way to work without my java?* Thinking quickly, you toss on your headphones and start to listen to a Beta audio recording on your iPod. The BBF tones feed into each ear, resonating underneath a bed of lively up-tempo music. Sure enough, within just a few minutes, your brain is chugging along at about 20 Hz, solidly in the range of Beta waves, and you feel bright and alert, without the cost of a $15.56 cup of mocha latté soy Frappuccino extra grande venti with a shot in the dark from Starbucks.

You go percolating through the day, energetic, alert and feeling pretty good, until your jerkwagon boss (the one who got pissed off at you for being gone too long in my time machine) reminds you about a project that is due. And he doesn't want it right, he wants it right now. Whipping out your iPod from your purse (okay, it's not a purse, it's a satchel like Indiana Jones carries), you turn down the lights in your crappy vestibule that passes for an office, close your eyes, and breathe like your favorite yoga instructor, while jacking into an alpha state BBF audio track with haunting minor key music and groovy ocean sounds for fifteen minutes, catalyzing an Edison-like state of mind *sans* ball-bearings. After reinventing the light bulb *and* the telephone, you remember that what your boss wanted was the specs for the new electric dog polisher. In the alpha state, you can hear every word of your muses and spontaneously solve the problem and buy small, inexpensive gift certificates for them as tokens of your gratitude.

After a tough day at the office channeling Tommy Edison, you decide it's time for some spiritual sustenance. You put on a Theta track with low harmonic musical tones and in fifteen or twenty minutes, you find yourself meditating at a depth something akin to Tibetan monks with twenty years of training. The more you listen to the Theta tracks, the easier it becomes to catalyze this deep meditative state, *whether you are listening to an audio or not.* With repeated listening, perhaps you find yourself calmer in stressful situations, more empathic with others, experiencing more intuitive flashes, and maybe even meeting angels or spirit guides and doing some astral cruising.

Now, it's seven thirty at night and your jerkwagon manic boss calls, but you are in such a Zen state, you don't panic: "You don't mind what happens." As it turns out, it's all good. "I *love* the work you're doing!" he screams into the phone. "The specs for the dog polisher are perfect. And I *love* the idea of running it with solar panels attached to the canine's haunches and taking advantage of the tail wagging to store kinetic energy. Genius! We're gonna *kill* in the green market with this! I'm giving you a raise and moving you to the corner office!" You smile broadly as excitement courses through your body. But as the evening wears on you wonder if you can get some sleep after all this drama.

Your mind is racing. How will your life be different if the Electric Dog Polisher gets picked up and marketed by the *As Seen on TV* folks? You reach for your ever present iPod and put on a Delta track with night crickets and slow tempo music that catalyzes long, low delta waves in your brain. You have learned to wear ear buds while you listen to the sleep tracks so that you can roll over on your right or left side without shoving a whole headset up your Eustachian tubes. You sleep soundly, dreaming of all the money you saved on Ambien and thinking that no matter what Big Pharma says about safety, people are sleep-driving on that stuff, and it really might be a "benzo in a chicken suit." You awake feeling rested, refreshed, and excited to blow your new paycheck and see your corner office overlooking the parking lot and the decrepit air conditioner on the roof of the nearby Dollar General: The Good Life is yours.

All thanks to BBF, your new BFF.

I am, of course, allowing for some hyperbole here. Thanks for coming along for the ride. I don't think that there is any guarantee that BBF audios will get you a corner office or help you to invent a Solar-Powered Electric Dog Polisher (although the one I bought on TV has some serious design flaws and somebody really needs to address this, and soon). But there are decades of research into BBF that suggest it actually does catalyze these states for people and can be used to deepen meditation, sharpen focus, boost creativity, and help people sleep. Is this all exaggeration? Here is UCLA neurophysiologist John Liebeskind talking about BBF research:

"It's difficult to try to responsibly convey some sense of excitement about what's going on . . . You find yourself sounding like people you don't respect. You try to be more conservative and not say such wild and intriguing things, but damn! The field is wild and intriguing. It's hard to avoid talking that way . . . We are at a frontier, and it's a terribly exciting time to be in this line of work."[4]

New brain scans are showing us just how powerful these states of mind are, and the incredible potential that resides in all us, if we can but catalyze these states.

Functional MRI and advanced EEG research have been conducted into different forms of meditation with the assistance of the Dalai Lama at the W.M. Keck Laboratory for Functional Brain Imaging and Behavior at the University of Wisconsin.[5] A lifelong meditator, who studied various forms of contemplation in the tradition of Tibetan Buddhism, demonstrated some startling results. (See, *Star Trek* or not, I told you I wasn't making this stuff up.) Not only did the meditator show lots of slower brainwave activity during certain forms of meditation, there was also a striking increase in a higher vibrational electrical activity above Beta: the newly-christened *gamma* and *hyper-gamma* waves, also seen in research at University of Birmingham. Current findings suggests that when there is a lot of gamma activity in the left prefrontal cortex of the brain, subjects report feeling energetic, joyful, bright, alert, and yes, exceedingly happy. This pattern was specifically linked to the kind of meditation he was doing, a technique to awaken compassion.

I can't help but wonder if this new kind of state of being that is both bright and alert and also deeply connected spiritually is somehow related to the optimal state of "flow" that star athletes, artists, dancers, and yes, witty therapists, experience when they are completely *in the moment.*

In addition, in a series of tests, the Buddhist meditator earned the highest recorded scores in his ability to recognize the emotional states of individuals in photographs *flashed for one fifth of a second or less.* Talk about theta states being able to improve empathy! And amazingly, our monk demonstrated something researchers had never seen before: the almost complete absence of a startle response in his facial muscles while in a meditative state when exposed to the sound of a gunshot at close range. In these tests, not even police marksmen with years of experience with firearms could suppress this startle response.

Wow, when a gunshot can go off next to your head, and you don't flinch, I guess you really "don't mind what happens." Truly, this is the peace that passeth all understanding.

Interestingly, newer iterations of BBF technology, such as Dr. Jeffery Thompson's Gamma Meditation System, capitalize on this recent research and entrain gamma and hyper-gamma waves. Imagine a mental workout that gets our mind in shape to think happy, compassionate thoughts, with no monthly gym charges, just a one-time CD or download charge. Plus, just think, you won't freak out so much when the next drive-by shooting happens in the neighborhood.

My experience with BBF has been quite positive. When I first heard of these audio recordings, I was so excited that I told myself I was going to listen every day. Well, that turned out to be three or four times a week in reality. But within a week, I noticed that I could stay more focused on my clients during sessions, my meditations deepened, and I experienced more intuitive flashes. Additionally, I found that my meditations were deeper, even *without* the headphones. Although I am new to the gamma and hyper-gamma audios, the first time I used them, I experienced a number of head rushes, similar to Kundalini-type experiences that I had had in other settings.

At times when I have had difficulty sleeping, I have found delta sleep audios a godsend, although I don't always *stay* asleep with them, they almost always *get* me to sleep.

Where to start?

A good introduction to this work is a beautiful CD by Dr. Andrew Weil, called *Sound Body, Sound Mind.* It has an almost hour-long track that starts in Beta, meeting you in regular waking state, gradually taking you down to Alpha and Theta, with thirty minutes in "the deep," a lovely little sonic tonic, that helps you relax, regroup, and may well boost your immune system. Then it gently returns you to your regularly scheduled program of waking consciousness in Beta. Whenever I feel myself getting sick, I use *Sound Body, Sound Mind* to head off colds and flus, and it usually does the trick. It's also helpful when I have grief I need to attend to. Yes, I know that is not the same as a randomized double-blind placebo controlled study that might constitute a bit more proof, but since we are getting so close, I thought you might like to know if it was good for me.

Dr. Jeffrey Thompson's *Brainwave Music System* offers the listener journeys into alpha, theta, and delta states in a setting of tranquil tones and the sounds of nature. Let's not forget *Hemi-Sync,* the company that pioneered the technology. Go to their website and you can peruse BBF CDs and downloads that offer everything from focus and concentration to (theoretically) astral travel. Sorry, but my out-of-body travel is limited to brief excursions catalyzed by listening to political pundits on TV.

But . . .

For more than twenty years, our government pumped millions of dollars into a remote viewing program in which trained soldiers, who had demonstrated potential intuitive skills, were to become so-called "psychic spies." After some preliminary preparation, the first place they sent trainees was the Monroe Institute, to listen to—you guessed it—Hemi-Sync audios to boost their psychic abilities. Legion of Merit award-winner Joseph McMoneagle, widely regarded as the most accurate of the military's remote viewers, also worked with Monroe audios using Hemi-Sync to both improve his abilities and also better control his spontaneous out-of-body experiences. After all, Cayce said that everyone "has clairvoyant, mystic, psychic powers" (Edgar Cayce reading 1500-4), but they had to be developed. Why not put the very best training tools in your corner?

Welcome to the future of your mind.

4

Past Lives, Future Lives, and the Afterlife: Understanding Your Karmic Arc

"[Under hypnosis] the conscious mind becomes subjugated to the . . . superconscious or soul mind . . . From any subconscious mind information may be obtained, either from this plane or from impressions left by individuals that have gone before."

Edgar Cayce reading 3744-3

Not So Sound Bites

The television camera was all but looking over my shoulder as I began to take my subject back to another lifetime. The conditions were hardly ideal. For starters, I was outdoors on the patio of a chain hotel; the Sacramento spring air was close and muggy, and periodically people were passing by. My client sat in a lawn chair, a last-minute volunteer whom I had never met, pressed into service by a bubbly young female reporter to "demonstrate" past-life regression therapy for a local network affiliate. To top it all off, the woman I was hypnotizing, a kind and gentle soul, was hard of hearing.

"It's okay," she said a bit loudly, when she volunteered. "I read lips pretty well."

That was of great comfort to me, given that most of the time she was hypnotized, she would be sitting there with her eyes *closed*.

I had flown into California to essentially keynote at a weekend event called *The Healing Arts Festival*, produced by my friend Marcie Mortensson. As the featured speaker, I would be offering a couple of abbreviated group past-life regressions as well as an exercise called *Discover Your Destiny*, that had helped lots of people intuitively grasp their life's mission and even apparently see a glimpse of their future. The trip seemed like a good idea at the time, especially when I had conspired with my best friend, Jack Morrison, to piggy-back some R&R after the conference. He would fly in and meet me, and we would drive over the mountains to hang at Lake Tahoe. Marcie had told me— no, *warned* me—that the media might be there.

Television is anything but a patient medium. Media today is all sound bites and snippets. Heaven forbid that anyone spend more than ten seconds on any subject. I knew I needed something visual. I decided on a rapid-induction technique I had learned when I trained under Dr. Brian Weiss, the leading authority in the field and the author of the best-selling *Many Lives, Many Masters*. Basically it was a technique that would put someone under hypnosis all but instantly . . . but not something that you would want to screw up on television.

Mary was seated in front of me, and I was standing. I asked her to place her open palm in mine and to look up at me. I tipped my head down, burning my gaze into her eyes.

"Look at me, Mary. Look at me. You are getting sleepy, sleepy. Your eyes are tired, heavy, limp, loose, relaxed. You can't fight them . . . " I said firmly. She began to glaze over slightly.

"Your eyelids are so heavy, so *very* heavy, you can't fight it—sleepy . . . heavy . . . limp . . . loose . . . relaxed . . . "

Her eyelids began to blink rapidly.

"*Sleep!*" I commanded.

Her eyelids snapped shut, her shoulders collapsing, her chin falling to her chest. As I recall, I literally had to catch her shoulder to keep her from falling out of the chair and onto the stoned pavement.

"Going deep, even deeper now, dropping down, way down, *so* easy, *so* gentle," I said quietly and rhythmically as her face softened even more. I could see the trance state taking hold. She took a very deep breath and exhaled. The camera, the patio, the cheap lawn chair beneath her, and the moist morning air were all falling away from her now.

"Just like a stone falling through clear water—going down, down, all the way down, even deeper . . . " I intoned.

I took Mary through a series of weigh stations on our way to her past life. There were additional deepening techniques to insure she was in a profound trance. I surrounded her with a brilliant spiritual light to guide her and create safety. Then it was on to a magnificent spiritual garden, a place of safety and sanctuary, where I would introduce her to a spiritual guide, who would take her on her journey.

It was only then that I realized the camera crew had not placed a microphone on her. Also, I had been so focused on Mary (as I should have been) that I completely missed the fact that the camera was no longer on us. Bored, I suppose, they had trotted off to get another bite of metaphysical news, somewhere else. Still, I had a client in front of me, and I felt an obligation to finish what we started. As we explored her past life, an amazing story unfolded.

She reported that she was a man, a Muslim, somewhere in the Middle East, perhaps hundreds of years ago. Yes, crossing genders happens sometimes from lifetime to lifetime. Although Edgar Cayce says that we typically incarnate as the same sex, we occasionally switch to check out what it's like to have different chromosomes. In that incarnation, as a male, she was on a special mission. She was given a sacred prayer mat that was to be delivered to some holy men for a very special ceremony. She believed that if she did not complete her task, and this sacred ritual went incomplete, then some catastrophe would occur. As she scurried across the city, through crowded bazaars, anxiously moving toward her designated meeting spot, she was suddenly waylaid and dragged into an alley. She was beaten and left for dead, and the holy prayer mat stolen!

As the last of her life flowed from her, her thought was not for herself, but that she had failed Allah and the Holy Ones. She wept with shame. Her life was a failure. Blood, tears, and eventually even her spirit, left her body.

We talked for a few minutes afterward. The intense regret and shame was still with her. In her incarnation now, she had always been concerned that she was fulfilling her life's mission. But in her current life, she had spent much of it composing, recording, and performing sacred Native American music around the country. Her work and spirit had touched thousands of people. Maybe, I said, she could forgive herself for what happened in her Muslim life. After all, she had died in the service of Allah. And in this life, her efforts to help bring spiritual growth to the planet had found success.

Mary quietly cried tears of relief and forgiveness. Smiling through her grief, she thanked me and told me that the regression was immensely beneficial and that it helped her make sense of a lot of her thoughts, feelings, and fears over the years.

"Most of all," she said, "I don't feel like such a failure anymore. That was an echo from my other life."

Later, the pretty and perky young reporter approached me and asked me to tell her what had happened to Mary in the regression. She shoved a microphone in my face, the camera light clicked on, and suddenly an electric white smile blazed on her face.

"We're here with Gregg Unterberger, a licensed professional counselor and a national expert in past-life regression. He has taken thousands of people around the country into hypnosis to see who they were in other lifetimes!" she said musically.

I didn't think I could match her 500-watt smile, but I remembered what my friend and producer Mike Gilg used to say, "Smile big for Mister Camera. Remember, this isn't real life, this is TV!" As we continued, I tried to share Mary's experience as briefly as possible. With my every sentence the reporter's skull nodded frenetically like a bobble-head doll on the dashboard of an '86 Oldsmobile with bad shocks. I tried to truncate Mary's story, but how do you encapsulate a transformative experience into a thirty-second sound bite?

Later, as I watch the recording of *Good Morning, Sacramento* with my friend Marcie Mortensson, I realized it hardly mattered. Initially during my interview, they let me talk about Mary and cut away to shots of my rapid induction as she collapsed into trance. It was a nice visual. But then as I continued with her story, the audio played an ominous over-the-top piece of music that would be best suited to a horror movie. Finally, they cut back to the anchors, mugging spookily while the lights flashed on and off in the studio and thunder sound effects played on the soundtrack.

Mary had a life-changing experience, and they had made a mockery of it.

I have (last I checked) a sense of humor about all this, of course. If you haven't figured it out, I think we can find some laughter in almost anything. But I think it is unfortunate that past-life regression therapy—something that has held up in court as a legitimate therapeutic intervention, a topic that has sold millions of books—should be reduced to a scary carnival ride by the media in this day and age.

I remember Dr. Brian Weiss telling me a story about someone who had a near-death experience (NDE). The person reported being tortured by demons and devils, something all but unheard of in the literature. A major network asked Dr. Weiss to regress the person to find out more details. Under hypnosis, the near-death survivor remembered being poked and prodded by EMS workers who missed his veins several times while trying to put in an IV and realized that the demons were a part of his delirium. Cameras recorded the session but, as you can imagine, when the media broadcast the report, they completely failed to include the hypnosis they asked for, instead going with the original interview with the man who said he had been tortured by demons, even though he had now refuted it! The network went with the story they wanted, not the one that was true.

Whether *you* believe in it or not, the majority of people on the planet believe in reincarnation or rebirth. Even in the Western world, according to polls, nearly a third of Americans and Britains believe in reincarnation—a substantial increase from twenty years ago. It's amazing when you think about it, since only one Christian denomination—the Unity faith—fully embraces reincarnation as part of their theology. That means that somewhere out there, there are a lot of people that are Lutherans, Methodists, Catholics, and (Holy Christ!) Baptists, who believe they may have lived before, despite their religious affiliation. You may be one of them.

As to beliefs about the afterlife in Judaism, my friend David H. Ehl, author of a remarkable book, *You Are Gods*[6], once told me that he asked a rabbi about the topic.

"He basically told me if you ask ten different rabbis, you will get twelve different answers," said David with a wry smile.

Still, according to Judaic scholar, Yaakov Astor, for most academics, reincarnation is unquestionably a part of mystical Judaism and is featured in the *Zohar*, a major source for Kabbalistic teachings. Indeed, Astor points out that many conservative scholars, not known for being sympathetic to mystical thinking, see reincarnation as a basic tenet *of mainstream* Judaic traditions, however unobserved.[7]

If a major network made fun of Baptist beliefs or Catholic beliefs, there would be a serious outcry.

Still, it was a wonderful weekend, overall. They pronounced my name right on television. Plus, a lot of people in my workshops remembered their past lives, and some discovered their destiny (*sans* the scary music).

And Mary isn't filled with shame anymore.

*   *   *

IN LOVE WITH A NAZI

What had I done?

"Get me out of here!" she all but screamed at me. All that Greta had seen were bodies: bodies upon bodies upon bodies stacked up like so much cordwood against the cold concrete walls. Her eyes closed, her head twisted about furtively like a tiny bird, frantically looking about in her mind's eye. "I can't find myself," she said with a ferocious urgency. "I . . . I don't know which one I am . . . Get me out of here!"

"Okay, okay, Greta," I said, trying to sound calm and focused while I felt like my heart was going to pound out of my chest. "As I count upwards from one to ten, you will slowly regain full waking consciousness. Here we go: ten . . . nine . . . eight . . . seven . . . six . . . " I recited, not realizing that I was counting in the totally opposite direction, *Way to go, Gregg!*

It was a good thing that Greta had her eyes closed, or she would have seen every red blood cell in my body rush to my face in embarrassment. In truth, that was the least of my worries. I had never seen anyone react so frantically in a past-life regression. Greta's sheer panic was overtaking her. I had never once had to count anybody out of a past-life regression because they were overwhelmed by the intensity of their feelings.

But then, I had never *done* a past-life regression before. This was my first.

Fortunately, I already *was* a licensed professional counselor, not completely unfamiliar with how to deal with an abreaction like the one Greta was having. I counted Greta the rest of the way out, still counting in the wrong direction, but Greta came up and out of hypnosis nonetheless.

She looked around, her eyes wide, the memory fresh. "I couldn't find myself!" she said with a thick German accent. "I was looking, but I could not find me!"

It took me a minute to get my bearings and figure out exactly what Greta was talking about, but slowly the tumblers were clicking into place. I had successfully hypnotized her and taken her into a past life. *Hey, at least I got that part right. Not bad for a rookie.* I told myself, trying to piece together a few shattered bits of my confidence, but cutting myself on the sharp edges. I had directed Greta to go to an important moment in that past life. But there was no way that either I or Greta could have known where she would go.

She had arrived in a lifetime in Nazi Germany, but not "in" her physical body. Moments before, she had been hung by her neck. Her body had then been taken away to some kind of warehouse for temporary storage along with other corpses. Greta was experiencing the aftermath of her life as a fifteen-year-old Jewish girl immediately after her execution. She was completely confused by the experience. She was deeply identified with her young body and panicked, her consciousness floating over the stacks of bodies trying to find the mortal coil that she had so recently inhabited. But then, it was too much, and Greta, rightfully, had asked me to *get her out.*

I snapped my fingers sharply, breaking the trance.

"Oh, mein Gott," she said, choking back the tears as I gave the final suggestion to arrive back fully in the present.

"Greta, open your eyes. Greta? Greta! Greta, open your eyes," I said in a firm voice. She responded, her eyelids fluttering rapidly, then becoming more present. She was breathing in short, sharp breaths, punctuated with chaotic moans. "That's good. Greta, look at me. Look at me ... *look* at me ... look at me." Her eyes finally went wide, as though she was seeing the bodies again. Then the rapid blinking returned as tears spilled down her cheeks. I was grounding her in the here-and-now by bringing her attention to my eyes and a safe presence.

"Greta, you are safe. You are safe. Do you understand me?" Her eyes were still filled with a lingering horror, but she nodded, still unable to speak. She whimpered and perused the room, as if to double-check if the evil was still present. She was here, at least in part.

"What you saw was horrible. What you saw was a horrible past-life memory. It was a very frightening image. And you are safe now. An image cannot hurt you. It can scare you, but it cannot hurt you. You are safe. You are back in Greta's life experience here, now, in the year 1999."

Greta took a series of slow, deep breaths and looked around the room, nodding, clearly wanting to believe me, beginning to believe me. The terror was still with her, but gradually she was orienting herself with my help in a large room that contained other counselors and therapists, paired off together, all practicing their brand-spanking new regression skills on their second day of training with Brian Weiss, a medical doctor with degrees from Yale and Columbia and perhaps the guy that was voted in his college yearbook as "Least Likely to be an International Authority on Past-Life Regression."

Brian, a largely agnostic, obsessive-compulsive, magna cum laude grad, who had authored more than forty scientific articles and book chapters, had his life turned upside down some thirty years ago when he put a patient, "Catherine," under hypnosis and directed her to go back to when the problem began, thinking she would land somewhere in her early childhood.

His worldview hadn't really prepared him for a patient spinning back hundreds of years to another lifetime and then having the audacity to heal the more she remembered her past lives. To top it all off, Catherine reported the presence of Ascended Masters on the Other Side, who gave Brian especially personal information that Catherine herself could not have known. It was time to take a personal time-out, and take a second look at the Cartesian worldview.

Brian had to, shall we say, *regroup*.

All of which led to the 1988 publication of *Many Lives, Many Masters*—Brian's international best-seller—followed by appearances on major networks and a string of successful follow-up books. Thus, regression came out of the closet and into afternoon TV, on *Oprah*, just like vibrators and men on the down-low.

I had seen Brian in person at a number of woo-woo conferences, but he wasn't woo-woo. He was honest, kind, peaceful, and authentic. He was real. He was funny. (A friend of mine aptly described him as Jerry Seinfeld on Valium. But I don't think that is his secret.) Mostly, he was totally credible, and I knew I would take the very first plane to his next regression training even if I had to hock the dog. You will be pleased to know that wasn't necessary; I got enough for the cat.

Oh, c'mon, you know me better than that by now.

When I tell people in my workshops about my first past-life regression, they always ask me, "Weren't you frightened?" And I always answer like the Wizard of Oz: "My Dear, you are looking at a man who has *laughed* in the face of danger, *sneered* at doom, and *chuckled* at catastrophe. Why, I was *petrified*."

On balance, I must say that if your first past-life regression is filled with extreme Nazi trauma like this one, then pretty much anything else after that is a piece of cake.

So, *thanks*, Brian, for pairing me with Greta. You know how to show a guy a good time.

Within about ten minutes, I had Greta firmly grounded back in everyday reality. She was still very shook up. I asked her if she thought we should go back in to complete what we started. She shook her head "No," vehemently.

"All right," I said, attempting calm, moving towards something that might loosely be called my center. "I want you to know that you never have to revisit that lifetime if you don't want to. Please be clear, I am okay with that. Having said that, your higher consciousness took you to that life for a reason, and at some point you may want to explore that. But that is completely up to you."

Greta smiled graciously. She clearly understood that I merely facilitated the memory and that I did not cause it. She graciously expressed her gratitude for taking such good care of her. Exhausted, Greta was only too happy to call it a night, and happy to leave that past life in the past . . . until she woke up the next morning with a bright red rash in a circle around the circumference of her neck.

Her body remembered the hanging.

A cold chill went through me as Greta tugged at her collar to show me the marks on her neck. In the pattern, I could almost make out the imprint of the braid of the rope. It was somehow simultaneously horrific and beautiful.

She smiled grimly. "I think . . . we had better go back into that life again." She mindlessly ran her fingers over the intense red mark. "It won't leave me alone, I think," her voice trembled with both anxiety and feigned good humor.

Later that morning, I placed Greta under hypnosis again, but this time I was careful to initially direct her towards a very happy memory in that lifetime in Germany. We needed some context, some background, and most importantly, a memory that wouldn't petrify her, at least not initially. Her most recent incarnation found Greta on the streets of a major German city, and she was about fourteen years old. It was a bright spring morning and the air was crisp as she walked hand-in-hand with her mother. The smell of fresh baked bread filled the air from a nearby bakery, and Greta felt the sun on her face.

The Nazi party was just coming to power, but Greta knew nothing of politics at her tender age. But as she looked across the cobblestone street, she saw a handsome young German officer. He looked so striking in his German uniform, all pomp and polish. He was firing off orders to several subordinates who snapped a salute before quickly leaving to do his bidding. Greta experienced feelings stirring somewhere deep in her body that she had not known before. Awed by his power and good looks, she was staring and caught his eye. Embarrassed, her eyes fell to the ground, but when she looked up again, he was still looking at her. He gave her a brief, if curt smile. She turned her face away, beet red with embarrassment, burying her countenance in her mother's threadbare cotton coat.

I directed her to go to another important moment in that lifetime. She was perhaps a year older now and once again found herself walking the streets, running errands with her mother. She saw the Nazi officer again, and it became obvious to both of us that this was a daily ritual. She would walk the streets with her mother hoping to catch a glimpse of this man who was her schoolgirl crush.

On this day, Greta watched her dashing young officer from across the street and saw an old Jewish woman approach him. Although she couldn't make out what the woman was saying, she could see that woman was animated—pleading and begging the young officer for something. Then, seemingly without warning, he struck her sharply across the face, frustrated by her cries for help. She fell to the ground, and he kicked her aside with a frightening nonchalance, appearing anxious to get on with his daily duties. Greta's hands went to her face, her mouth agape.

Just at that moment he looked across the street and caught her glance and fiercely looked at her as if to say, *See who you are in love with?* Looking deeply into his blazing eyes, Greta took a sharp breath.

"I know this man. I *know* this man." Greta became increasingly agitated. "He was my husband Klaus in my current life. In my current life, he was a good man . . . a good man, but now he is a monster!" Her hand rose to her mouth in horror.

"My Klaus is a monster!"

After using some calming techniques, I asked Greta to move ahead to the next important life experience. Her shoulders contracted, and her expression became grim. Her face was pale.

"It is the moment of my death," she said grimly, her voice barely a whisper.

I assured her that she was safe to observe her own death, that her soul was eternal and these were echoes or shadows of her past.

"I understand that," she said softly.

Now, I can look back at the thousands of past-life regressions I have induced since then, and I have been pleased to say that experiencing a death in another lifetime is rarely traumatic and is usually liberating. Very typically, subjects feel no pain and, upon leaving their body, are glad to be free of it, feeling peaceful and even joyous. However, the first few moments after leaving the body are usually an adjustment, especially if the death is sudden and unanticipated. There can be cursory leftover concerns about those who are left behind. But amazingly, most people come to terms with the death of their physical body quickly and have an underlying sense that everyone who is left behind will be okay.

I remember leading a group regression in Atlanta. I instructed the audience to go to the moment of their passing. A heavyset gentleman in his fifties immediately groaned as his chest heaved forward, his head whipped backward, like a ragdoll. I checked to see that he was okay and continued on with the regression. When it was over, I asked him what happened.

"When you asked us to go to the moment of our passing, I was suddenly hit with a spear right through my chest."

"Did it hurt?" I asked him. He frowned considering the question.

"No, it was more like a shock, a sudden pound on my chest. It wasn't so much pain as it was surprise. I literally didn't see it coming," he said with some amazement. "It actually took me a little while to realize that I was dead. But I hated being a soldier, and it wasn't long before I felt relief and an incredible freedom."

Greta's feeling of terror after dying, I would soon learn, was very atypical. She said she felt no pain when she left her body, but there was a sense of shock and surprise as she discovered that her consciousness and awareness continued to live on. Curious, she floated up high over the rooftops of the city in which she lived. She was offered a panorama, a completely novel perspective she had never known in that life as she looked down on rows of familiar houses and shops with smoke billowing from their chimneys, drifting up into a deep blue sky.

Then she "remembered" she had a body . . . but where?

Suddenly frightened, she returned down to the scaffolding where she had been hung, but her body was no longer there. This is exactly the moment where we had "entered" her past life in our first regression. No wonder she had been so terrified and confused.

Following some kind of internal homing beacon, she found herself in a cold concrete warehouse where the bodies of dead Jews had been stacked. It was uncomfortable, but less painful to experience on this, the "return visit." She became frustrated, because she could not see the faces on the bodies.

She eventually identified her body by her shoes.

"I spend some time looking at my feet and my body and all the bodies," she said, her voice breaking. "I don't know how long it is. Maybe a few minutes, maybe several hours, but then I become aware of a light—a beautiful, brilliant golden light that seems to enter the left-hand corner of the warehouse. As I look up at the light, my heart feels drawn to it, and I have a sense that everything is going to be okay. I realize that somehow, I am going to be okay, too."

She released a heavy sigh. As she floated deeper and deeper into the light, her facial muscles relaxed. Then suddenly, she brightened.

"It's Klaus!" she said excitedly, "not the Klaus from back then, but the Klaus from this lifetime. Oooh, it is so wonderful to see you." Her face wet with tears, the words came rushing out in a tumble. "He is hugging me, and he says he loves me, and he says he was a monster last life, but he came back to prove that he didn't have to be one in this life, so Klaus wasn't a monster."

"He wasn't a monster this lifetime?" I asked, echoing her words.

"Oh no, oh no, no, no, no, he was a good man," she said emphatically. "Well," she said, giving it a second thought, "he was a hard man. He was a *stubborn* man." Then her face broke into a smile again, "But he was a good man, and he loved me, and he provided for me. He is saying that he will be waiting for me. On the other side, you know," she said clarifying. "Klaus died just last year from prostate cancer."

"I am so sorry," I said softly. "How wonderful to know that his spirit lives on and that he loves you still."

But suddenly Greta's joyous reunion was transformed as she faced yet another goodbye.

"But Klaus," she said to him, beginning to blubber, "Klaus, how will I go on without you. What will I do? What is my purpose?"

Tears were streaming down her face. I knew this was a pivotal moment, but one completely out of my control. The ball was in Klaus' court. I could only hope he had a ready answer. I never would've guessed what came next.

Greta broke out into a fit of laughter.

She continue to guffaw and giggle for several minutes. For a moment it seemed like she might never stop laughing, and I found myself chuckling right along with her, though I had no idea what was so funny.

"Oh, that Klaus! He was such a kidder, what a kidder he was," she said, barely able to catch her breath. "Prince Albert and Schotzie," she said aloud, as though that would make perfect sense to me.

"I'm sorry . . . Prince Albert and Schotzie? I asked.

"Yah, Prince Albert and Schotzie," she said, this time emphatically.

My face screwed up in confusion, even though she couldn't see me.

"They are our two dachshunds! He says, 'Who would take care of Prince Albert and Schotzie if something happened to my Greta?' Oh, he is laughing too. He is such a kidder, but I understand what he means. I still have to look after the dogs. There are, of course, my children and grandchildren. Although they live far away, I still have lessons at the earth school, he says." She giggled. Then her demeanor changed, her face becoming utterly serious. "Again, he says he will wait for me." She paused, and I sensed a moment passing between them, a communication beyond words. It was quiet. And then, her voice a whisper, she offered her beloved Klaus a tender farewell.

"I will see you soon, my love."

A tiny, final tear slipped from the corner of her eye.

Apropos of nothing, I suddenly felt two thumps on my back, like I was being hit by a rubber mallet the size of a small skillet. I was temporarily distracted, but refocused, resolute that I would count Greta out of hypnosis, this time actually getting the numbers in the right sequence. After a few minutes, she got her bearings, opened her eyes, and smiled at me.

"I feel better," she said. "It's done now. You know, most Americans don't realize how much shame and regret the German people still carry for the Nazi atrocities, even now. When Klaus and I were married in our current life, I could see that we carried that regret but for different reasons. Now, I know that I had a deep empathy for the German Jews, because I was one in my last lifetime, and Klaus felt some regret, because he had been a Nazi officer, although I can assure you in this lifetime, he was a kind, loving, and just man." She paused, putting it all together. "He made different choices this life," she added with a smile of admiration.

Greta and I spent a few more minutes talking about the experience, and finally I had a sense that it was time to wrap up, but I had to ask a last question. "If Klaus liked someone—say, a male friend—how would he express that?" I asked.

Greta giggled. "Oh, Klaus never was—how do you say it in America?" She paused a moment with the quizzical look of a fifteen-year-old girl. "He wasn't *touchy-feely!*" She laughed out loud. "He was not a hugger. But if he thought someone did a good job, he would clap them on the back. Usually a bit too hard, I think."

I grinned at Greta, and suddenly felt a warmth rush to my chest. I think maybe Klaus gave me a couple of thumps of approval that day just to let me know that I did a pretty good job—for a rookie, anyway.

Greta and I smiled at each other with knowing glints in our eyes. I wondered what kind of karmic connection Greta and I had that we might bring such a deep and profound experience to each other. Perhaps one day, as I float above Gregg's body, those answers will be revealed.

*   *   *

THE MURDERER INSIDE HER

Natalie had awakened in the middle of the night with a profound sense of evil surrounding her. She felt like hell itself was burning in her belly as a rage like she had never before experienced went through her. The young mother wondered if she might be possessed. *What if I hurt someone?* she asked herself.

Natalie was just twenty-six years old, and her four-year-old son, Donny, was asleep just a few doors down the hall. In desperation, she prayed feverishly, repeatedly, hoping against hope that the feeling would dissipate, while her husband John slept blissfully unaware of the murderous rage that had erupted in his petite wife. Could this evil somehow spill over into the other room? She would spend the rest of the night unable to sleep, wrestling with this question.

Natalie, attractive and fit, dressed in the latest designer clothes, showed up in my office asking me for a past-life regression some two weeks later. Whenever someone comes in asking about a specific therapy, I usually ask why. I want to make sure that I am tailoring my approach to my client's needs. If someone is having marital problems because they have poor listening skills, it seems a little silly to trot off into another lifetime to try and track down the problem.

Running her hands anxiously through her short red hair, Natalie told me about her encounter with the dark side. She said she had repeatedly seen and heard my name in her meditations in connection with a past-life regression. Although I was certainly open to the idea of Natalie being divinely guided, I wondered if this interest might be due more to the fact that Natalie's cousin had seen me several years before for a past-life regression. My reputation wasn't completely unknown to her, and I was concerned that she thought a regression would be a quick fix.

But Natalie began sessions twice a week; she was experiencing the frightening feelings almost every night. Sleeping pills helped, but often left her drowsy and exhausted all the next day. The cycle was beginning to take its toll on her. I taught Natalie some relaxation techniques and some ways to tame the anxiety tiger. I knew these were temporary fixes, but Natalie tried them and did get some relief. We had to dig in and get something done soon, but I was reticent to do a past-life regression until I knew more.

In one session, Natalie told me how she had "made a scene" at a Chinese restaurant. She had been having a plate of noodles with her son and her favorite aunt. The aunt playfully asked her son for a kiss, and he bashfully turned away. "Aw, c'mon Donny, give Auntie Billie a little kiss," she pressured, as Donny tried to crawl under the table. Billie began making kissy noises and ducking her head under the booth to try and reach Donny when Natalie exploded. "Stop it! Stop it! He doesn't want to be kissed! LEAVE HIM ALONE!" Her aunt froze—as did most of the diners within three or four tables. Natalie, realizing her overreaction, felt her face blanch as she looked blankly around at the other patrons, nearly as shocked as they were.

"I just don't know what came over me. I just freaked out and started screaming at the top of my lungs." I thought for a moment and gave Natalie a chance to compose herself. Even in the telling of the story, she was clearly agitated.

"It sounds like it was a very uncomfortable and embarrassing moment," I said.

She nodded, feeling understood. I paused for a moment.

"Natalie, do you have any memories of sexual abuse?" The blood drained from her face, and she slowly nodded. "I can't help but wonder if this has to do with everything that is happening to you."

"But I am so frustrated! All I have are these vague memories—I tell myself that it didn't happen. But maybe it was my grandfather. My parents were also members of this weird swingers group; about every two weeks or so they would go down into the basement with other couples." She sighed heavily, a long world-weary, hopeless exhalation. "I don't know . . . " She trailed off and looked at me bewildered. Then suddenly, she teared up. Natalie sat up instantly in her chair, agitated. "I just want it to all go away. Is there some way you can hypnotize me and just make it all go away?"

"I'm sorry, Natalie. I wish I could. It's not quite that simple." I said.

"But if I can't remember it, how can I ever get over it?" she said, her voice cracking, an octave higher.

"Well, there is good news. Some of the techniques I use can be very helpful in resolving these issues, even if we don't have a specific memory to work from."

Her chin down, her eyes tilted up, hopefully. "I just feel like I am going *crazy*."

"I don't think so. I actually think you are getting better."

"What?" asked Natalie, incredulously.

"I think that evil you felt in you wasn't some kind of dark spirit. I think it is more likely that it is the rage that has been pent up in you for years."

As I continued to go through her family history with Natalie, she talked at length about her parents, who were largely absent. Her dad worked all the time and was rarely seen, except to dole out criticism and punishment. Her mother, Natalie reported, rarely even cooked dinner for the family and took root on the couch every night. Many nights Natalie went to the refrigerator only to find it empty. "I might as well have been invisible for all they cared."

"Do you ever get upset with your husband John? Are you afraid *he* doesn't see you?" I asked.

"Oh, all the time! He is a great guy, and I know he loves me, but he can get so wrapped up in his job or a football game that I think he forgets that I am in the house."

"Given your childhood, can you see why that would upset you?"

"Yes, of course . . . but John really *does* see me and cares about me. He is different from my parents. But he says I am overly dramatic about everything. Maybe he is right. What's wrong with me? He probably doesn't deserve that I am so hard on him sometimes."

"Maybe not," I said gently. "But I can certainly see why it would be touchy for you."

At eleven years old, Natalie moved in with her Aunt Billie and things got much better.

"She was the mother I never had."

"I am glad that you found some respite from your parents and the swingers. When you were little, what do you think would have happened if you had gotten angry at your parents?"

"Are you kidding me? They would have just made fun of me. Mom probably would have hit me. It would have made everything even worse."

In a subsequent session, we used a Brainspotting technique to desensitize the "fire in the belly" anxiety that had plagued Natalie for months. (We will explore brainspotting at length in Chapter Seven.) As we worked, I asked her to notice what was happening in her body physically. She reported an energy, almost nauseatingly sick, that wanted to come up, while another energy in her fought to keep it down.

"I HATE this part! I wish it would go away!" she growled, her eyes tearing up.

"How far back has this battle inside you been going on?" I asked.

"As long as I can remember!"

"What would happen if you let this energy out?"

"It would be awful, terrible, something evil would happen," Natalie revealed in horrified tones.

"Like what?"

"Someone will get hurt," she said menacingly. "I just want to kill myself."

"Why?" I questioned.

"Because, I am so evil!" Natalie was utterly convinced.

"What if you are not evil? What if you are just angry?"

Natalie couldn't answer that, but by the end of the extended session, the pain and intensity of the fire were dramatically reduced. Natalie said the emotions were all still there, but the physical discomfort had been cut in half. She felt better for the first time in months. I told her that there was still more work to do, but I thought it was likely that she would feel even better when the emotions settled down and she got a good night's sleep. In my experience, there can be a raw quality to more intense therapy sessions when they were immediately finished that fades within a few hours. But on the off chance that she needed me, I gave her my cell phone number and told her to call me.

That Friday afternoon, I had no idea how glad I would be that Natalie had my cell phone number.

I was halfway through cooking one of my famous Saturday morning homemade omelets, when the phone rang. It was Natalie. "Oh my God! It's back. *The evil is back!* John was teasing Donny and playing "tickle monster," and when he came after Donny, I just freaked out. I mean, Donny was smiling, he wasn't upset . . . but all of a sudden I wanted to kill someone when I saw that . . . and then I wanted to kill myself!"

I tried to think on my feet, wishing I had put an extra scoop of French Roast in the coffeepot. I was in Chef Gregg breakfast mode, not quite ready to staff the suicide prevention hotline. But reaching into my psyche's closet, I managed to grasp my therapist ball cap and snap it firmly on my head.

"Natalie, take a deep breath," I said, taking one myself. "I am so sorry. I know this is frightening." I could hear her exhale. I needed to take her temperature. "Do you really think that you will kill someone?"

She paused thoughtfully.

"No, I mean . . . I would never kill anybody. It's more like I am AFRAID that I am going to kill someone, and then I just want to die. Does that even make sense?"

"Perfect sense," I replied.

"What do you mean?" she asked, her voice choking. I could hear the sheer panic in her expression. "Do I need to go to the hospital?"

"No, I don't think so, but I think we need to meet as soon as possible," I said. "Is John there?" I asked, a firm urgency to my voice. "Can you have him drive you to my office?"

Natalie said he would and to expect them in twenty minutes.

I slammed down a second cup of coffee and jumped in my car, praying for guidance as I drove to my office. Although I certainly had not ruled this out, it was hardly what I expected. As I unlocked the doors of my office and flicked on the lights, I raked through the memories of her last session: Natalie said the physical manifestations of her anxiety had gotten better, but her emotions felt the same. As it turned out, although we had accomplished some level of desensitization of her trauma, nothing had "settled" after the session. Seeing Donny chased by his dad had probably triggered memories of her own abuse and justifiable anger. But Natalie experienced this as the "evil" within her surfacing, and when she saw it in herself, the shame and guilt overwhelmed her. She wanted to die.

I knew we had to somehow release that rage from her system. But as long as she thought those feelings were her mortal enemy, how could we do that? I remembered that in the last session she had shrieked, "I HATE YOU!" when we touched in on this energy within her. How were we going to resolve this?

Minutes later, Natalie was at my office. She looked visibly shaken. It was hard for her to sit still in her chair, and she wrung her hands nervously. Words tumbled from her mouth like an avalanche.

"It happened again. I woke up in the middle of the night, just overwhelmed with panic. My heart was racing. All the things you taught me to help with the anxiety just flew out the window. All I knew is that I was furious, angry. I wanted to do something bad to someone. What kind of horrible monster am I?" she exclaimed, her eyes wet with tears. Her question was sincere.

"I don't think you are a monster, Natalie," I responded very quietly.

"But I *do!* It was almost like some part of me was taunting me, daring me to do something really evil."

My mind raced. Voices taunting her? Was this schizophrenia? Somehow, it didn't quite click.

But this was tricky. As most therapists know, when someone hates themselves enough, there is the possibility that they will take their own lives. But for my clients who are parents, I can always gently remind them that their children *need* them. Many a patient has decided not to commit suicide because they don't want to see their children suffer the pain of their death. But if Natalie was really convinced that she might hurt her son, she might justify the suicide as a way to keep him safe.

While these thoughts streaked across my mind, Natalie simply looked at me with expectation. Something about her expression brought me out of my thoughts and into the room. She looked down at her hands before quietly remarking, "I really do think this is connected to another life."

I took a moment and inhaled a deep breath. My immediate response was that she needed to express the pent up rage. And yet, in previous sessions, we had tapped into at least some of her fury, but it was still accompanied by a sense of shame. Every time she would start to experience anger, another part of her mind threw cold water on the experience. The anger that needed to be honored was tamped down by a terrible shame. It was the kind of double-bind that could stall therapy for weeks or months. Maybe Natalie's gut feeling was right. I was still convinced there was probably some kind of abuse in her current life that "drove" the traumatic responses and her panic.

But maybe there was something from another time that we needed to look at.

I took about thirty minutes or so to talk to Natalie about what to expect in a past-life regression. Many of my clients have unrealistic expectations for the experience. They seem to think that they will "see" things in their mind's eye like a three-dimensional IMAX surround-sound movie experience, when the reality is that regression is often like looking through the bottom of a coke bottle. Some things are clear, some aren't. Some individuals "sense" or "feel" the memory, while others see it; some aspects are in focus, while others are not. Edgar Cayce was once asked why we couldn't remember past lives, and he glibly responded that we don't remember when we learned to add two and two or how to spell "c-a-t, cat." Why then should we be surprised if we don't remember all the minor points of another life?

I always remind clients that we may not need to know all the details. What you had for dinner in the sixteenth century probably isn't nearly as important as whether you were starving in that life or you were eating regularly. Descriptions of clothes and locales are of less value than details about who you were and what you did that you most regret or appreciate about your former life. So, as it turns out, we don't really need all the details anyway.

I also remind clients that I will keep them safe. I always offer an extended white light imagery and a prayer of protection to bond them with their Higher Power as they understand it. Never once has any "dark energies" or "entities" bothered my clients or workshop participants in regression.

That is not to say that regression clients don't sometimes encounter painful memories. Think about it: If I were to direct your memory, right now, to some of the most important moments in your current life, many would be ones of loss and transition; many would be loaded with emotion, good and bad. It is no different when visiting another lifetime. But, no matter how horrific they appear, these memories of the past cannot "get" my clients now, any more than a bad guy in a movie can jump off the screen.

I also made sure that Natalie knew that, unlike those childhood moments of abuse, she was completely in charge of the session. If she wanted to say "stop" at any time, she could, and I would bring her safely up and out of hypnosis.

Natalie listened, but it was clear she was already someplace else. She fully understood what I said, but part of her consciousness seemed to be already headed towards a foreboding era, decades in the past.

*   *   *

"He stinks! God, he is so disgusting!"

We were about forty minutes into trance. I had already helped Natalie to relax and had used deepening techniques to take her to a state of hypnosis. We had used some white light/Higher Power imagery to cleanse her and keep her safe as she "made this internal journey." I had guided her in her mind's eye toward a radiant garden, a place of peace and great beauty. But Natalie's unconscious, apparently anxious to get to the root of the problem, had ignored my suggestions. Instead of a magnificent garden, she saw a dusty rocky landscape, populated only by a lone dark figure, a man in his late twenties or thirties, disheveled, unshaven, grubby, and unkempt.

"Oh, my God. He is evil. He is a bad, bad man. He hurts people . . . he kills people. He rapes. *He is evil itself.*"

Natalie froze in her seat. Though her eyes were closed, it was as though she was recoiling into the chair, somehow trying to meld into the upholstery to stay as far as possible from this horrific vision.

"This is an image from a past life. You are safe now to look at it." I said in a gentle, reassuring voice.

"*No, I am not!*" she shrieked. "He says I am just like him. He says I will kill and rape, too! Oh, Jesus, he is so revolting. He is smiling, devilishly. He is taunting me. He is saying, 'You will see. *You will do it all again.*'" Natalie covered her face with both hands and whimpered.

"Natalie," I said in a calm but firm voice. "Do you remember the Light that surrounded you a few minutes ago?"

"Yes," she said breathlessly.

"Let it surround you now. Feel its peace and its safety. This evil cannot hurt you." Natalie took several deep breaths. Her body relaxed, and she settled into the chair, though her face was still contorted. "He's here. Jesus is here. I feel him by my side." I noticed Natalie softening a bit more. Then she smiled ever so slightly. "And Nicole is here, too."

"Nicole?"

"Nicole was my dog. I loved her so much. It's so good to see her."

This was good news, I thought. It is always reassuring when a loved one or loyal pet appears spontaneously to help with facing something frightening in a client's mind. Whether it really is the essence of the being that has passed or it's the client's imagination, these impressions always support the client and give them strength against the frightening aspects of themselves or their history.

But suddenly, the imagery took a surprising turn.

"She's gone now." Suddenly, the smile vanished and Natalie started shaking. "She's gone now, and I killed her." She started whimpering. "I killed her. I KILLED her!"

I was completely unprepared for this revelation. But I wanted to know more.

"I am so sorry, Natalie. I know you miss your Nicole. Tell me what happened."

"The Bad Man is laughing, like some kind of maniac. He says I killed her, and I will kill others, too. He says I am evil just like him, and I will see!"

I knew I needed the specifics.

"Natalie, what happened to Nicole?"

"Oh, she was a wonderful dog. She was so sweet and loyal. I miss her so much. She had puppies, but the pregnancy was so hard on her. So I took her to the vet. They said she shouldn't have any more puppies so I took her to be spayed. But I killed her!"

"How did you kill her?"

"She died in the surgery. She wouldn't have died if I hadn't taken her to the vet, but I *killed* her!"

"Didn't you take her to the vet, because she might die if she got pregnant again?"

"Yes," said Natalie, sounding bewildered. "But she died there!"

"Why did you take her to the vet, Natalie?"

"Because I wanted her to live . . . I didn't want her to suffer with another pregnancy . . . or to die!"

"Listen to yourself, Natalie! You didn't want her to suffer . . . you didn't want her to die! Does that sound like someone who is evil?"

"No," she said, her voice trembling on the razor's edge of believing me. "But *he* says I wanted her dead!"

Something began to shift as she realized the Dark Man had twisted everything. Natalie started crying tears of relief . . . and tears of release. This went on for a few minutes when she suddenly paused, taking a sharp breath.

"Nicole is back! She is telling me it is all right. She is saying it wasn't my fault, that all I wanted to do was help her. She says I am forgiven. I mean," she chuckled, "it's not like she is *talking* to me, but she is communicating it to me in my mind. Oh, Nicole . . . " Natalie started laughing and crying at the same time. "I am petting her. She understands. She loves me . . . she still loves me. It's not my fault."

Natalie's hands moved in the air as though actually petting her dog. For all I know, she *was* petting Nicole. I gave Natalie a few minutes to be with her beloved Nicole, a wonderful and happy reunion. She seemed to settle down more and appeared less panicked.

But then, the Dark Presence returned.

"He's back. The Bad Man is back. Oh my God, I can smell his foul breath and his body. He smells like fecal matter and sweat. He has this wild, evil look in his eyes—like he is capable of anything!" Her face contorted with nausea. She gasped and froze.

"Breathe, Natalie."

She gasped a quick breath.

"Is Jesus still with you?"

"Yes, I can look at the Bad Man now, and it doesn't scare me so much. But he is still taunting me. Jesus is holding my hand. He says I am *not* the bad man. I am not *him*!"

"That's right, Natalie. You are NOT him. Tell him, Natalie. *Tell the Bad Man that you are not him*," I commanded.

"Oh my God. Oh my God . . . but I WAS him!"

Chills raced up and down my spine.

"This is Alabama . . . it's the 1930s, and I just drifted from place to place . . . I killed people, molested children, stole from others . . . oh, I am such an awful person . . . "

"No, Natalie, that is not you now. You might have been awful in that lifetime, but that is *not you now*. Tell him Natalie, *tell him!*"

"I am NOT YOU! Do you hear me? I am NOT YOU! I will NOT BE YOU this lifetime!" she screamed at the top of her lungs. "I will NOT kill! I will NOT hurt anyone!" she said with a new conviction.

Not wasting a moment, I jumped in. Natalie had a foothold against this evil, and I wanted to continue the momentum.

"Tell him that it was awful what he did in that lifetime, and you refuse to go back to that kind of life. Tell him maybe that was all *he* had to live for, but you have a husband and a child, and he is *not* going to take your joy and happiness from you!"

Natalie continued with quite a monologue, screaming aloud and drawing distinctions between the Bad Man and herself. As she shouted, she was taking herself back by increments from this horrific past life. Jesus stayed by her side, gazing at her with pride, while Nicole barked protectively. Finally, the Bad Man hung his head, and Natalie, her face wet with tears and red with rage, took a long, ragged breath. He was beaten.

"He is hanging his head. He is ashamed. All his bravado is gone."

She paused, her face contorted, confused.

"It's funny, he doesn't seem so frightening now. He is just kind of . . . pathetic."

And then there was a moment of quiet—a brief calm. But I knew something that Natalie didn't know. This was the eye of the storm. There was someplace else that we needed to go, something else that I knew Natalie needed to see, so she could fully put this life behind her.

"Ask the Bad Man to take you back to when all this began."

"I am afraid," she said nervously. "Can Jesus and Nicole go with me?" she queried with all the innocence of a child asking a parent if they can keep the stray dog that followed them home.

"Of course, Natalie," I said in kindly voice. She smiled sweetly. "Go back to what made the Bad Man this way."

She took a deep breath. Natalie's brow furrowed. She looked concerned, her eyelids tightened as though she were trying to focus or make out something in her internal vision. Her eyes darted about under the lids.

"There are people all around him. He is just a boy. And they are . . .

oh, God, they are hitting him. They are *hitting* him with metal bars; I think the bars are iron. Rebar? He's just a kid! He didn't *do* anything! I don't even know why they are doing this to him. They think it's funny or something. They are cruel. He doesn't even cry. It's as though if he does they will make more fun of him and hit him more. I want to tell them 'Stop it! STOP IT!' but they can't hear me. It is so awful!"

"How long does this go on?"

"Hours. But, it's like this isn't the only time it happens. This happens again and again. Eventually he runs away and does whatever he can to get by. It's all he knows. That poor little boy." Tears began to roll down both her cheeks

"He was angry. He was so bitter and angry. He did exactly to others what had happened to him."

"What do you want to tell him?"

She took a deep breath. "I understand now why you did those things. Bad things happened to me, too," she said looking the Bad Man in the eyes and thinking of her father's beatings. "But I don't have to make the choices you made. I can choose differently this lifetime. In fact, I *am* choosing differently this lifetime."

There was another important piece that Natalie had to complete to really put this behind her. But I knew it was one she wouldn't want to acknowledge. I was walking on eggshells now. Still, I knew it was something we had to pursue. I rolled the dice.

"How is it that you can choose differently this lifetime, Natalie?"

She paused, confused for a moment. She frowned and then slowly grimaced, her eyes tight, tears leaking from the corners of her eyes. "It's . . . it's because . . . " She couldn't get the words out.

"You need to say it aloud, Natalie. You can do it."

"It's because . . . of him?" she said haltingly, as though reporting to me.

"Tell *him*, Natalie." She turned her internal focus toward the rank, disgusting, pathetic ogre in front of her.

"It's because of you," she said awestruck that the words could escape her mouth.

She sat, transfixed, frozen for what seemed like an eternity. We were at the very edge of the precipice. She had to make peace with this Dark Figure or the internal battle would continue. Her nights would be forever haunted, unless she could embrace this truth. But how could she ever be grateful for this horror?

She swallowed hard, and addressed the Dark Figure in her mind.

"It's because of *you* . . . that I can make different choices," she whispered, haltingly. And then the words came in a rush. "Oh my God, I can't believe I am saying this, but it is true. I mean, what you did was wrong, but you did it because you were hurt and angry; I understand. But because you did it that way in your lifetime . . . " she gulped air, getting the enormity of the moment.

She paused, correcting herself.

"Because *we* did it that way in your lifetime, we learned," she exclaimed, her voice choking, tears streaming like rivers down her face, a bizarre attempt at a smile on her face, as though to cheer up the disheveled figure before her.

Beauty and the Beast, I thought.

"We can make a different choice this lifetime. It's okay to be mad, but we don't have to hurt anyone this time. And if we're not bad this lifetime, then we don't have to feel the guilt that you felt when we did all those things, isn't that nice?"

He was hanging his head. She was sobbing uncontrollably now and somehow finding a way to talk in between desperate gasps for air.

"We can do it differently, because of you! I know that I never, ever want to do it the way we did it that lifetime, because I learned!" Natalie's convulsions slowly gave way to quiet tears as she became swept away by the thought that this evil person that she had been was somehow her savior in this lifetime. She had a chance to make new choices this time and learn from his mistakes.

"Thank you. I mean that. Thank you," she said to the Bad Man.

"What do you see in his eyes?"

"He is crying. He is so ashamed of how he lived that life. He didn't have a clue; he really didn't know any better. But he is so glad that it wasn't in vain, it wasn't all a waste! He is hopeful; *I am his future*."

I am his future. It had rolled out of her mouth before she really had time to consider the ramifications of this truth that rang like Big Ben in her head. She stopped cold.

"Somehow, if I can do it differently, he is happy, too." She frowned, quizzically. "It's weird."

On one level, the whole interaction seemed bizarre. Where was she? Who was she? Sometimes when I watch people heal, there is the timeless sense that I am helping them use symbols to push concepts around in their minds, until they can find some order that they can live with. I flashed on Einstein's famous quote that past, present, and future are all an illusion, however persistent. Somehow it all made sense to me. Maybe I had ordered my own concepts.

A strange half smirk came over Natalie's face. She was reacting to something she was seeing.

"He is thanking me for not caving into his rage, but also he needed for me to understand him. It's like he wanted me to know there was a *reason* why he was so angry. And I know that feeling in this lifetime too. But I learned from you, Gregg, what *he* never learned—that it is okay to feel angry, and I can express it in ways where no one is hurt. And my anger for the evil that was done to me, does not make me evil too. I can acknowledge it, and it will pass. It is not evil, it is human!"

That day turned out to be a watershed in Natalie's healing: a quickening. She left that three-hour session completely exhausted but slept all night for the first time in months. Things were immediately and markedly better for Natalie. There were, of course, other areas we had to pursue in therapy. She had been a victim in her childhood, and she had to reclaim a new sense of identity as an autonomous survivor. She literally had to "grow into" the idea that she could make her own decisions and that it was okay to stand up for herself. Alongside of that, she had to let go of the hope that others could (and should) make her life "magically" happy, a common fantasy as a little girl. And, just as I had expected, some specific, if half-formed memories emerged of sexual abuse from her current incarnation.

Even outside of her past life, there was still a lot of justifiable anger she felt toward her parents, and Natalie felt ashamed that she was so filled with rage about the way they treated her. As long as she thought that expressing those feelings would cause her to become a murderer, there was no way we could release them. But now her resentments were readily and rapidly addressed.

Much of these patterns were worked through relatively quickly, using trauma-release therapies like Eye Movement Desensitization and Reprocessing (EMDR) and Brainspotting, which I will be discussing at length later in the book. Without the shadow of the Dark Man, these important issues became eminently treatable. Almost immediately, Natalie's twice-a-week therapy became once a week for several months, and finally about once a month, for "tune-ups."

A skeptic might well argue that Natalie's imagery merely reflects an externalization of a murderous rage that lived within her in response to childhood abandonment and abuse. It's a reasonable hypothesis, and one I won't rule out. And, for people who are open to reincarnation, it's possible that her anger from her current life "piggy backed" on those past-life memories, making them even more implacable.

But what is important to me are results: Her work in therapy accelerated, her life got markedly better, and her need for medication was drastically reduced. On the other side of her regression, her appreciation for her son and her husband blossomed. In fact, her new clarity took on a new activism, working as a child advocate in the courts to try to prevent the kind of cruelty that she had experienced in both incarnations. The echoes of her past life, real or imagined, no longer keep Natalie in shackles, and she readily embraces her life in the now, as a mother, wife, and charitable volunteer.

* * *

VISITING HEAVEN

As I continued over the years to regress people individually and in my workshops, I found people mentioning an author again and again. His book was *Journey of Souls*, and his name was Dr. Michael Newton—a regression therapist who specialized in taking people to "life between lives," the dimension or plane in between lifetimes, or what some in the West call "heaven," and what the Tibetans call the *bardo*.

For over forty years, Dr. Newton explored life-between-life (LBL) regression therapy. He and his associates compiled over 3,500 cases in which clients have been regressed under hypnosis to the "life between lives," giving a potential glimpse of the afterlife. In extended sessions, lasting at three to eight hours, Dr. Newton has taken hypnotized individuals back to their most recent past life, then through their death and into the afterlife. Although there are some variations, individuals report a surprising number of similar experiences in their otherworldly journeys.

The "Cartography" of the Spirit World

Based on thousands of regressions, Dr. Newton has suggested a rough outline for the soul's journey in between lives. Here is a greatly simplified version of the soul's potential progression through the Spirit World:

- **Leaving the Body**: The soul leaves the material body on or about the time of physical death and feels a "pull" away from the earth. They may experience brightness all around them or in one area of their vision, the now-famous "tunnel" with the light at the end.

- **Meeting a Spirit Guide**: After floating toward (or through) a gateway or portal, a being of light—usually accompanied with a feeling of familiarity—greets the soul—renewing its energy, and sometimes offering a preliminary review of the life lived.

- **Energy Shower**: As noted, this energetic renewal, a shower of revitalizing light, is sometimes offered by the Spirit Guide. For others who have been particularly emotionally traumatized, or for those who have committed acts of cruelty, the soul is taken to what amounts to an intensive care unit, where it is attended to by helpful beings who renew, remodel, or revivify the soul.

- **Reuniting with the Soul Cluster**: In what amounts to a "spiritual homecoming," the soul joyfully reunites with other spirits it has incarnated with before: lovers, family members, business partners, and friends. According to Dr. Newton's research, a part of each soul's energy always remains in the spirit world, typically allowing returning souls to make contact with all the essential soul mates and comrades, even if they have reincarnated. Remember, Cayce said that soul mates are relationships in which "there is an answering of one to another . . . where they are a complement to each other . . . not [merely or necessarily] from physical attraction, but from the mental and spiritual help [they offer to each other]" (1556-2) It is important, then, to remember that the term "soul mates," as Cayce used it, refers to more than just romantic partners or spouses and can be any of our relationships, even difficult ones, in which we learn and grow spiritually from each other.

- **Meeting with the Council of Elders or Masters**: The soul then appears before a group of Higher Beings, spiritually advanced entities that help the soul to both evaluate his or her most recent life and plan the necessary karmic lessons for their next incarnation. Often, they are accompanied by their guide. These entities are compassionate and constructive, and one never feels judged or ashamed in their presence.

- **Life Selection**: At what one subject called "The Ring of Destiny," the soul looks at images of locations and potential host bodies for their next incarnation and are able to see a variety of potential karmic possibilities. While these opportunities are broad, they are not without some limitations. Beings—who may be either guides, members of the council, or others—supervise the selection, though the soul has free will to choose.

- **Embarkation**: The soul returns to the earth plane, initially streaking through veils or layers, to finally enter through the same means it left, sometimes through "a long hollow tube" or "tunnel."

In reading Dr. Newton's work, it sounded (even to me) a little far out.

Councils of Elders?

Energy showers?

Rings of Destiny?

But after I thought about it, it dawned on me that maybe these realms didn't exist, so much as they reflected a symbolic experience of something in temporal terms that we can't wrap our space-time minds around. In other words, maybe this is our way of understanding as presented by a Higher Power giving it to us through some kind of three-dimensional metaphor.

Dr. P.M.H. Atwater is one of the leading researchers in the field of near-death experiences (NDE). She actually has had several herself. She "died" three times in 1977, and wrote a book about it called . . . wait for it . . . *I Died Three Times in 1977.*[8]

Clever, huh?

When I asked her about LBL regressions, and even NDEs, and proposed that they might be completely symbolic, she readily agreed that this might be a valid way of understanding these experiences. She went on to remind me that children who have NDEs often meet spirit guides, like their grandmother, baby-sitter, or a favorite teacher on the other side *who are still alive*. It begs the question, how can they be on the other side if they are still alive? Potentially, these could be thought of as symbolic representations for the child—love in a form they can understand.

Accommodations, P.M.H. calls them. (And here I thought that was the luxurious Quality Inn that I usually get booked into when I give a presentation on the road.)

After researching Dr. Newton's work at length, I wondered if it might be possible to take groups into their life between lives. I had no idea if anyone else had ever tried it. In 2009, I was booked to lead a workshop at the international headquarters of the Association for Research and Enlightenment, or Edgar Cayce's A.R.E., located in Virginia Beach, Va., along with P.M.H. and Dannion Brinkley; a NDE experiencer and author of the best-selling *Saved by the Light*. (Dannion calls Dr. Atwater PMHWSRT. Someday soon, I am going to get my secret decoder ring in the mail from Captain Crunch, and I will find out what it all means.) I decided to attempt the regression.

I had specifically warned my hosts that this was generally done *individually* at sessions that were *at least three hours*. When someone is regressed to a past life, they at least know that they will be in a body and wearing some kind of clothes in some sort of earthly location. But between lives, what should they expect? Floating around in the universe?

I anticipated that it would be hard for them to get impressions, plus I had only an hour for the regression, not three. I must have been nuts. I briefly considered that taking over a hundred people into the *bardo* simultaneously might be pure folly.

It was.

When the regression was over, nearly ninety percent of the participants were getting impressions of their most recent incarnation, but only thirty percent got anything about their life between lives. I was devastated. I remember going out for a drink with an associate, vacillating between, "Why didn't it work?" and "What kind of fool am I to even try this?"

But . . . something about the whole thing tweaked my curiosity. I decided to rework the material somewhat and extend the induction time—the part of the regression that deepens the trance state. We need more theta waves in the noggins of the audience, a deeper state than I had taken the Virginia Beach crowd into. I changed the music and tweaked the balance between the spoken guided imagery and periods of silence. I made the regression the experiential centerpiece of a one-day workshop called *The Unseen Worlds: Past Lives, Future Lives, the Afterlife*, that explored a "map of heaven" based on mystics, near-death experiences, and current research.

First in Kansas City, and then in city after city, seventy percent, eighty percent, even ninety percent of audiences were getting glimpses of their spirit guides, soul clusters, even memories of choosing their current incarnations and karmic lessons.

And low and behold, what used to take three hours or more in an individual setting could be done in a group of a hundred or more in an hour and fifteen minutes.

It was, in a word, a *quickening*.

(I thought you might like that.)

In fairness, some people got stronger impressions than others, to be sure. But in any given workshop, I could look out and see tears streaming down the faces of many participants as they reunited with the spirits they had been with in incarnations many times before. People saw themselves planning their current life and its lessons, re-experiencing the glory of energy showers, and enjoying the limitless freedom of being without a physical body.

Stories emerged: A well-to-do gentleman who had always carried some guilt about his success remembered a life on the Trail of Tears as a mistreated Native American and remembered choosing his current incarnation of comfort as a break and a chance to use his wealth and connections to forward metaphysical growth through his philanthropy. A young woman remembered a soul agreement that she had made with her mother before incarnating in which her mother wanted to attempt the parental role, something at which, in life, her mother had failed miserably. And yet, the young woman said tearfully that she could see at a spirit level how badly she wanted to be an appropriate mother, and it became a doorway for true forgiveness. An older gentleman related how he recognized that he had *chosen* many of the pitfalls in his life at a soul level to learn specific lessons, and that he had not been a "victim" at all!

But my experiences were not to be limited to past lives and the *bardo.* On occasion, people had asked me in individual settings to "progress" them to future lifetimes. When I trained with Brian Weiss, he said that future progressions were "potential lifetimes" and were, in effect, too nebulous to pursue. That is, until he wrote a book, *Same Soul, Many Bodies,* about his work with future life *progression* in 2005. Okay, Brian, but you may have some serious karma for holding out on us on this one.

Consequently, I did work with individuals and groups in the longer format of a three-day workshop to take them into future incarnations. Often, progressions are helpful, as they show a potential "destination lifetime," if the soul continues on its present course. As you might imagine, the future lives either show the potential for how an individual might evolve into as a blessing for the world, or offer a dark harbinger of what may come, a la Ebenezer Scrooge.

While, on occasion, I still progress individuals and groups into their next incarnations, I have come to think that Brian was right in the first place: while interesting, future lives are too unreliable and inaccurate. A courageous book from the 1980s called *Mass Dreams of the Future* by Chet B. Snow progressed a number of people into their future, and there was a phenomenal amount of agreement: Many saw a bleak, post-apocalyptic future for the United States.

Hang on.

Before you go investing in overpriced gold from one of those late night infomercials, the individuals were progressed into the *1990s.* Last I checked, there was no wasteland in that decade, unless you count network TV. Long live streaming video.

Free will is still at play when we look toward future incarnations and perhaps the timeline has shifted into the future and that apocalypse is yet to come. But I believe most clients will benefit much more by looking at where they have been and what they planned for their current life to best understand their life journey and karmic connections.

If you have read other books that include past life regressions, you may have noticed that they tend to skew towards more dramatic experiences: people murdered violently in the Middle Ages, mothers and children separated from each other, the everyday horrors of subsistence living.

In my estimation, there are probably two reasons for that. First, the author is selecting exciting and dramatic cases that make for good reading and demonstrate the potential for the therapy. The stories I have shared with you so far are no exception. But second, and perhaps more importantly, the truth is, when people come for regression therapy, their higher mind often directs them to traumatic past lives, whose loud echoes spill over and impact their current incarnation. Though intense, these sessions usually offer a bounty of healing.

But on occasion, someone remembers a tranquil life that still contains the seed for a profound shift.

*   *   *

JOY IN BALI HAI

Her actual Japanese name was something I couldn't pronounce. But all of her American friends just called her Joy. Joy, like many people after discovering that I am a past-life regression therapist, came to me for what I jokingly call "one-stop shopping." In other words, an individual is curious about whom they were in a past life, and they schedule an extended three- or four-hour session. I do an abbreviated history, brief them on past-life regression, and then they spend ninety minutes to two hours in hypnosis exploring a past life. Then we usually have fifteen or twenty minutes at the end of the session to help integrate the material and make connections. As Edgar Cayce pointed out, " . . . to find that you only lived, died, and were buried under the cherry tree . . . [in another life] does not make thee one whit a better neighbor, citizen, mother, or father . . . " (5753-2); it is what you learn from the experience. This way, the memory is not simply a magical mystery tour, but it's something useful: a quickening.

Her husband Bill, a lanky Caucasian man with a neatly trimmed beard and a shy, infectious smile, had escorted her to my office. The three of us talked briefly in the lobby. Bill seemed quite enamored of Joy, maybe even a bit love-struck, but she seemed to take every opportunity to cut him off at the knees, making sarcastic comments and periodically rolling her eyes at his remarks. It was a bit uncomfortable to watch. I had to remind myself that no one had hired me to do couples therapy in my waiting room; Jan was here for a past-life regression.

We stepped into my office and began our work. Outwardly, Joy was a pleasant young lady with a gracious smile, perfect skin, and long black hair. On a Visa, she had trained to be a physical therapist in the United States and had met Bill and gotten engaged. They had only been married a year.

As I got to know her better, I came to understand that she hadn't exactly "fallen" for her husband. In describing her choice to marry Bill, she would say things like "he is a good match for me" or "we will parent well together," but there was none of the romantic affectations that I hear from many of my young female clients. Joy seemed to see marriage almost like a business partnership, and Bill brought to the table what she needed. But I consciously stepped back from my assumptions about Joy. I knew there was more to learn.

Her family history was painful, if not remarkably so. She said both her culture and her father had extreme expectations of her. There was no question, she said, but that she would be successful in business, marry, and have children. For better or worse, her life (to date) was not about her individual desires, passions, or even her needs. She was to play her proper role in her family and society. I did not have to scratch the surface very deeply to discover a core of bitterness and resentment, despite a gracious veneer.

Joy was a good hypnotic subject, and within about thirty minutes she found herself in a tribal lifetime. We never did find out exactly what year or what country she was living in. But it kind of makes sense. Just imagine, it is one thousand years ago, and you are climbing in some icy mountains bundled up in four animal skins tied with cords. If you are completely inside that experience, you don't know whether you're in Norway, Sweden, Greenland, or Antarctica. What you know is that you are cold and hungry.

"Don't worry too much about the minor details," I typically tell my clients. "It's a lot more important that we spend the time exploring the traumas and joys of the lifetime than trying to determine whether you were eating dinner with utensils or your hands."

But Joy knew she was in a tropical setting. It was idyllic with palm trees, white sand, and gentle breezes. As she described it, I could almost hear *Bali Hai* playing in the background. The weather was usually warm with the highs and lows of the seasons being very tolerable. Her first memory was of being a young girl, and being matched by her family with her husband, who could not have been more than twenty, while she was about twelve. She was pleased by the choice that her family and tribal elders had made for her and seemed genuinely attracted to her husband.

The next scene we visited was several years later. Now it was summer, and her nomadic tribe had migrated to higher altitudes where the weather was more comfortable and food more plentiful. She was still "married" to her husband. She had several children, and even though she had lost a child to illness, she had adjusted and life was happy. She took pleasures in simple day–to–day experiences: watching her children play, eating simple fresh meals, seeing the smile on her husband's face. Finally, she found herself back on the beach again in what amounted to some kind of palm shack. She was much older now and had been ill and was getting ready to die. But she didn't seem to be the least bit upset by this.

"I am old," she told me, "and it is my time. It is the way of things. My children are happy, and I have been a good wife and mother. I have nothing to regret."

She told me that her passing was peaceful with very little pain. Surrounded by family and friends, her soul simply lifted gently out of her body and floated upwards.

After I brought Joy out of hypnosis and into formal waking consciousness, we talked about her experience.

"Why do you think you went to that particular lifetime?" I queried.

She frowned and thought for a moment. "I don't know . . . " she said, almost apologetically, "I was happy. Things were easy, it was very pleasant. Maybe not exciting, but not really uncomfortable either."

"Joy," I said, curiously, "what makes you happy now?" She looked at me like I was from Mars. "What makes you happy?" I repeated.

"Honestly," she said, "I don't think about it most of the time. But I will tell you what I don't like. I'm tired of being pushed around. I don't like being told what to do, but nobody ever gives me any choice. It's never about what I want. It's always about what they want. But it doesn't matter . . . because I just don't matter," she said flatly.

I couldn't help but notice that Joy didn't relate this story with any sadness. Instead, she remained stiff and resolute, obviously angry, but resigned to her fate.

"But you were happy then in that lifetime. What was that like?" I asked.

As she began to think about her life in the tropics, her icy stare slowly melted. She warmed, and I saw a flash of innocence. *Maybe*, I thought to myself, *this is the aspect of Joy that Bill fell in love with.* She wore a gentle smile.

"I was so happy" she said. "It was very strange. I've read about tribal existence being difficult, but for us, life wasn't typically a terrible struggle. We were surrounded by people we knew and everyone supported each other. There were seasonal festivals and tribal customs. We always had plenty to eat, and we took joy in nature."

As she discussed the experience, she had a dreamy, gentle look on her face. It was as though a soft light had fallen on her countenance.

"How would your life be different if you took the same attitude you had in that lifetime into this life?"

It was if a switch was suddenly flipped, and she became someone else.

"They are completely different," she said curtly, waving her hand dismissively.

"Joy, do you ever stop to savor and appreciate how much Bill loves you? Do you ever take time to enjoy the Texas Hill country and the lakes around us?" I asked earnestly.

"I don't have time for that." she said, stone-faced.

"Maybe you could make time for that. Maybe the past–life memory came to remind you that life doesn't always have to be a struggle *against* something—your father and his expectations . . . or Bill," I remarked.

"Well," she said abruptly gathering up her purse and her belongings, "It was certainly an interesting experience. I have a lot to think about," she commented with a cool smile. I glanced at my watch. We still had another twenty minutes in the session.

She was clicking back into gracious mode. I had touched on a truth that was, at least for now, too uncomfortable to explore. Were her eyes moist or was I just imagining it, wanting, hoping that she could get the healing she came for?

She left my office without saying goodbye.

There was more that I wanted to discuss with Joy. I wondered if the reason why she thought of marriage as a "package deal" had some-thing to do with her arranged marriage in the tribal lifetime. And what of her feeling constricted by her father's vision for her life? In aboriginal cultures, specific roles were fixed, often even rigid, but they allowed for the very *survival* of the tribe. In her tropical lifetime, it may have served her and the tribe very well to play within the subscribed roles of mother and gatherer. But in her current life, she could make her own choices without threatening the survival of her parents who lived in another country.

I suspected that unless Joy could find at least some areas in her life where she could step outside of her parents' expectations, she might continue her life as a bitter victim and project her experience with her father onto Bill. Joy had said that in her current life, she didn't know what brought her happiness, but instead was busy fighting against what *didn't* make her happy, real or imagined. Battling against a life you *don't* want is different from moving towards a life you *do* want. I believe it was no accident that Joy went to the tropical lifetime so she could remember what it was like to be happy in the moment.

I heard through other clients that Joy and Bill went on to have a delightful precocious daughter, only to acrimoniously divorce a few years later as she became more and more critical of Bill and both of them became unhappy. I couldn't help but wonder if she had taken a bit more time to explore what she had learned in her past life if that might have been avoided.

Joy's story can be a reminder to all of us that when a quickening invites us to take the next step on our spiritual journey, we cannot simply hear the call, we must answer the invitation.

5

Vanishing Trauma:
The Magic of EMDR

"Among those who already have a spiritual connection, we see time and time again that with EMDR there is a letting go, a softening and a strengthening of that spiritual connection, allowing for peace to emerge. For those that have never thought in spiritual terms, we often see this happening as well. It is actually a hallmark of EMDR therapy when those spiritual connections happen."

Francine Shapiro,
Developer of Eye Movement Desensitization
and Reprocessing Therapy (EMDR)

In this chapter, I want to share some profound breakthroughs for my clients as I worked with them using Eye Movement Desensitization and Reprocessing (EMDR). Yeah, I know, it's a real mouthful. The first three hours of the training is learning how to say it aloud.

Some of you may be saying, okay, I understand how shifting consciousness so that I might tune in more readily to the Divine might help me "leap ahead" on my spiritual journey. And, of course, if I understand my past lives and my karma, that is going to give me a lot of clarity and direction on the mystical path. But, now you are diverting into therapy. What does one's psychological journey have to do with the spiritual journey?

My answer is simply this: Everything.

When clients enter into therapy, it is because they have discovered that something isn't working in their lives. Pain is their teacher. However dimly, something begins to break through their unconscious denial.

None of my relationships work . . . maybe it's me.

How many more jobs can I lose . . . maybe I am drinking too much.

Everyone seems to love me, but I feel like I am worthless . . . maybe I don't see the good in myself.

Arguably, nearly everything that brings individuals into counseling is rooted in the individual's inability to express themselves as the spark of God that they are, although few would categorize their issues as such. Their light, their creativity, their authenticity has somehow become stifled. Something blocks their ability to love themselves and others. And if our spiritual journey is to learn to love our neighbors as we love ourselves, then this is an inability that we really must remedy.

If we agree to the major mystical tenet that we are a part of the Infinite, then everything that blocks the expression of underlying unity is a barrier that must be removed to continue forward. Dr. Brian Weiss explains it this way: If you find a Coleman lantern that is encrusted with mud and light it, you still can't see its radiance. The problem is not that there isn't enough luminescence; the problem is the mud on the glass. Removing that mud then allows the light to shine.

What is that mud? The ego, a false identity, which blocks our awareness of our connection to the Divine. We are too busy being ashamed or self-important to see ourselves as a Radiant Light of God. So, the spiritual journey is one of undoing, by increments, those impediments (self-condemnation or self-glorification) that lead to a self-delusion.

As *A Course in Miracles* directly states in its introduction, "This course does not aim at teaching the meaning of love, for that is beyond what can be taught. It does aim, however, at *removing the blocks to the awareness of love's presence* which is your natural inheritance." (italics mine.) The *Course* boldly suggests that there are ultimately only two thought systems: love and fear. Most of us are ruled by fear: fear that we are not good enough, fear of failure, fear of abandonment, fear of condemnation, fear of punishment, and of course, fear of death. All of us, in our own ways, do a lot of bizarre things to cope with that terror: working ourselves to death, shopping, eating, and staying busy or numb—not to mention the usual suspects: sex, drugs, and alcohol. (I mean, not *you*; you are a spiritually enlightened being, but, the person you live with.)

Our fear then blocks the expression of love, which is our natural inheritance. These fears go way beyond clinical phobias. A level of alertness and concern is certainly a gift on a busy highway or a walk near a treacherous cliff. But many of us click into panic mode or anxiety many times each day, overstressing ourselves, cratering our immune systems, collapsing into shame or lashing out in anger, all in an attempt to cope with that fear. So, letting go of fear, clearing out the mud from the lantern, is a lifetime journey. Maybe many lifetimes!

Jesus said that "perfect love casts out all fear." Our journey is not one of pulling in, but casting out. Our journey is not one of doing, but undoing. If our essence is love, it is the removal of the fear that blocks it that is the heart of the spiritual journey. Don't believe me? What if I told you just this: You are perfect love.

Now, watch your thoughts.

All your resistance came up! *No, I am not; I am not very loving at all!* You probably thought. Or, *Yeah, I'm loving, but hardly perfect loving. My Grammy, she was perfect love, not me!* Or even, *Gregg, you obviously didn't see me in traffic today!*

Now, I will be the first to tell you that I cannot always live my life as the *expression* of that Perfect Love. And you don't always either, especially when you get around your in-laws. And that is because fear takes over. It's the mud on the lantern. So the spiritual journey is removing the mud. Again, not a doing, but an undoing!

Many people who have had mystical experiences (including near-death experiences) speak of a moment of recognition that literally *there is nothing to fear*. They were in the presence of a Perfect Love or Perfect Peace. They returned from their peak experiences remembering this truth, however imperfectly, and it made them more fearless and, therefore, more loving in their day-to-day lives. Hence, we should put a premium on moments of transcendence or mystical revelation that "cannot be taught," but can be *known* through experience. This is the heart of Zen.

This is a hard concept for Westerners who put an emphasis on the intellect. But there are limits to what the scientific method can measure. No one has ever "seen" a love, as one of my professors at Texas State University pointed out. We don't know how many gallons a love is, or how wide or how tall love is, or how much it weighs. We can, and should, study the *effects* of love, using the intellect. But for those of us who have experienced a powerful love, romantic or platonic (and I certainly hope that includes you, Dear Reader), know it can be life-changing. It is an experience, but its wisdom cannot be taught or explained. Even poetry and music do not try to explain the truth so much as catalyze an experience of truth. But again, these artistic endeavors are not of the intellect. Not surprisingly, much of this book looks at igniting those kinds of transcendent experiences that are beyond learning.

So love has its place as an agent of change and not merely some sort of Cosmic Big Love. The psychologist Erich Fromm believed that his patients began to heal as they discovered that he loved them. Similarly, the influential psychologist Carl Rogers was absolutely clear that connection to the client was an integral part of therapy, though he was shrewd enough to call it "unconditional positive regard" and not "love." (Okay, Carl, whatever you say, but if it walks like a duck . . .) This positive regard was seen by Rogers as a necessary component of the healing process. Of course, most therapists' "unconditional positive regard" for their clients may not be the perfect love that casts out all fear—but they are often caring enough to create a fertile space for healing. And of course, their training—that is to say *how* they express that love—certainly comes into play.

Hearing this information from titans of psychology may sound nice, but can the importance of love as an agent of change be supported empirically? Over forty years ago, a meta-analysis of 375 studies at the University of Colorado explored the question of what kind of therapeutic approach was most effective.[11] The answer?

Broadly speaking, all of them!

The study suggests that after crunching the numbers prodigiously in a statistical review of the research, individuals in therapy—any kind of therapy—improved by seventy-five percent more than those who went untreated. (Please tell that to your father-in-law who says things like "counseling is a waste of time" and "real men don't do couch.") Again, the authors found no statistically significant differences in the outcomes, regardless of the *kind* of therapy that was being practiced. To be clear, that doesn't mean that you, personally, might not respond better to one approach than another. The authors of that study later concluded that the importance of a good relationship with the therapist—that would include trust, confidence, and mutual regard for each other—is likely the key component for healing, and not necessarily technique.

Dr. Irvin Yalom, emeritus professor of psychiatry at Stanford, is the man who (literally) wrote the book on group therapy. His tome *The Theory and Practice of Group Psychotherapy* is regarded as the seminal text on the subject. Yalom famously told his students that there were three things that they had to remember about therapy: "It's the relationship that heals, it's the relationship that heals, it's the relationship that heals."

Even if you have never been to therapy, you could probably tell me dozens of stories of people who loved you and influenced you. They believed in you, and their love made you want to be a better person. Or, perhaps, they loved you *and* mentored you, creating a space of possibility for you to step into.

My mother, the late Dr. Betty Unterberger, was the first female full professor at Texas A&M University and a winner of the Distinguished Teaching Award, an honor proffered by students at the University. I met a number of her pupils, all of whom told me basically the same thing: "She was one of the toughest teachers I ever had and one of my favorites. She really cared about us." Because the students knew she loved them and expected the best from them, they worked their butts off for her.

So, when someone is "working through" their issues with their parent and their family of origin, you may think of that as counseling, and it is—but it's really about forgiveness, a vital skill on our spiritual evolution. When someone feels broken and unwanted due to sexual abuse, and they discover themselves as worthy, they are really rediscovering themselves as valuable and seeing themselves the way God sees them. When someone lets go of a lifelong phobia, they are "casting out fear" and gaining a sense of peace—their birthright as a child of the Universe.

The psychological journey is one of removing that fear so as to know ourselves and others more deeply as the natural radiance that we are at the core of our being. And so is the spiritual journey! Thus, although therapy is not a requirement for the spiritual journey, it has the potential to be an extremely powerful ally. And, as you will read onward, you will see how spirituality can spontaneously and overtly intertwine with therapy—often when it is least expected.

* * *

NEEDLES IN THE HAYSTACK

Vanessa was an executive secretary to the president of a major corporation. Her job required a big toolbox: not only the usual secretarial skills and interaction with high-level employees and clients, but also the ability to run interference for her boss, planning, organizing, and much more. Her marriage was strong, life was good, and she was in control. But a recent trip to the doctor brought her bad news. Her doctor thought that she might have cancer and said further tests were necessary. Blood tests. But, strangely, it wasn't the cancer that scared Vanessa.

It was the tests.

As far back as she could remember, needles terrified her. Now, her life was threatened by disease, and perhaps the only way she could save herself was to have some blood drawn in order to have tests run. But she knew how it would go.

On the way to the doctor, she would begin to panic. Then, the waiting, the waiting, the seemingly interminable waiting of the waiting room. The nurse would finally call her name, and her stomach would pitch, and she would go back to the tiny closet called an examination room. And then she would see the needle and the syringe. Her heart would pound, her hands would sweat, the room would spin, and Vanessa would become faint. *I am a grown woman, what's wrong with me?*

It was embarrassing. No, worse than that, it was humiliating. She avoided doctors at all costs, but this time the cost might be her life.

Vanessa was a smart and shrewd businesswoman who was more than just "a little scared of a little needle." The fear was overwhelming. She briefly considered not going for the tests, but then thought better of it. Firmly, in her executive mode, Vanessa had called me, explained just the facts, and then interviewed me: Could I help her out? Exactly how many sessions would it take? How much would it cost? And, oh, by the way, the blood tests were next Wednesday. *Wonderful,* I thought to myself, *I have a whole week to somehow cure a twenty-year phobia.*

Thanks a lot, I thought to myself. *Would you like a side of world peace with that?*

I always try to be realistic with clients. Yes, I told her, many of the techniques I use seem to be able to accelerate healing, but a cure in a week? I couldn't promise that, but I was hopeful that we could desensitize her phobia, at least to some degree, and make the whole experience more tolerable for her.

"Maybe we can get it to the point where it's not so frightening, so you can have the test done, even if you have to white knuckle your way through them. After all, Vanessa, it could be your life at stake."

Phobias are usually rooted in traumatic life experiences. Someone gets locked repeatedly in the closet as a child by an abusive parent and this induces a long-term fear of the dark or enclosed spaces, even ones that aren't really dangerous. "The cat, having sat upon a hot stove lid, will not sit upon a hot stove lid again," Mark Twain observed, "but he won't sit upon a cold stove lid, either." I set up an initial session that lasted about an hour and then we scheduled two additional two-hour sessions before her appointment with the doctor. I wondered if I were up for the challenge. I had five clinical hours to somehow undo a couple of decades of fear.

I used the therapeutic modality called EMDR. Dr. Francine Shapiro, who developed EMDR, noticed that when someone thought about something distressing, and then moved their eyes rapidly back and forth, there was a natural desensitizing effect—the person felt somewhat calmer. So, she combined a lot of cutting-edge thinking about trauma with these eye movements and discovered that she could turn down the volume of the panic-button fear response and reprocess the way the brain thinks about a traumatic trigger. And, in relatively short order. Or, to borrow Mark Twain's idea, the cat can learn that it can sit on a cold stove and be safe, but still has enough sense to stay out of the kitchen when Estella is cooking tortillas.

(And let me say, right now, do not attempt this at home, kids. There is much more to the therapy than eye movements. We'll talk about what you can do at home in later chapters.)

Roughly speaking, one theory suggests that these eye movements are associated with the same rapid eye movements, or REM, that take place while we sleep (not to be confused with the band or the town in Hungary). It seems that every night, our meat computers sort through the stack of mail of happenings from our day. Our brains toss out the memories that don't seem relevant (the "you may already be a winner" experiences) and hang on to the salient stuff (hey, I didn't use my blinker at the stoplight today and nearly got T-boned by that eighteen-wheeler . . . don't wanna forget that) that are useful, especially for survival. Something about the eyes moving back and forth underneath our eyelids may help us process memory, rhythmically firing the right and left hemispheres of the brain to create a balance between the emotional and intellectual parts. So, someone traumatized in a car wreck with a red Corvette could emotionally and intellectually make the distinction between the car that hit them and a red sports car in the parking lot. They could look right at it and not get panicked.

As Dr. Robert Stickgold points out, using some more clinically appropriate jargon, "We believe that EMDR induces a fundamental change in brain circuitry similar to what happens in REM sleep—that allows the person undergoing treatment to more effectively process and incorporate traumatic memories into general association networks in the brain. This helps the individual integrate and understand the memories within the larger context of his or her life experience."[12]

I kind of like my explanation of my meat computer going through junk mail in my mind and deleting the superfluous crap, but I guess that kind of talk wouldn't exactly wash at a professional convention, which is why Dr. Stickgold is a cognitive neuroscientist at Harvard and the leading researcher in his field and I am just a lowly therapist, a pawn in the game of life, as the sage Mongo once said.

So, like the man who fell off the Empire State Building said, "I've got to get back to my story."

In my initial meeting with Vanessa, we went over her history, her symptoms, and her concerns. Frankly, she explained, she was anything but convinced that I could make a difference, but I had come highly recommended. As we talked, I saw how, in brief moments, she would drop her professional veneer. I got a glimpse of a real live human being with fears and joys. But it was clear that this was uncomfortable for her. I explained that she might have to feel some of the uncomfortable feelings associated with her phobia, but I would do my best to keep these emotions from being overwhelming.

Using EMDR to desensitize trauma does not mean that we can avoid painful memories associated with phobias or PTSD. But it does mean that we don't have to fight them for a lifetime. In EMDR, people face them, feel them, and process through them *in truncated fashion*, speeding to the day when they can talk about an earlier trauma like it was yesterday's lunch.

Imagine being able to say aloud to someone, "That was the day my mother died in a car wreck" or "That was the day my step-father raped me" and it carried all the emotional charge of, "Yesterday, I had a cheeseburger," but without dissociating, numbing out, or repressing your feelings. You can see the appeal of EMDR. You can leave the past in the past. You can also see why there might be resistance—from both clients and the therapeutic community, even after twenty-five years of clinical use—to this amazing therapy. It just seems too good to be true.

In our next session, Vanessa and I agreed to focus on her most recent bout of panic brought on by hypodermic needles. I asked her to close her eyes, focus on the memory and the feelings of that day, and describe in detail how it felt in her body. Then I introduced eye movements by asking her to follow my hand as I passed it before her eyes, back and forth, almost like a windshield wiper. As the session progressed, she agitatedly remembered her encounter with the nurses. The panic and tears weren't the worst of it—it was the insensitivity of the nurses and the shame she felt at "being a grown woman, acting like a baby." It was a struggle to act as if everything was "okay," when it had taken everything in her not to run screaming from the room.

As it was, she remembered swooning in the office, and the nurse attending to her while the ceiling spun in circles. No doubt if people at her office had seen her—the boss' confident, strong, right arm—they would have hardly recognized her. But within just a few minutes, the eye movements stimulated the brain to sort through what was relevant. Initially, I had asked her how disturbing the image of the needles were on a scale of zero to ten. She said an "eight." But now, her body, while still tense, was much better, and she reported a distress level of only "four." She spontaneously remembered other doctor visits that were less stressful, filled with kind and sympathetic nurses. These visits were not without discomfort, but Vanessa realized that truly not *all* of her needle encounters had been overwhelming.

By the end of the first EMDR session, she could focus on the image of needles in her mind and her distress level maintained at about a "four."

"I still don't want to go to the doctor," she said adamantly, sounding as though she expected I might hold her at gunpoint.

"That's okay. This is only one session. But notice how the numbers have begun to come down. You are, right now, in effect, half as uncomfortable with seeing the doctor as when you walked in."

"I know," she said grimly, not really believing it herself. "But there is something deeper, something really frightening in there." I sent her home with some self-soothing techniques and a promise to call me if things got overwhelming. But at her next session, Vanessa reported that while she felt a bit stirred-up over the weekend, it "wasn't a big deal."

Now, I had only a two-hour session to make things tolerable for Vanessa. As we did EMDR, other memories came: a sidewalk accident on a bike, early trips to the dentist. When EMDR is at work, it's almost as though the mind is going through a fat mental file of traumas that have become symbolically linked. In EMDR, these individual experiences are called memory nodes that composite into a larger amalgam. Dr. Stanislav Grof calls these knotted-upon-knotted traumatic clusters a "COEX," short for systems of COndensed EXperience.[13] The mind emotionally reviews a memory in a shorthand manner, only to go on to the next item.

Sometimes these linkages can be quite odd. In a training video, I saw a woman who was processing the terror of an earthquake, and then within a few minutes she was flashing on a memory of getting served with divorce papers. She teared up, and her eyes got wide with shock. "It was like the ground came out from beneath my feet that day." Her mind had linked the (literal) earthquake with the shock of the divorce (symbolic).

One of my clients was processing a memory of almost drowning in a shallow pool of water as a child when he was rescued by his sister.

Suddenly, as he watched my fingers, he found himself thinking of a television show in which the leading character's mother put out a hit on her own son.

"Why am I thinking about this?" queried my client. "This must be resistance. I think I am trying to avoid the trauma."

"Maybe not," I said supportively, "Keep following my fingers."

Memories of other episodes of the show followed until he suddenly put it together when another memory from his childhood came.

"Oh, my God! When I came home from almost drowning that day, my mother was drunk, and all she did was complain about the mud on my clothes. And she hadn't been there to save me. I think, I believed as a child that this must mean she wanted me dead, just like the guy on the show!"

Of course, in reality his mom did not want him to die, but at the time, that was his conclusion. And much of the client's life had been lived in a way that had certainly tempted fate and taken him close to what he believed was his mother's wish. It was very important to realize this unconscious interpretation and to dispel and desensitize the experience to see that, literally, *it was okay to be alive.*

Similarly, Vanessa followed out a number of memory nodes all associated, however tangentially, with her needle phobia. But then she got extremely quiet. I felt like we were hitting pay dirt.

"I am with my mom in the hospital," she said haltingly. "I'm just a little girl. They haven't let me visit her much. I don't really understand what is going on. A lot of big people are going in and out of the room, and I have to be quiet. I feel like I am in the way." Vanessa's breathing became more labored.

"A nurse just came into the room." It dawned on me that Vanessa was talking in present tense, as though the event was happening now. "My mother is very still. There are tubes and machines everywhere. Beeping noises. The nurse gets out a syringe. It seems to me the needle is huge. She is sticking my mother with the needle; I can see her wince and hear her moan. She doesn't like it. I don't understand. I thought nurses were supposed to help!" Vanessa began to cry, her face taking on the expression of a very young child. Even the sound of her sobbing was that of a young girl.

"I am so sorry. You are really scared. You are worried about Mommy,"

I said quietly, addressing the child that was energetically present in the room.

She nodded her head vigorously, the corners of her mouth turned down violently. Suddenly her face screwed up. Vanessa was puzzled. She began breathing in and out, very quickly. "But they are not giving her medicine! They are *taking* something from her. They are stealing her blood in the glass jar!" She could see the syringe in her mind's eye, drawing back, the bright red color filling the vial, the same bright red she had seen on the street when she fell off her bike and it hurt so much.

"Why are they stealing her blood?" she said in a panicked voice.

She had shrieked aloud in the room, but an adult had told her to be quiet, shushing her, pulling her back from the bed, back away from Mommy. She was helpless to stop the awful nurse who was hurting and stealing from Mommy.

Five minutes later, her mother was dead. It was the last time Vanessa saw her alive and the last thing she saw was the needle. The needle had killed Mommy, and it would kill her, and she would never, ever forget.

Initially, Vanessa reacted, her body going into a freeze response, then over the course of minutes and several sets of eye movements, she alternately cried and gasped. Some trauma theorist believe that when clients re-encounter the trauma that they are not being re-traumatized at all but merely feeling and releasing energy and emotion that has been locked up in their psyche by the freeze response. The energy is then released, and if the event is reprocessed, the amygdalae resets itself. Within minutes, Vanessa was much calmer and regaining her composure. Her breathing became less labored. She opened her eyes and look at me with surprise, as though suddenly rediscovering me in the room.

"Well . . . " her professional persona stepping back in to take over. "I have made quite a mess here, haven't I?" she commented, wiping her cheeks and her eyes.

"I used to charge by the Kleenex," I said with a wry smile, "but nobody could afford me, so I went with a flat hourly rate."

Her face brightened with a warm and genuine smile. It was a mixture of relief and gratitude. We talked for a bit, and I grounded her.

Then I asked her to once again focus on the needles. I asked her to tune into her body, to watch her emotions and her thoughts, and tell me what she noticed.

"It's gone." Her eyes popped open. She looked agitated. I knew what was coming next, and I took a deep breath. "It's gone, Gregg. But it can't be. I've had this for years, and it's gone, and it can't be!" she said flatly. "I don't believe it," she said adamantly with a subtle toss of her head. It was almost as though she was irritated with me. "It doesn't bother me at all, and that can't be."

I remember a fellow therapist telling me a story of a patient who was afraid of flying. He learned all about EMDR from his therapist and told him, "I am completely convinced that EMDR will cure my phobia. But then I will get on a plane, and it will crash, and I will die, so I have decided not to get treatment."

Similarly, I imagined that Vanessa had grown used to this way of being and was rooted in the belief that it would never go away. So, if it "appeared" to go away, then it must be a deception, and I was a deceiver, and I should be treated with great suspicion, which was what I was seeing on Vanessa's face: distrust. Somehow, I was trying to con her out of her loyal ally that would keep her safe from death, and I was the enemy. Not that any of this was conscious for Vanessa. I felt sure she experienced all of this as simply a reaction, a feeling that something was wrong and that if she gave up this strategy then she would be in danger. And I genuinely appreciated her honesty. This was not a setback or a permanent obstacle. It just demonstrated where I needed to work.

So that fear became the next thing we would desensitize. "I understand, Vanessa," I responded very quietly.

"It just seems impossible. How could this happen? How could this just 'go away'?" She nodded resolutely, momentarily "forgetting" that this was the relief that she had prayed for in therapy, and that she was upset that she had achieved it.

"On a scale from 'one' to 'seven,' where 'one' is completely false and 'seven' is completely true, how true does this statement feel, 'I can be okay with needles.'"

"I want to say a 'five,' but I don't trust it. I will probably go in on Wednesday for the tests and freak out."

"Okay, Vanessa, imagine going in for the tests, make it as real as possible and notice what you feel."

We did about ten minutes of EMDR, and her belief that she could be largely unafraid strengthened.

"Gosh, it really doesn't bother me that much. Could this be true?"

"I don't know," I said coyly. "Could it?"

"It feels true, I just don't know if I believe it, but I guess I do." Vanessa opened her eyes and smiled at me. "But I am still holding back judgment until I go to the actual doctor!" She was giggling now; this was more of a swipe at me than disbelief. She didn't want to be fooled.

"Ask me how I feel when I get blood drawn," I said.

"Well, wait a minute . . . you have a phobia, too?" She asked.

"No," I told her, chuckling, "but ask me."

"Okay," she said, doing her best therapist imitation and stroking her chin. "How *do* you feel when you get blood drawn?"

"I don't much care for it. My anxiety level goes up, not to a ten, but maybe a 'two' or a 'three.' It's unpleasant, and sometimes they don't get a vein on the first stab. Not fun," I said matter-of-factly.

She smiled. "Okay, I get it. A 'two' or 'three' is to be expected. That's what normal folks whose Mommas didn't die after a blood test would feel."

I nodded. The fact that she could joke about this demonstrated how much we had desensitized and reprocessed it.

"That's right. You should expect a little anxiety. Welcome to Life. But the carousel probably won't start, and your heart will stay in your chest, and you will be able to breathe. Just remember to breathe, okay Vanessa?"

"Okay," she said with genuine warmth.

I never saw Vanessa again after that, but not because she died. (This one has a happy ending. I bet you knew that.) Vanessa did have some very mild anxiety, mostly leading up to her doctor's appointment. But the room didn't take her for a spin, and it was no big deal, just the way she had seen it in her mind's eye when we rehearsed it. Vanessa got her tests, which came back clean. I talked to her briefly on the phone after her appointment and later when she was cleared of any diagnosis.

Now, when Vanessa needs to go to the doctor, she can go without overwhelming fear.

And she lived healthily ever after. The End.

*   *   *

So what happens when we experience trauma? Let's imagine for a moment that you served in a war. You've seen some mortar shells go off and watched your best buddy die right before your eyes. The billions of neurons in your brain go to work to make sure that you don't forget the experience. The brain says, *HELLO! This experience is important! This is a matter of life and death: BOOM equals death, and death is very bad!*

The brain has two hemispheres. Roughly speaking, the right hemisphere is the emotional, creative part of the brain, and the left hemisphere is the list-making, linear, CPA brain. Generally, both hemispheres have a conversation with each other. Now, I've never been inside of your brain, but in my brain the dialog goes something like this:

Emotional part of the brain: I sure would like to eat that whole bag of jelly doughnuts!

Linear part of the brain: How many calories do you think are involved with that? Lots!

Emotional part of the brain: Who cares? They are all gooey and tasty and sugary! YUM!

Linear part of the brain: You are out of control; you stop that right now!

Eventually the emotional part of the brain negotiates a deal and gets a partial win, and I find myself compromising and eating one jelly donut.

It's almost like the little angel and the little devil on your shoulder, just as they portray them in movies, only it's not that one part is good and one part is bad. They're just different ways of thinking about life. My emotions aren't very helpful when it comes to balancing my checkbook, and my linear brain's not very good at explaining why I love somebody. So, optimally, the two parts of the brain work in concert, in so-called *whole-brain thinking.*

However, when a life-threatening situation happens—like a mortar shell going off on the battlefield—the brain sometimes creates a shortcut, sort of an emergency plan, to deal with a specific threat. This is not so different from the shortcut that is on your computer or iPad, when you have an icon on your homepage that you can click and go right to a program or a document. When you're exposed to danger, real or imagined, your amygdalae, the little almond shaped organs in the center of the brain, get triggered by the right hemisphere. This is the seat of the so-called fight-or-flight response. Recognizing imminent danger, the body secretes stress hormones, such as cortisol and nore-pinephrine. These neurotransmitters gear the body for danger, increasing the heart rate, flooding the bloodstream with glucose (which fuels the body), and surging blood to the muscles of the skeleton. These hormones also direct additional oxygen to the brain to make sure we can focus our attention and think on the fly.

In the extreme, the speech centers of the brain all but shut down to allow for more glucose and oxygen for other parts of the body. Have you ever been so scared you found yourself tongue-tied and speechless? Fortunately, you don't need to say much more than "ARRRRRGH!" when running from machine gun fire. You may even . . . how can I say it diplomatically? *Secrete* bodily fluids, vacating the bladder and bowels. It's all about survival. You can run faster if you aren't carrying a load of . . . stuff. (Yes, it's not just an expression; you really can have it *scared* out of you.)

If you have ever been about to give a speech or presentation in front of a group and had to go to the bathroom three or four times, you know exactly what I am talking about. Maybe you have seen the Quentin Tarantino movies where someone at gunpoint wets themselves. They aren't wimps; their amygdala is triggered. It says, "Just dump the ballast and the blimp can go higher." So, in the face of trauma, your blood is up, your mind is focused, and your muscles are coiled like a snake about to strike.

You are ready for action, baby.

Bring it, says the amygdalae.

The body stands prepared, and the amygdalae, the emergency officers of the brain, offer some immediate options.

FIGHT: "There's gonna be a dustup," as we say in Texas. For those of you north of the Mason-Dixon Line, that means a fight. In the presence of the exploding mortar shells, you rush toward the danger, picking up a flame thrower and a grenade launcher, screaming—a la Sylvester Stallone—something intelligent like, "Arrrrgh!" (because your speech centers are offline), and firing at the enemy. Or, in slow motion, guns blazing from both fists, you heroically charge toward the bad guys.

But probably only if you are a Medal of Honor winner or a movie star in last summer's action flick.

More likely it's . . .

FLIGHT: This is the *feet-don't-fail-me-now* strategy, the "He who fights and runs away, lives to fight another day" approach. Get the hell outta Dodge, and I don't mean maybe.

Dr. Walter Bradford Cannon coined the phrase "fight or flight" in 1932, but the euphemism misses a third and final option of the amygdalae, which is . . .

FREEZE: This is the, "I will stand completely still and maybe the T-Rex won't eat me" moment from *Jurassic Park*. This is the proverbial deer in the headlights. This is a four-year-old child who senses their violent, angry, drunken father is just waiting to knock them into next Wednesday for the slightest thing. So they stand there, eyes wide, feet frozen, knowing that if they don't move or say anything, they just might survive it. If the predator can't see the prey . . . or isn't provoked by it . . . maybe he won't kill it.

Something physically changes in the brain when this happens. The right hemisphere "hardwires" the experience to the amygdalae—after all, this is about survival—and now any time a mortar shell goes off, the body goes on hyper-alert. And well it should. On the battlefield, there's no time for leisurely conversation between the linear left brain and the emotional right brain.

Imagine an explosion in combat. "Say . . . " the analytical left brain wants to murmur, "maybe we should assess this loud noise, think it through." The left brain slowly scratches its chin thoughtfully. (Okay, maybe its temporal lobe.) "Are you *sure* it's not a flashbulb going off, or lightning or something?" The left brain muses. "Maybe we should take a moment and not act rashly," it says, sounding a bit like Thurston Howell III. And so you light up your pipe and put the kettle on, to ponder over whether you should run from the incoming shells like a CPA pouring over taxes.

Of course not. The amygdalae grabs the reins, hijacking the central nervous system before the left brain can even light its pipe or the kettle whistles, and you are fighting or flighting or freezing.

The organism is now re-wired for survival and ANY loud flash and sound will be attended to as though it is a life-or-death circumstance. This works great on the battlefield or if you are growing up in a home where Mom or Dad can get "set off" into a rage at any time. Of course, the more often we are triggered into a traumatic response, the more often we are triggered into a traumatic response. The psychobabble term for this actuation of neural networks is *long-term potentiation* and it refers to the repeated synchronous firings of neurons that literally strengthen their abilities to chemically communicate with each other. What was once an old dirt road becomes a six-lane superhighway of urgent neural firing. In other words, as psychologist Donald Hebb observed more than sixty years ago, "*The neurons that fire together, wire together.*"

Dramatic events are easier to remember and access, because they involve a sense of learning that involves survival, and it is very adaptive for organisms to learn and act quickly on strategies that will allow them to live!

Thus, a bomb going off and blowing your friend to smithereens hardwires down to the amygdalae, setting up a shortcut: a giant neon sign hanging in the mind that says, WARNING: BOOM EQUALS DEATH. STANDBY TO RUN OR FREEZE OR FIGHT LIKE HELL.

So, great, thanks to the amygdalae's immediate response, maybe you survive your time on the battlefield or your childhood in an abusive home. Now, let's be clear. Once this neural net has been hardwired into the brain, it doesn't go away easily, which is a good thing the next time a bomb goes off in a war zone. You go on alert, which is exactly what you should do. Each subsequent trauma reinforces this survival response, and there's a lot of "firing and wiring" going on. The superhighway gets bigger and faster. But what happens when you get back to your peaceful homeland?

You take your son to the Fourth of July celebration and the fireworks go off: BOOM! The neural net gets triggered, the amygdala goes off, and you find yourself wanting to run and hide underneath your pickup. Later you slam tequila shots, smoke a couple of joints, eat a pint of Häagen Dazs, and drop two Valium. Anything to try and calm down the fight or flight response that has you feeling jacked up like one million volts are going through your body. And then you tell yourself, *I can never go to a fireworks show again.*

Not surprisingly, the Department for the Army estimates that anywhere from ten to eighteen percent of combat veterans will return from wars from Iraq and Afghanistan with PTSD.[14] And of course, factors like exposure to death of their comrades, length and number of deployments, low morale in their unit, and prior exposure to trauma in their lives only increase the likelihood and severity of PTSD.

Learning How to Give People the Fingers

I can remember like it was yesterday, my first experience with EMDR at my training in 2000. One of the teaching assistants, I'll call him Bill, told an amazing story. He was working at a Veteran's Administration (VA) Hospital and had already been trained in EMDR but was very reticent to use it, because it seemed so strange. What would a veteran say when he told them that the way they would get over battle trauma was to watch somebody wag fingers back and forth? He was sure that he would get laughed out of the room. But then, Bill got a call from his supervisor about a client who was in desperation. A Gulf War veteran was on the brink—her marriage was falling apart, she had been all but sleepless for months—she had horrible nightmares and constant flashbacks; she felt utterly hopeless. Bill's supervisor told him, "Try anything, do that eye movement thing, do something; this woman needs help!" Bill was not at all sure he could help, and he felt even more powerless when he heard her story. The woman, whom Bill called "Trudy," had been in charge of cleaning up the interiors of tanks.

"Now," said Bill, gazing around at his small group of EMDR trainees, "that may not sound like such a traumatic deal to you, but here's what you may not know. Modern ordinances are not engineered to blow up a tank completely, like you see in Hollywood movies, with huge orange fireballs." His face became grim. "Remember, the idea is just to kill the enemy inside the tanks. The military, in its infinite wisdom, designed shells to penetrate the tank's armor and, in effect, rattle around inside the cockpit and do as much damage as possible." Slowly it dawned on us what this meant. A few students gasped audibly.

"Trudy's job," he said, his tone completely flat, "was to clean up the viscera and body parts inside the captured enemy tanks. She did that . . . day in and day out."

There was silence in the group.

"And," said Bill, "this woman lands in my office, and although I'm trained, I have never done EMDR before, not really. So, no kidding, I break out the manual on my lap in front of me and start doing the worksheet and explaining the eye movements. And this woman is so far gone, she doesn't even care, she says she'll try anything. I spend about an hour and a half with her, and I'm not really sure whether I did anything, but she seems a little better. A few hours later, I get a call from my supervisor, and boy, am I worried! He says, 'What the hell did you do to her?' And I said, 'I did the EMDR just like you told me, why?' And he says, 'Well, she is absolutely freaking out!' My stomach pits, I'm thinking holy shit, what have I done? But then I think better of it and ask him, 'What do you mean?' And he says, 'Trudy just came to talk to me in my office. And for the last two hours, she has been sitting in the park across the street, thinking about everything that happened, the blood, the carnage, the stench, and *she can't trigger herself anymore*. I think she wants to like it, but she can't believe it. She tells me the whole thing feels more like it's just something awful that happened a long time ago, but it doesn't bother her right now! How the hell did you do that?'"

Bill looked around the room at our astonished faces. "And that's when I knew; I was really onto something. The nightmares and the flashbacks went away, she got back with her husband, and after a few more sessions, she never came back!" He was beaming, a true convert. It was a powerful story, and it was still hard to believe that anything could work that fast.

Bill supervised my session with another trainee. I was to play the role of the client, and my partner would wave his hand in front of my face and play EMDR therapist. Bill asked me to think of a moderate trauma, something that bothered me in the "five" to "seven" range on a scale where "ten" was the biggest trauma I could imagine. I picked a very distant memory from when I was about eight years old. My brother, the family rebel, was about sixteen and tall for his age. He was yelling angrily at my father, who was six foot one. My father was yelling back. Soon, they were fighting, screaming at each other, when—*crash*—father and brother locked together and careened into the front window, which shattered. I think there was blood. I couldn't remember the details—what they said, or how it resolved. And when I thought about it, it really didn't trigger me all that much. But I could feel some pitting in my stomach and a little knot in my throat.

"How distressful is that as you think about it now?" asked my "therapist."

"Oh, I don't know, about a 'five,' I guess," I replied casually.

He began to move his fingers in front of my eyes, stimulating the processing. Within minutes the feelings intensified. I was choking back tears; the distress had gone to an "eight." I was little, my brother and father were huge—giants, in my eyes—screaming and thundering! Here were the two most important men in my life, my brother and my father, both of whom I feared and adored. How could I make them stop? How could I pick a side? What could I do?

Nothing.

I was in the classic traumatic double bind—a life-threatening circumstance (as far as I knew) was in front of me, and I was powerless to stop it.

Waves of different emotions coursed through my body. First, panic—they were screaming and fighting, and glass was shattering. Next, fear—*what if they hurt each other? What if they hurt me, too? Maybe they wouldn't want to hurt me, but they were so out of control, I could get hit or one of them could fall on me!* But my feet were anchored into the tiles in the entryway. I was frozen. Then, guilt: *I should do something. I have to do something, but what? And how can I do anything when I can't even move or speak?*

It was amazing. I was simultaneously allowing and experiencing the emotions that had been frozen in me, but somehow, I was also "watching" the whole scene from a larger perspective, not from the child's point of view! It was sad and terrifying and amazing. I felt almost as though I had gone back in time to talk to eight-year-old Gregg and allow him to feel his fear, his panic, and his guilt. It was as though some Higher Mind was looking at him with compassion, as if to say, "I'm sorry. This is awful! How frightened you must be! You didn't do anything wrong, you did not cause this, you are loved, and you can't and don't have to fix this!"

I was crying, rocking, remembering with intensity how painful that day was. And I kept watching the fingers go back and forth.

And then it seemed to vanish, almost as quickly as it came. I was quiet. I was sad that it happened, but not sad or upset in the Now. I could hardly believe it. I told my partner, "Wait a minute." I closed my eyes, went back inside my mind's eye, saw Little Gregg, offered compassion, played the violin for myself . . . and, like the Gulf War veteran, *it was gone!* I was sad that it happened then but now I am okay.

EMDR: **Eye movement**, then **desensitization** (but not before reconnecting with the emotions lost in the freeze response) and **reprocessing**: *Oh, it's over, and I'm safe now. I'm an adult. If that happened now, I could enter the fray or call the police or step back to be safe or yell to get their attention* or a dozen other things came to my mind.

I looked at my watch. Seven minutes had gone by since the first set of eye movements. Several waves of emotions had come and then gone. And now, I was left with a pesky "two" on the distress scale. Something still kind of gnawed at me.

"Follow my fingers," said my partner, waving them again in front of me.

As I did, another memory came. In this one, my brother was twenty-four years old, and I was seventeen. I adored Glen and looked up to him, but he was driving his 1970 black Oldsmobile, "The Tin Indian," in the Texas Hill Country, going far too fast. As we cornered on the twisty, curvy road, the tires squealed hideously, and we came perilously close to limestone cliffs with hundred-foot drop-offs.

It was two in the morning. Only a cruel sliver of a moon illuminated the black road and a distinct absence of guard rails. We were almost out of gas. He was drunk. My heart began to pound and my shoulders tightened. *What if we went off the road? I don't have a clue where we are. What if we ran out of gas? How will we get home . . . and when? If we had a wreck, what would I do?* My brother, whom I was sure had all the answers, was drunk and wouldn't be able to help. My distress level went to a "seven," but only for about two minutes. My mind processed the experience: it was in the past, I was now safe, I wouldn't do that now, no, *hell no*; I don't get into cars with people who have been drinking.

Then another memory: I was in my early twenties. I had flown in from out of town and a relative picked me up at the airport. She was drunk, and I didn't know where we were going. No map in the car, no GPS, no money for a cab; I felt completely at her mercy—like I had to ride with her or get out and walk to God knows where. To top it off, my relative had no idea how to drive a stick shift, and when she tried to change gears, there was a horrific crunching noise as the gears tore at each other.

"Ha–ha–ha–ha!" she laughed, spraying me with saliva, a glazed manic look in her eyes. "If you can't find 'em, grind 'em, that's what I say!"

And that's what she *did* say, over and over, as though it would some-how be funnier the tenth time than it was the first, as we drove the two hours to our destination, the car lurching spastically and weaving like a ribbon snake in and out of the opposite lane. Once again, I was frozen, stuck in a traumatic double-bind.

But this time, I was not as reactive as I watched the fingers move back and forth. It was as though my mind was saying, *Oh, I get it now. We are revisiting these horrible things to see that they are over and we are safe and that we don't get into cars with drunken people anymore.*

And then it was suddenly over. It was far from just the absence of terror or sadness or regret. It was a feeling of well-being, a new clarity. I had dropped some baggage that had been in my unconscious for decades. The likelihood of any of those things happening now was miniscule, because now I would respond differently. I was safe. I felt like I had more power—like I was an adult and not a helpless child.

"What is your distress level now?" I heard my partner echo from some other dimension.

I turned inward. *What was it?* I looked at my brother and my father fighting and at the two memories with drunk drivers.

I felt . . . fine.

"Zero?" I asked incredulously. I didn't trust it. "Okay, okay, just wait a minute here!" I proclaimed adamantly. "I can't be at a zero, that was some awful shit that happened that day—*those* days!"

It was almost as though I was upset that I had surrendered my right, *my right, dammit,* to be hurt and angry about these things! If I was no longer hurt and angry, then did that mean it was okay? If there isn't any effect called a Hurt Gregg, then what does that mean? Does that mean what they did was okay? But, it wasn't okay, and I was determined that they would not get off that easily. My suffering was the proof of their sins, and if I let it go, there would be no evidence of their injustices.

And it was in that moment, I saw that *I had a commitment to hanging on to my pain.*

I took a deep breath.

Wow.

And here I thought I wanted to leave these awful traumas behind me. But a part of me *wanted* this pain, *wanted* to point at it and say to those others in my mind, *See what you did to me? See how much hurt you brought me? I hope you feel awful like I do! I hope you always feel guilty and ashamed and never forget this.*

Truth is, I said to myself, *I don't want this pain any longer. It's just not worth it.* And then I heard in my head a very famous line from *A Course in Miracles.*

Do you want to be right, or do you want to be a happy?

And I decided that I wanted to be happy. At that point, it literally was a decision. And as I made that decision, *as I alone chose* to let it go, I felt a softness, a warmth in my chest. I felt like it was the right decision for them *and* for me.

I could just open my hand and let it go, like a tiny, white down feather being taken up by a gentle summer breeze.

I let it blow away in the cool wind of my mind.

But my intellect started buzzing. This whole thing just wasn't possible in one sitting. I still wasn't convinced that I had completely released the trauma. So, I went back inside my head and focused on those traumatic moments. And it was horrible then—horrible that day my dad and my brother were fighting, and horrible being held captive by drunk drivers.

It was horrible *then* . . . but okay now.

It wasn't that what they did was right or appropriate or kind or loving, it was that in this moment, it didn't bother me. *They were things that happened.* It was in the past; why would I want to waste a lot of energy getting spun up about it now? It seemed useless.

"What does it feel like in your body right now?"

I scanned my body. Not only were there no tight places or pitting or tears, I felt okay, no . . . more than okay, I felt . . . unburdened, genuinely peaceful. I asked myself in that moment if I felt any grievances toward those people who had hurt me, and I didn't, at least not for those particular moments. *Forgiveness*, I thought to myself. If I am no longer struck with terror and anger, then I can choose to forgive them.

"So what is your distress level now?" my therapist radioed from somewhere on Planet Earth.

"My distress level is . . . uh . . . zero?" Eyes still closed, I found myself nodding, answering my own question. "Yup. Zero."

I opened my eyes, somehow surprised that the conference room complete with trainees was still all around me and my partner in front of me. I felt like I had been gone. Everyone was looking at me, breathlessly awaiting a report from inside the experience. I looked directly at my training partner, who'd been nervously playing my therapist. Everyone leaned in waiting for me to speak. I couldn't resist.

"Oh, Auntie Em, is it really *you?*" I said in a desperate falsetto, rapidly batting my eyelashes. The group collapsed into laughter, the tension broken. Grinning broadly, I patted my partner on the arm. "That was amazing! But I am sorry I ate up so much time!"

"Look at your watch," said Bill, blithely, who had been supervising the entire role play. It had been only twenty minutes since we started.

I was hooked.

* * *

DINNER WITH JESUS

Nicholas was the kind of man who never met a stranger. Within five minutes he would have you talking to him like he was your best friend. Tall, slender, and good-looking, he was charismatic with a pearly white smile that could win over the most stubborn person. Not surprisingly, Nicholas worked in sales. I had the impression that not only could he sell ice cubes to Eskimos, but he could probably convince them to buy an upright freezer as well. He was a very successful new car salesman, but the longer I knew him, the more I saw that he did not fall into an easy stereotype.

"Do you know why I'm so successful?" he once asked me earnestly. "It's because I listen to the customer. I give them what they want. I don't care how much commission I would make on the car, if I thought the customer would leave unhappy. And that is why people keep coming back to buy cars from me again and again. They send me their friends and relatives too."

Looking into his eyes, I could see it was a point of pride for Nicholas. He was a family man, married for fifteen years, and a staunch, committed Catholic. Nicholas had only one major problem.

He liked to shoot dope.

Five years ago, it had come to a head, and his entire life crumbled before his eyes. Over the previous several years, there had been a gradual descent into the hell of addiction. It started as an increased use of alcohol, which was never really his "drug of choice." Then, it was snorting "just a little" cocaine on weekends. But slowly, Nicholas wanted more intense highs. Soon, he was injecting speed. He began to turn his natural sales abilities towards marketing drugs, initially just to support his habit. But soon, he wasn't just strung out on drugs; he was addicted to the lifestyle.

As he put it, "I became the biggest badass on the block. I may not have been loved, but everybody respected me when I walked into the room. Everybody stopped and turned to look at me, only me. Some were afraid of me. Many wanted what I had. There were women who would give me anything—and I mean, anything, any way I wanted it—for what I could give them: money, sex, the glow of power. I had it all, baby."

But having it all almost cost him everything. Only after he got fired from his job, overdosed, and nearly lost his wife did Nicholas wake up and smell the coffee. On the brink of a divorce, no longer living with his family, Nicholas crawled into my office, a shell of the man he once was. Slowly, we built a relationship.

His father had abandoned his mother when Nicholas was a baby, initially by drinking himself into oblivion every night and eventually disappearing from his life. He often left little Nicky with his elder sister, who resented having to take care of him and expressed her displeasure by beating him and demeaning him. Nicholas' happiest memories were times spent with his mother who had primary custody. But her periodic absence made connecting with her an agonizing paradox: It was heaven to be with her, but hell to be away from her. Ten years earlier, his beloved mother had died from a vicious cancer in a matter of months. It seemed to amplify a lesson he learned at an early age.

"There's only one person I can count on," he would often say to me tersely, his eyes blazing, "and that's me."

If there's one thing I knew Nicholas liked, it was making money. I knew he would balk at going to twelve-step meetings if I suggested it. I fully expected the usual litany: they didn't work; he didn't have time; he thought they were stupid. I told him I had a friend who could hook him up with a unique business opportunity. When I asked him if he could find just an hour a week to make $150.00, he answered an emphatic yes. I told him that since we had established that he *could* find an hour a week if it was valuable enough, then he could find time for a twelve-step meeting.

"Nicky," I told him. "Think of the thousands of dollars you lost when you were out of work. Think how much you could lose in a divorce, or how much—at your lowest ebb—you would have paid to win your wife and children back. This hour a week could be worth far more money in the bank than you could imagine!"

Nicholas laughed, "All right, you got me there. You closed me, I'm buying," he replied as only a salesman could. Years later, he would jokingly tell his friends that I "tricked him into recovery."

It took time, but slowly Nicholas began to recover from his addiction. Initially, he threw himself into twelve-step programs. But after a few months, he admitted that he didn't always go to Alcoholics Anonymous (A.A.) and Narcotics Anonymous (N.A.) meetings like he should. And he certainly didn't do as much therapy as I thought he needed. Only sporadically did he work through a few of his many childhood traumas, often missing sessions or arriving late. But he had found a way to do enough to somehow get by. His complacency concerned me, but the longer he was clean, the easier it got; until one day, fate nearly knocked him off the wagon.

Nicholas found himself in my office and in jeopardy. "Accidently," he told me, both of us knowing none of this was accidental, he found himself going back into the neighborhoods where he could get "sharps," (needles) where he might be tempted to score an eight ball (of cocaine). *What am I doing?* He would ask himself. Yet, as any person in recovery will tell you, there are times when addicts are completely powerless over their addiction. Nicholas would pray the serenity prayer over and over, but increasingly he felt like he was white-knuckling his sobriety, and it was only a matter of time before he would get waylaid by the addiction.

"I knew I had to come back to see you, Gregg. You got me started on this path to sanity. You've got to help me get through this again." I was wary. Why did I get the impression that Nicholas was unconsciously setting me up as his savior? I was destined to disappoint. His unconscious schema was that no one would be there for him. I knew I needed to move ahead cautiously.

Nicholas pulled up his sleeve, and pointed to a place on his inner forearm. There were small, white lumps of scarred flesh, vestiges of the days when he used to shoot up.

"It's weird," he said, "all I have to do is barely touch them and the cravings come back. If I could shoot dope right now, I would. I swear to God, Gregg, if I had a needle in my hand, it would be in my arm right now," he said emphatically.

When Nicholas had seen me originally, we had used EMDR to work through some of the trauma that we came to believe, at least in part, drove the addiction. Without question, it was a powerful ally, along with twelve-step programs, toward Nicholas' sobriety. But I anticipated that it would take multiple sessions for me to be of much service to Nicholas and his urgent "jonesing" to shoot up. Fortunately, I'd had some cancellations that afternoon, and Nicholas had the day off.

"Could you do three sessions right now?" I asked him earnestly.

"I'll do anything!" he said desperately. "*Anything!* Just make it stop!" he said, his eyes moist.

There it was again. Could it be Nicholas wanted me to be his cardboard super hero who was supposed to save him? Then he would knock me down and tell me how I had failed him, just like his father.

Here be dragons.

It was a chance I felt like I had to take, but not foolishly.

"You understand I can't heal an addiction in three hours, Nicholas. There is no magic wand. And you've got to put some skin in the game. You have worked with me before. This is going to get messy. But I do think I can help."

Nicholas nodded his head repeatedly. "You got me this far, Gregg. Don't stop now."

"I won't," I said firmly, locking eyes with Nicholas. "But you can't either."

I asked Nicholas to focus on the cravings. He said, "That's easy. All I have to do is touch the scars on my arm, and it's like electricity going through my body." Nicholas extended his right finger and let it dance over the track marks on his left arm. "I can't tell you how badly I want to use right now. I feel like if I don't shoot up right this minute, I am going to explode." I nodded.

"If zero is feeling completely free of the desire to use, and ten is the most you've ever wanted to use in your entire life, where are you right now on that scale?" I asked Nicholas.

"Damn, that's easy, I'm at a ten."

"Nicholas," I said, "feel that ten in your body; what does it feel like?"

His words began to rush together frantically. "It's like electricity everywhere. My stomach is pitted out. My whole body is uncomfortable. It's like this huge ache, and I just want it to go away, and the only thing I can think to do is to shoot up to make it stop!" he replied, in genuine anguish.

"Follow my fingers," I said, hoping that the sooner his eyes got in gear, the sooner the relief might come. But that wasn't what happened at all.

"Oh God, I don't know if I can even do this!" The eye movements activated the doubts he had repressed so deeply. They were rushing to the surface. Nicholas began to thrash in the chair. He cried out, his right hand shooting to his shoulder with a sudden ferocity. "OW!"

"Are you okay?" I asked.

"It's just like these sudden pains moving around in my body," he said through gritted teeth. "I can't stop it. OW!"

He doubled over in the chair in front of me, grabbing his abdomen. He cried out time and again for a good twenty minutes. I watched Nicholas have purely physical reactions to his cravings. It was strange, because Nicholas was not in withdrawal. He had three years of sobriety. But the sharp pain would hit suddenly, and he would reach behind his lower back or up to his chest, reacting to the torture. It was as though there were demons stabbing him with pitchforks.

Then, I watched astonished as Nicholas entered some kind of delirium; screaming, mumbling, coughing, groaning—his whole body jerking like it was plugged into a wall socket. Was he talking to himself? Was he talking to his addiction? Was he talking to the drugs?

I couldn't tell.

I have learned that—even when things don't always make sense to me—my clients are usually working something through at a deeper level. A lot of therapists pride themselves on the thought that they know exactly what is happening in the session or that they're even controlling it. But when I work at deep spiritual levels, I can't always afford that luxury. It's as though they have to go right to the edge of their most intense emotions and break through to the other side. The lyrics of an old song by Seal flashed through my mind: " . . . but we're never gonna survive, unless we get a little crazy . . . "

"I hate this. *I hate this!*" Nicholas said repeatedly. "Awwrrr, I *hate* me, I hate me, I hate this *fucking* addiction, when are you going to leave me alone? Aaaaaaaaaaaaw!"

His whole being twisted violently, grotesquely, veins popping out from his neck—only to segue into his body going rigid like a board—almost as though he were having a seizure.

"When are you going to stop it? I hate you. I hate you!" He crashed his fists repeatedly into his muscular thighs, rock-hard with tension. "Oh my God, just leave me alone! Pleeease! Stop it! Stop it! Leave me alone, *Goddamn it*, leave me alone, *STOP IT!*"

The thrashing in the padded recliner and the screaming continued, his head slammed first left and then right, reaching a fever pitch.

"AWWWWWRRRRRRR!"

Then suddenly, silence.

It was almost like someone rang the bell at a boxing match. All of the violence stopped cold. The only sound in the room was the deep rhythmic sound of Nicholas' breathing, like a runner at the end of a marathon. His chest heaved dramatically and fell. With every ragged inhalation, I could almost imagine Nicholas trying to suck his life back into his body. His exhalations got louder, almost like grunts, as though he was trying to push out the demons.

The tears came. His whole body convulsed. Somehow, he found his voice again.

"I don't want to blow this again," he said in a voice just below a whisper. "I will lose everything. I don't want to lose everybody." Then suddenly, the volume went up again. "It's not worth it, do you hear me? I know it's not worth it!" he sobbed uncontrollably. "I've almost lost everything once. Why do I want to do this again? It's crazy!" Right in the middle of the sobs, another scream would escape from his mouth as he would grab his chest, the torture returning. For another ten minutes, Nicholas alternately sobbed and screamed. Finally, the physical pain appeared to be morphing into raw emotions. Nicholas wept from his gut.

Then, I noticed something different. I have an intuitive sense about emotions. I can often see when the client is experiencing both anger and sadness, somehow simultaneously. But for Nicholas, for just a few moments, for the first time in the session, I saw something different. He wept. And all that was there was pure, unadulterated grief. It was not mixed with frustration or anger, or hopelessness. He was just sad, only sad.

And then Nicholas got very quiet. A subtle smile accompanied the grief.

"My mom is here," he said very softly, tears gently rolling down his face. "I can see her face. It's glowing. It's the face of my mother, like when I was eight years old—when she was at her happiest; when she was at her very best. She loves me. I can see it in her eyes. She's telling me that she loves me. Oh, Momma, I've missed you so much," he said, sobbing.

"Oh, Mom, somehow you could always make it all better," Nicholas said to her, "no matter how bad things got. I wish you were here to-day." He stopped and looked puzzled at the image in his mind's eye, for a long moment.

"She's saying, 'I *am* here, and I believe in you, Nicky. I am *so* proud of you. You got clean and sober. You've become a good husband and father. You learned to say something that your father never said to you. You can tell your children 'I love you,' and I'm so proud of you for that. You're a good boy. You can do this. I believe in you.'"

I could see the pain slowly softening as I looked at Nicholas' face over a period of minutes. His face became peaceful and serene as he continued to watch my fingers move back and forth. His breath became very easy and gentle. Something magical was happening for Nicholas, but I wasn't exactly sure what. Something was changing in-

side of him. Nicholas closed his eyes and cried softly, obviously overwhelmed by something beautiful. Then, he slowly lifted his face as
though he were looking toward the sunrise. He stretched his arms out
halfway in front of him, holding his palms up as though receiving
some kind of divine radiance from above. Although I was curious,
something told me not to question him. This internal experience continued for twenty or thirty minutes. There was no weeping now. Instead, his face seemed to glow, and tiny tears would periodically spill
out from under his eyelids. A soft beatific smile remained on his face.
There was amazing stillness and peace in the room.

I found tears were rolling down my face, too, not fully understanding why, but I trusted Nicholas and whatever was going on for him.

Finally, his hands gently descended to his lap, and he slowly
stretched his body as though waking from a long nap. He opened his
eyes and initially looked around the room. But when his eyes finally
came to meet mine, they slowly tilted towards the floor.

"You're not gonna believe this," he said, in obvious disbelief himself,
rubbing his forehead with his thumb and fingers, "but I was with Jesus."
Nicholas took several very short sharp breaths, fighting back the tears,
trying to get his mind around it.

"I was there, and Jesus was there. *I was there* . . . I was at the Last
Supper."

I looked in Nicholas' eyes and face. If he was imagining this experience, he was certainly completely convinced. He hesitated, incapable of
forming the words. It felt almost blasphemous to say it aloud. "Jesus . . . "
He stopped, seemingly unable to speak it aloud.

"Jesus knelt before me and washed my feet . . . " Nicholas' face went
all but blank. He was dumbstruck, staring out a million miles away in
disbelief. "He told me I was forgiven. He said I was worthy."

"He washed my feet," he said again, "like I was one of his disciples . . . "
I smiled and nodded. I began to wonder if maybe . . .

"I mean, it wasn't like a past life, Gregg. I don't even know if I believe in those things. No, I was there like me dressed in my Levis and
my Longhorn shirt . . . but he welcomed me . . . like . . . like I was one
of his own."

"How do you feel Nicholas?" I asked.

"I feel a peace—a peace like I've never known before." He smirked.

"Way better than any drug I've ever done." Then his smirk became a smile. His smile was not the smile of a world-weary car salesman in his late thirties, but the smile of a five-year-old who has just been told that tomorrow is his birthday. His voice even took on a child-like quality. "I feel fresh, and I feel all clean, like I just slept the best sleep of my whole entire life, and I just woke up," he said in utter astonishment.

I sat with Nicholas for a long time. Finally, he met my gaze. We just beamed at each other for several minutes. Then he looked away toward the window of my office. I have learned to recognize the sacred silences in my clients' processes. I have come to understand that if I ask too many questions, I can shatter the moment. I have learned not to violate sacred space with words.

I don't always have to know what is going on in order to know that healing is happening. The faraway look and subtle smile on Nicholas' face continued unabated for quite some time. Then, as though sensing it was complete, he took a deep breath, exhaled, and looked toward me with a different kind of smile.

"Go ahead, ask me," he said with a knowing look. Nicholas knew that I needed to check with him to see how the cravings were.

"Okay, Nicholas," I said, trying to sound more like a therapist and less like someone completely awestruck in the presence of a man who just touched Jesus. "Close your eyes, and imagine that you're driving to the part of town where you can buy drugs," I said. "Remember how much you wanted them and needed them. Imagine that urge inside you. Now, reach over and tickle the scars, the injection sites, and see how your body responds."

Nicholas quietly chuckled. And then, it got bigger, expanding. Finally, he laughed aloud, a loud guffaw, as though I were Will Ferrell, Eddie Murphy, and Bob Hope combined.

"You don't *get* it, Gregg. I might as well be scratching my ear right now," he said with a broad smile, continuing to finger his scars. "I don't feel anything, zero, nada, nothing! There are no cravings, Gregg, *the cravings are completely gone!*"

"Nicholas, come back to the image of driving through the neighborhood where you can get drugs. Go ahead and keep tickling the scars. I want you to scan your body for that physical pain, for that tension, for that electricity you felt earlier," I said.

"I'm telling you there's *nothing there*. It's gone; it's all gone!"

Nicholas and I spent a few more minutes reflecting on the experience and talking about what it meant to him. In the years since this session, although the moments of temptation have sometimes returned, Nicholas has not used drugs or alcohol. Not only has he told me that but, to the best of my ability, I have been able to corroborate that ethically through a number of other sources.

Nicholas continues to rebuild his marriage and has miraculously regained the trust of his children. He still goes only sporadically to twelve-step meetings and has not returned to regular therapy, both potentially dangerous choices. No matter how powerful a single experience may be, recovering addicts (and the rest of us) would be wise to continue some kind of consistent healing pathway. On balance, he has taken a major leadership role at his church, where he has become not only respected, but beloved.

I told him, "Nicky, you used to settle for being feared, when what you really wanted was to be loved!"

Eyes blazing in mock indignation, he furrowed his brow, steeled his jaw, and feigned his best drug–dealer "badass face." "When I walk into the church," he said in a gravelly voice, "everyone turns to stop and look at me, only me. I have something that they want." He paused for effect. "But now, it's for all the *right* reasons! Usually, they want me to head up the all–you–can–eat pancake supper!" And he threw his head back and laughed.

In the twelve-step tradition of A.A., the final goal is having a spiritual awakening, like co-founder Bill Wilson did; not simply to overcome addiction, but to lead a transformed, spiritually grounded life.

For Nicholas, that spiritual awakening took the form of a powerful emotional and energetic release: a visit from his mother who had passed ten years before, and an invitation to the Last Supper with Jesus the Christ, all in one day.

That day was Good Friday, 2006.

* * *

For more than fourteen years, I used EMDR and continued to be amazed at the changes in my client's lives. I saw people come back from car accidents, sexual abuse, and horrific childhoods. I am not alone in this wonderment. Ask anyone trained in this modality who has used it faithfully, and you will hear another dozen stories of "miraculous" healings.

EMDR worked best when there was a single uncomplicated trauma. But I also saw it work effectively with complex trauma; however, it required more time. One client who had lost her second husband in an industrial accident came to me for grief counseling, and the longer we worked together, the more intense experiences she spontaneously remembered. I asked about other traumas in her life.

"Well, there was the time my first husband beat me. Actually, more than once. And did I tell you I was date-raped when I was sixteen? Oh, and I told you I was in New York for 9/11 and saw the towers fall, didn't I?"

I rolled up my sleeves.

I had never worked with a client with so much cumulative trauma. We processed through with EMDR week after week, sometimes twice a week, knocking down trauma after trauma. Some traumas took several sessions to desensitize. It was painful and sometimes grueling. But after a year, she said, she felt better than she had in her entire life.

"It's like I have been wearing a lead jacket for decades, and you helped me take it off," she said. She even came to appreciate the role that her husband's death played in her awakening.

"The learning that came from his passing was the best gift I never wanted," she said with a smile in our final session.

I was convinced that EMDR was an important key to healing not only trauma, but a useful tool for reducing anxiety, depression, grief, and improving peak performance in a space of time heretofore thought of as impossible. But I would soon learn that EMDR could be applied in ways beyond *my* imagination.

My clients began to talk to dead people.

6

Induced After-Death Communication: Touching the Afterlife, Healing the Grief

"The Prince of Peace was born to reestablish the condition of love by teaching that communication remains unbroken, even if the body is destroyed, provided that you see not the body as the *necessary* means of communication."

A Course in Miracles

It was a bolt. It probably weighed just a few ounces, something you could hold in the palm of your hand—nothing anyone ever thought of as frightening. But when it bounced out of the back of a pickup going seventy miles an hour and whistled through the windshield of Sheila's Lexus as it drove in the opposite direction, it became a lethal weapon that instantly killed her husband, Howard.

As Sheila sat in my office, it had been seven years since that horrific night. She was in her late forties, an attractive woman, dressed conservatively. Even though she was remarried and had gone on with her life, she was haunted by those images. As she recounted the tale, she alternately cried, violently shook, and rocked herself. At times, she would cover her face with her hands, and at other moments she would stare off into the distance, eyes wide—the panic palpable, as though she were trying to see through the bookcase on the far side of my office. This is the hallmark of trauma: the feeling that something that happened *then*, is happening *now*. It is a memory so real that we feel we are there all over again—this is a flashback. At its most devastating, the flashbacks overwhelm the survivor at the slightest provocation. A song, a picture, a commercial, triggers the intense memory, and they are no longer "here-and-now," they are "then-and-there." They try to explain the experience to others only to be told, "That happened a long time ago, don't worry about it." Their friends and family don't realize that for the untreated trauma survivor, the terror never ends. Once triggered, they cannot control or stop the excruciating panic-button response. So survivors learn to not talk to anyone and instead suffer alone in silence, often retreating more and more from a chaotic world that triggers their old wounds and people who don't understand them. In the extreme, untreated, they sink into a deepening whirlpool of depression, despair, and addiction. The National Center for PTSD estimates that about eight percent of the population, nearly twenty-five million Americans, will suffer from post-traumatic stress disorder, or PTSD[9], at some point in their lives.

I gently reminded Sheila that we were not revisiting this memory to frighten her but to bring healing, and that her feelings were welcome. In some ways, it can be argued that in traumatic moments we don't fully experience our emotions. Survivor instinct kicks in when we are in life-threatening situations and the fight-or-flight-or-freeze response engages as the body readies for action to do battle, to escape, or to stop dead in our tracks—like the proverbial deer in the headlights. Survival becomes the primary goal and, emotionally, we just go numb. But those feelings have to go into the psyche *somewhere*. Today, I knew the healing was beginning as the intense, frozen emotions were starting to thaw. I was trying to gauge how upsetting the memory was for Sheila so that we could both comprehend its intensity and monitor if we were making any headway as the session continued. On a scale from zero to ten, I asked her, "How painful is the memory right now in this moment?" In other words, how much was she being "triggered?"

I knew the answer before she said it: Ten.

Shelia had come to me for a new therapy called Induced After-Death Communication (IADC). The therapy was developed by Dr. Allan

Botkin at the Chicago Veterans Administration Hospital. For years, Dr. Botkin had treated veterans using Eye Movement Desensitization and Reprocessing (EMDR), a breakthrough technique that engages both the emotional and rational parts of the brain to "digest" trauma rapidly and allow survivors to let go of their painful pasts. But in a two-week period in 1995, three of his clients spontaneously had apparent visionary contact with others who had crossed over during their EMDR sessions, resulting in dramatic reductions in their PTSD symptoms and grief. While Dr. Botkin was unsure whether these experiences were real or imagined, he was astonished by the relief they brought and developed protocols to duplicate the experience with other clients.

In Dr. Botkin's initial study, he found that over ninety-five percent of his IADC clients achieved a resolution of their "core sadness" around the loss of the loved one in a single extended session. Experiences of apparent contact ranged from subtle sensations of the presence of loved ones who had passed to tactile experiences in which they felt hugged or touched. Prior to their sessions, only eight percent of these clients believed that contact was even possible, so it was unlikely that the experience was some kind of unconscious wish fulfillment. In addition, while not "proof" of an afterlife, ninety-eight percent of his clients believed their experiences of afterlife contact were real, even those who considered themselves atheists or agnostic! To this day, if someone asks Allan whether he believes, he simply says, "Ask the people who had one." For Dr. Botkin, in the final analysis, it doesn't matter whether they are real or not; what matters is that they are healing.

Strangely, it wasn't until I first heard about IADC that I realized I had already done one.

The Cowboys Ride Away

I worked with Harris several years before I'd ever read about IADC. Harris was a balding, beefy middle-aged African-American man who had been running some construction equipment at a job site when two of his co-workers had perished before him in the machinery. He was forty-eight, but looked much older. *It's not the years, it's the mileage*, I thought to myself. I immediately liked Harris, a salt-of-the-earth kind of guy, not given to sharing his emotions. He didn't want to burden anybody. He wanted to go on with his life and was as mystified as his friends that he couldn't just "get over it." But I could see the pain in his eyes. Harris was the kind of guy that worked his butt off and took pride in his efforts. All his friends said it was tragic that he had to deal with this, and it wasn't fair. He didn't deserve this. "I just want to be able to go back to work, man. My family counts on me. Just get me back to work," he said, emphatically, over and over again.

But as I found out more of his story, I wondered if I was up to the task. I was newly trained in EMDR, and Harris had experienced his two co-workers dying right before his eyes, crunched to pieces by his equipment. He knew their names. Although his friends had reassured him it wasn't his fault, somehow he just couldn't believe them. He began to suffer from acute traumatic stress: Harris was unable to sleep most nights. Work was impossible. He felt overwhelmed with panic at various times during the day. He found himself crying and despondent, pulling away from his wife and children. He felt unworthy of their love, and seeing what it did to his family only made him worse. He hated himself. Real or imagined, Harris told me he thought his wife was frustrated and really might leave him. When he finally collapsed exhausted at three or four in the morning, he dreamed of the men, hearing their bones snap as they screamed over and over in never-ending agony, the moment suspended in time. His anxiety only increased when the state conducted an official investigation.

Harris was given leave from work for three weeks. Thanks to a referral from a co-worker who had worked with me, he showed up in my office, hopeless and frightened that the memory would never leave him and that he could never again work in construction. After an extended session getting Harris's history, I told him about EMDR, and a few days later we were working to desensitize the painful memories. I was encouraged that within several sessions, Harris was feeling considerably better. He was sleeping and eating again, but still had intrusive thoughts about the accident, and still felt responsible, even though he admitted that it didn't make sense. Then the news came in from the investigation: He had been officially cleared! But this appeared to have no impact on Harris. "'I mean it's nice to know, I guess," he said tentatively. "But I still can't imagine going back to work. I will have to climb into my cab on the same site and put my hands on the same controls that killed them!" Harris hung his head and shook it slowly, his breath shallow, his eyes widening as he imagined that moment. He was still unable to accept his innocence.

We were running out of time. His leave of absence was all but complete; Harris would have to return to work in the next week. He was improving, but it felt like there was still a piece unfinished. I knew that with particularly intense experiences, multiple EMDR sessions are not unusual. So we approached, yet again, the moment of the catastrophe. Harris released wave after wave of regret and sadness. Then he closed his eyes. His face slowly changed over a matter of minutes. It took on an appearance of profound peace. "I can see them," he said, barely mouthing the words. "The two guys . . . they are standing right in front of me."

"How do they look?" I asked.

"They're fine, they're just . . . fine." I knew that it was progress that Harris could even *think* of these men without getting overwhelmed. But that he could be at some level of peace with their images in his mind? We were making enormous headway.

"What do you want to tell them?" I asked.

"I want to say to them simply this . . . " he remarked in a voice barely above a whisper, "I am sorry. I am so sorry. I was just doing what they told me."

I expected another wave of weeping, but instead, he sat in my office transfixed for several minutes. His breath was very slow and very deep as a kind of reverence fell over the room.

Then he spoke quietly, with little emotion. "They say, 'Don't worry. It's cool, we forgive you. It wasn't your fault. You were doing your job, just like we were doing ours. You were following the foreman and the supervisor's instruction. You were doing what you were supposed to have been doing, just like we were doing what we were supposed to be doing. *We were all just doing our job, man.* It's cool.'" Harris sat calmly and perfectly still, pondering all of it for a long moment, dumbstruck.

"What do you see on their faces?" I asked.

"It's weird. They're smiling. They're okay. They aren't mad at me; they understand." He sat quietly, intent upon whatever he was seeing.

For a change, I knew enough not to open my mouth. Minutes ticked by.

"They're going now." He chuckled. "You know how the cowboys ride off in the end of those old movies? It's kind of like that. No horses, though," he said with a funny smile. He extended his arm and pointed towards an imaginary horizon, his eyes moving rapidly under his lids. "It's like they are turning back towards me and waving." He paused. "And now they are walking into the sunset. They're cool with the whole thing. It's all good."

He was smiling, his eyes moist. Then he took several deep breaths and opened his eyes. We sat together silently for what seemed like an hour but was probably four or five minutes. During that time, Harris alternately stared out into space, gave a little smile, or shook his head in disbelief.

Harris closed his eyes again. Finally, as we were nearing the end of our time together, I broke the silence. "Harris, that's amazing. I think it's wonderful that you can imagine how they might feel."

Harris opened his eyes and looked right through me. "I wasn't imagining," he said, without missing a beat. "They were here."

While I wasn't sure that Harris had really talked to anybody on the "other side," it was immediately apparent his anxiety and guilt were gone. Harris returned to the same job site where the accident had happened, puts his hands on the same controls, and went back to work. Can you imagine?

I touched base with him by telephone and asked him if he was okay. I was worried that even if he could "white knuckle" his way through his first day, it might be tough. But Harris calmly said that it was "no problem." Nothing had come up. His first time back on the job was "just another day" at the office. We had done a total of ten sessions over three weeks, and now his acute stress disorder, which had threatened his job, his marriage and family, maybe even his life . . . was virtually non–existent.

Is it appropriate to contact those on the other side? Cayce made it clear that spirit communication not only *should not* be forced, but *could not* be forced. However, he suggested that it can be *invited*, and then, "The willingness and the desire from both is necessary for the perfect communication . . . " (5756–4) Interestingly enough, in the civilian population, Dr. Botkin has estimated that IADC typically garners apparent contact in seventy percent of patients on the first attempt.

Sitting with Sheila, I remembered how I had seen IADC work effectively many times before. After reading Dr. Allan Botkin's compelling book, *Induced After Death Communication: A New Therapy for Healing Grief and Trauma*[10], I immediately flew to Chicago and trained directly with him. As the fifteenth person in the world certified in this cutting-edge therapy, I experienced myself riding the crest of this revolutionary healing modality.

One of my first IADC clients was John, who came to me because he felt his father, who had died years before, had never really loved him. John explained that the day he left the country and went overseas to serve in the military, his father had gone to the bathroom and hadn't even said goodbye. In a tearful IADC, John reunited with his father in an internal vision. His father explained that he had started to cry and hid in the bathroom, because he was so ashamed of his "unmanly tears." John's father had been a stiff-upper-lip kind of guy, but from the other side, he apologized and told his son he did love him. John said *he physically experienced hugging his father* during the IADC.

In 2007, in Seabeck, Wash., I had consented to do a live onstage demonstration of IADC at a retreat (sponsored by the Association for Research and Enlightenment). After carefully screening and interviewing about a dozen volunteers, I decided to work with Janeen, who had lost her husband after a long chronic illness, only to lose her only child in a car wreck weeks later. Weeks before, I had talked to Dr. Botkin about doing this demonstration. Allan thought I was crazy—what if the volunteer didn't make contact? Wasn't I concerned about looking like a complete idiot? Even Cayce himself had remarked on the pitfalls of spirit contact, saying, "We find individuals [who have passed over] at times communicative. At other times uncommunicative. There are moods and there are moods. There are conditions [for spirit contact] in which such conditions are easily attained. There are others that are hard, as it were, to meet or cope with . . . Those in the astral plane are not always ready. Those in the physical plane are not always ready." (5756-4) This would certainly account for why not all of my clients who attempt an IADC make contact. I had to concede that Cayce and Dr. Botkin had a point. There would be no guarantee of apparent spirit contact. But as Allan himself knew, the underlying therapy is so effective, so healing, that it typically brings phenomenal relief in a single session, *even when the client doesn't make apparent contact.* I was convinced it was a risk worth taking to demonstrate the healing potential of this unsung modality.

I had no real idea what I was getting myself into.

As I began to work with Janeen onstage, waves of grief poured from her. She missed her husband Juan, and the loss of her daughter on the heels of his death felt like a cruel twist of fate. More tears. She felt homeless and orphaned. What was the point of living? How could she ever start again? Sobs came from somewhere deep within her, wails of pain. While I was focused on Janeen, I was also keenly aware of the audience as the therapy continued. Over an hour had gone by, as Janeen worked though agonizing after agonizing aspect of her losses. Was this too much for onlookers? I was trained to deal with trauma, but they weren't. Many were crying, while others looked shell-shocked. I could feel them getting restless. I imagined the audience members talking after the demonstration. "Gregg said he could help her, but all she did was cry, and her husband and daughter never came through. All he did was torture her." Maybe Allan was right; this was insanity. It was foolish of me to even try. Was I just torturing Janeen, freaking everyone out, and making an utter fool of myself?

But then it happened.

It was subtle at first, but the *kind of crying she was doing changed.* Janeen began smiling through her tears. "It's Juan! Oh my God, it's him!" Then she began laughing, and with her eyes closed, she began talking to Juan in her mind's eye. Watching Janeen was like watching someone have a phone conversation, only without the phone. "I'm telling him I am sorry that I wasn't there the evening that he passed," she said regretfully. "I let him down!" Then there was a long pause. She frowned and then smiled. "He says, 'What makes you so sure that I *wanted* you to be there when I crossed over!'" She laughed, and said, "He is telling me that he didn't want to leave me with that kind of trauma, so he waited until I left that afternoon, and he appreciates all the days I came to sit with him at the hospital."

How many times had I heard that story from clients! "After three days of staying in their hospital room, I just went downstairs to have a cup of coffee, but when I came back, they had just crossed over!" I have come to believe that, like Juan, many of our loved ones don't want to leave us with the agony of their death and somehow arrange to postpone their passing until we are out of the room. Or perhaps, the idea of someone close to them witnessing their death feels like a loss of dignity. Let's face it, although death is a natural part of life, so is going to the bathroom, but that doesn't mean I want an audience while I do it!

After a few more minutes, Janeen seemed to wrap things up with Juan. I had a brief flash in my head of Juan kissing Janeen on her cheek. I tucked the image into my hip pocket behind my left temporal lobe.

Janeen's smile was short-lived as she became focused on an image of her daughter Denise in her coffin. "I can smell the roses on her casket," Janeen announced with amazement. "I can actually smell them . . . " she said with conviction, "but . . . but, I just can't take my eyes off the open casket. Her body is . . . well . . . " Her lower lip quivered furiously as her voice choked with emotion, her attempt at a deep breath reduced to a series of tiny, staccato intakes. "You see, the car . . . " she gulped air, trying to approach the horror of her next statement, "her car . . . *the car was accordioned between two other cars and . . . "* she gasped, *"Oh my God, the body in the casket . . . oh God, they did the best they could . . . but, but it doesn't even look like her!"* Janeen fell forward in the chair, her face plummeting into her cupped hands. "IT DOESN'T LOOK LIKE HER!" she shrieked into her palms, shaking her head. She wept violently into her hands. I glanced briefly at the audience; they were with her, most in tears, many in prayer, still others stared with eyes glazed over, filled with compassion as Janeen sobbed for several minutes. Then, eyes closed, Janeen's head mysteriously rose up out of her lap, a marionette lifted by some invisible string. I knew something else was happening. She paused for a moment. "Denise is telling me that she is up here," Janeen revealed in a flat, emotionless voice, gesturing towards the ceiling, "and not in the casket. She wants me to look up here."

In one of my more brilliant therapeutic moments, demonstrating my keen sense of the obvious, I offered a novel intervention: "Janeen, why don't you just look up?" Eyes closed, Janeen tilted her head up towards the corner of the ceiling. A smile gently dawned on her face. Her eyes were shut, but she clearly "saw" Denise, radiant and whole.

"Mom," Denise told her, "I'm not down there in the casket. I'm up here."

Janeen's face turned toward the floor again, towards where the casket was in her own internal vision. Her face wrenched with anguish. "But, Denise your body is crushed!" she told her daughter, choking back the tears.

"Mom, you don't understand. I am up here. I am not down there. I am like the roses on the casket. You can crush the petals, and they will fall to the floor, but you can still smell the fragrance. Mom, my fragrance will always be with you. *My fragrance will always be with you!*"

Tears streamed down Janeen's face as she communed with her daughter for a few more minutes and then bid her goodbye. You would think that saying goodbye to someone you had lost—yet again—would be terribly painful. But typically, my clients tell me they feel very peaceful at the end of the session—that something feels organically complete, and they can more readily let go. Janeen was no exception, and I wrapped up the onstage session and grounded her energetically.

"Before you leave the stage Janeen, I can only imagine that some people in the audience are saying. 'Wow, poor Janeen just got up there and cried for ninety minutes. I can't wait to do some of this therapy myself!'" I said sarcastically. The audience laughed, grateful for the welcome break in the intensity. But Janeen was not amused.

I gave her a moment before asking, "So, Janeen, sincerely, what was this like for you?"

She narrowed her eyes at me. "Don't you dare joke about this," she said with an unexpected ire. "I have always believed in an afterlife. But now I am absolutely convinced that my husband and my daughter are okay and their spirits live on. *This is the single most important experience of my life.*"

I was simultaneously taken aback and touched, but quickly found my footing. I nodded apologetically as a hush fell over the audience as they took in the enormity of her comment.

"I understand," I said. "Thank you for your courage, Janeen."

The audience, wiping their eyes, suddenly started cheering and applauding. Smiling, I caught Janeen's arm, just as she was about to leave. I had remembered my internal vision of Juan kissing Janeen earlier and wanted to satisfy my curiosity. I whispered away from the microphone, "Before you broke contact with your husband, did he kiss you on your cheek?"

Janeen, astonished, smiled at me and blushed, "How did you know?" I just grinned and said, "A little birdie told me."

I knew then exactly what Dr. Botkin was talking about when he discussed "shared IADCs" in which the therapist or another individual in the room shares part or all of the client's internal vision or experience. I believed it was possible, but it was the first time it had happened to me.

All my history with IADC was percolating in the back of my mind as I began to work with Sheila. I was concerned. Sheila didn't just see someone die in the hospital after a protracted illness or the death of someone she knew casually, although those certainly qualify as clinical trauma. Hers was a whole new level of trauma. She had witnessed the particularly sudden, violent death of the single most important person in her life. Like some kind of cruel magic trick, one minute her husband was alive, sitting next to her in the front seat of their car chatting, and then presto-chango, he was dead. Would IADC work on something this extreme? Could I really desensitize this level of trauma? To top it off, Sheila had come from out of town to see me: We only had three hours together.

As we engaged the IADC procedure, *unprompted*, she emotionally shared a series of terrifying memories of her husband's death: hearing the windshield crash, and looking over to see the devastation to Howard's head; the arrival of EMS; hoping against hope that he might be saved, only to see the look of horror on the medical technician's face; the trip to the hospital; sharing the news with her friends and family; and the agony of telling their children. It was as though Sheila's mind was leafing through a scrapbook of painful scenes, initially overwhelmed by sadness and terror, and then making peace with one page, only to go on to the next. As intense as this was for her, I knew this was the mind engaging the IADC process, digesting the trauma, grinding through the most salient memories, and then arriving in a place of acceptance in an accelerated fashion. With each memory revisited and acknowledged, Sheila became more and more relaxed, even peaceful. I knew that the entire trauma could be left in the "then" and it would no longer haunt her "now."

Finally, the memories slowed and a beatific look came over Sheila's face, her eyes closing. Her voice, almost monotone, announced softly,

"He's here." Then tears appeared, like tiny diamonds in the corners of her eyes. A long pause. "It's Howard!" she suddenly sobbed, her voice rising. "It's Howard, and he's hugging me. I can really feel it . . . oh, oh, Howard." She wept unabashedly, simultaneously grinning from ear-to-ear. "It's really him . . . it's so good to see him . . . it looks like him in his prime, there's not a scratch on him! He's telling me he's okay and that he loves me, and he watches over the children." She suddenly laughed. "He likes Bob, my new husband. He's *glad* I've gone on with my life. He's really happy for me," she exclaimed giggling through her tears.

Suddenly, Sheila lowered her voice. "I was so worried he would be hurt that I remarried," she said to me conspiratorially under her breath, as though if she whispered he would not hear her. "But he is not! And he says Bob is a great father to the kids and that is such a relief to him! He says I chose well! He is proud of me!" She announced, beaming. Her internal communion with Howard lasted about ten minutes, and then gently faded from her awareness. "He's gone now," she announced, her grin fading to a gentle smile. "But it's okay." We sat in the silence for a few minutes, her face glowing.

To wrap up the session, I asked her to envision the original fright-ening memory of the moment the bolt came through the windshield and through her husband's head to see if it still affected her. As with all of my IADC clients, although it seemed unkind to ask her to return to this painful image, I needed a reality check. Could Sheila look at the same mental picture in her mind without being so overwhelmed by terror?

"I can't even picture it anymore . . . all I can see is his face, glowing, smiling at me, and hugging the kids. I'm not terrified when I think of his death. It was awful, but it's over now."

Sheila opened her eyes and looked directly at me. Her countenance appeared five years younger than when she came in three hours ago.

"I guess I'm not at a 'ten' on the terror scale anymore, Gregg," she said, her eyes twinkling, astonished at her reaction. "I'm at a zero. See, I now know that in some special way, he will always be with me."

The Stories Continue

People often ask me, what's the wildest thing that has ever happened in an IADC? I am tempted to tell them about the woman who lost her pet, who felt her "dead" cat jump up into her lap and could feel her fur as she petted him. I could tell you about a session I did with a young woman who lost a family member, who repeatedly saw a telephone ringing in her mind's eye for something like ten minutes. Exasperated, I finally said, "Answer it!" and the woman picked up the phone. "Oh," she said blithely, "it's her!" and went on to have a twenty-minute conversation with her sister, who had been dead for ten years.

Sometimes I think about the skeptical red-headed woman who jumped out of her chair in the middle of an IADC, as I sat eight feet across from her, and asked me if I had touched her. I said "no" and she replied emphatically, "Well . . . somebody did!" To which I said, "It looks like your husband is trying to come through!" Or I could tell you about an atheist who saw her father and her brother on the other side who is still unconvinced about God—but does believe in some kind of afterlife.

But mostly what comes to mind is a young, slight woman named Nonnie, who had lost her brother Daniel and desperately missed him . . . or so she said. She came to see me at a lecture and was so incredibly grief-stricken that I agreed to see her immediately after my presentation, even though I was bone-tired. It had been a long day for me, and to top it off, the workshop had been plagued with audio-visual problems; my PowerPoint was on the blink, and we had trouble with the music. "Sorry folks," I had apologized, "just a tough day at the office, I guess," and they had laughed understandingly.

Nonnie arrived promptly at my hotel suite at seven p.m., accompanied by her cousin, Cynthia. As we engaged the IADC process, a theme emerged: She had been "pissed off" at her brother in life, and now that he was gone, she was pissed off at him in death. Time and again, she recalled "what a loser" he was. I half wanted to ask her if she hated him so much why she even wanted to talk to him.

Daniel had been ten years older than Nonnie. At sixteen, he had left home and Nonnie behind to pursue his career as a painter. Over the years, there had been good and bad times between them, along with copious amounts of alcohol and drugs.

Then suddenly, right in the middle of our session, the alarm clock in my suite began to sound furiously: *BEEP! BEEP! BEEP!* I apologized to her profusely, I literally had no idea why the alarm was going off—I certainly had not set it—and I could see she was more than a little annoyed. I was completely baffled. I hadn't touched the clock and had no reason to set it for eight thirty p.m. or a.m. for that matter. Long ago, I learned not to trust hotel alarm clocks and always scheduled wake-up calls. I briefly wondered whether the last guest might have left an alarm scheduled, only to remember that I had been in the suite at eight thirty the night before and no alarm had sounded.

As perplexed as I was, there was no time to play Sherlock Holmes when I was in the middle of a very disjunctive IADC. But not five minutes after we re-engaged the procedure, the alarm system for the *whole hotel* went off! We were once again, shall we say, *alarmed* by the deafening sound, but they announced on the hotel PA system that it was a malfunction and there was no real threat. Only after covering our ears for about five minutes, did it finally get quiet . . . only to go off again ten minutes later! Though all of this was completely beyond my control, I once again told Nonnie how sorry I was and joked that it *really was* a tough day at the office.

Finally, the session wore down to the last few moments and there was no apparent contact from Daniel. Maybe this was one of those Cayce instances where either she wasn't ready on this side of the veil or he wasn't ready on his side, and there would be no contact.

"Just like in life!" she barked, throwing her hands in the air, clearly irritated both at him and me.

"All I wanted him to do was to show up and tell me he was sorry! But even in death, he couldn't get it right!" she said angrily.

"Well, he kind of did . . . " said her cousin nervously.

The odd expression on Cynthia's face gave me pause. My brow furrowed. Nonnie shot Cynthia a terse glance. "What is she talking about?" I asked Nonnie.

"Well, I had prayed for him to give me some real evidence that he was here, watching over me. I told him, if he still loved me that he had to 'make you' say the name of his most famous painting in your lecture today."

Apparently, I must have looked puzzled. "He is known for his impressionistic art, but he also could be very whimsical with it," said Cynthia with a nervous smile. "Maybe you have seen the famous painting of the businessman in blue, all turquoise and cobalt, slumped over a computer?"

I shook my head.

"It's called *Tough Day at the Office.*" My eyes widened as the blood drained from my face.

"Yeah," said Nonnie, dismissively, "but he couldn't get the alarm right!"

"*Excuse me?*" I said, more genuinely confused than angry.

Nonnie pouted and refused to respond.

Cynthia spoke up, unable to contain herself. "In her meditation this morning, she told Daniel to set off the alarm in her hotel room if he loved her."

"*WHAT THE HELL DID YOU WANT AS MORE PROOF FROM THIS POOR BASTARD?*" I screamed.

Okay, so I didn't actually say that.

But don't think it didn't cross my mind.

Instead, I took a deep breath and set that thought aside. As it turns out, my graduate degree and years of meditation come in handy now and then. I understood that Cynthia carried a lot of anger, and it was becoming apparent that at an unconscious level she was desperately trying to avoid any evidence of her brother's love. Instead, I said quietly, "Nonnie, do you remember how I said at the beginning of the session to try and accept Daniel's way of showing himself to you, and to try not to second guess it too much?"

She nodded and crossed her arms.

"Maybe this was his way of coming to you" I said, leaning over and touching her shoulder. "It strikes me that he did what you asked him."

"Yeah, but the alarm didn't go off in *my* room," she said, dripping acid.

"The alarm went off in the *whole hotel!*" I said.

She looked at me blankly.

"What hotel are you staying in?" I asked Nonnie.

"This one. But so what?"

There was no getting through to Nonnie. She left in tears, still angry, and still feeling victimized and abandoned. Cynthia shot me an apologetic look on the way out the door. Maybe Daniel had been unkind in his life and there was good reason for her rage, but it sure seemed to me that he was using whatever spiritual influence he had to move heaven and earth to reach his sister.

Nonnie was stuck in a frame of mind that she was worthy to be abandoned, and her brother was cruel, and there would be no changing her mind, regardless of the cost to her, or him.

"He who has ears to hear, let him hear," said Jesus.

I guess there was just a lot of wax in Nonnie's ears that day.

* * *

Let's be clear. IADC cannot reanimate bodies or bring anyone back from the dead. It cannot guarantee reconciliation with anyone who is not open to that possibility, any more than therapy between two *living* individuals can. Nor can it take away a certain level of garden-variety grief of losing a loved one. There will always be some pain on that first holiday without them, the anniversary of their passing, or those bizarre moments when we think of them and then "remember" they are dead. If we will but allow the grief to surface at these times, we will move through the hard times and increasingly arrive at a place of acceptance. Although Cayce always reminded those in times of trouble to trust and lean on God, several readings suggested that some "purging" is necessary, a veiled reference to the importance of releasing painful emotions. IADC seems to be excellent at reducing the "core sadness," the overwhelming terror, devastating grief, and shock associated with death. In my estimation, it truly can break the paralysis of intense pain after the loss of a loved one.

As Dr. Botkin points out, new models of grief recognize that when someone dies, the goal is not to simply recognize their death, end the relationship, and "move on." To the contrary, the relationship to the person who has passed *continues* but takes on a new and different form. For most people, that means they relate to that person in their mind and memories. But many IADC clients report a sense of their loved ones continuing to "be around" or still connected to them in some way psychically well after their experiences. Even those who don't make contact in an IADC session sometimes report dreams or other synchronicities that they believe are contact at a later time.

Currently, research continues on IADC therapy at the University of Virginia. Very soon, we may have better clinical evidence of IADC's effectiveness, and thanks to electroencephalography (EEG) studies, we may even discover what is happening in the brain when apparent contact is made.

This is your brain.

This is your brain on dead people.

While it is unfortunate that IADC has been slow to catch on in the United States, where clinicians see it as too "woo-woo" or as too-good-to-be-true, the European therapeutic community has no such qualms. Dr. Botkin tells me that in the last few years he has certified hundreds of therapists in Germany, and there are more lining up to be trained.

IADC therapy suggests that much of that intense suffering around death may be truncated. To the degree there are unresolved issues with the person who died, or if there is trauma or a sense of over-responsibility for the person's death (a common occurrence), these exacerbate the suffering of the survivors. And, as I said earlier, IADC seems to be able to help resolve these issues in an accelerated fashion, *even if contact is not made.*

As one of my clients remarked about their lost loved one, some six months after their IADC, "I still miss them. But IADC took the ax out of my stomach. The guilt, the regret, the fear I somehow failed them is all gone."

7
Brainspotting: Changing Your Brain to Change Your Mind

"Brainspotting is a very important leap forward in helping people resolve trauma ... a remarkable, sophisticated, flexible addition to the therapeutic toolkit of any psychotherapist. I know because I use it regularly ... many traumas and symptoms can be rapidly relieved."

Norman Doidge, MD, FRCPC

In the fall of 2007, I was going through a difficult period in my life, when my friend and colleague Jack Morrison suggested attending a training program in Santa Fe, N.M. It was about *Brainspotting*, something of which I knew nothing at the time. The brochure was filled with a lot of neuro-psycho-babble, but it said the training was given by Dr. David Grand. I had read his book *Emotional Healing at Warp Speed: The Power of EMDR*[15], and had attended his workshop at an International EMDR convention. I was impressed with his bearing and character. And frankly, the idea of getting the hell out of Dodge for a few days in Santa Fe with Jack appealed to me, no matter what the excuse. Little did I know that it would change my practice completely.

It was the dead of winter in Santa Fe, and a blanket of white covered the city. The stark Pueblo architecture carved stunning beige silhouettes into the blue-gray sky. The cold gripped my face the moment

I stepped out of the airport, bringing me out of my malaise and into the immediate moment, as if to say *Wake up! Pay attention!*

At the training, Jack and I learned extensively about Brainspotting. Without boring you with too many technical details, the modality includes working with trauma or negative beliefs by treating them with two distinct eye positions or Brainspots. The first is an eye position called a *distress Brainspot*, which allows repressed trauma to surface and be expressed. You may remember we talked about the amygdalae—the brain's panic button—offering only three options: fight, flight, or freeze. Let's be clear, this Brainspot doesn't *cause* distress, it allows the client to *access* distress that is already in the system, but unprocessed. For many people, the emotional response to the original trauma is somewhere in the deep freeze of the unconscious, and activating a distress Brainspot allows the buried material to come to light— expressed, reprocessed, and put in its proper place in the memory banks. Something happened that was bad, but it happened a long time ago, and it's no longer a current, acute threat.

The other kind of Brainspot is called a *resource Brainspot*, and it refers to an eye position that theoretically activates the most resourceful, adaptive, and positive neural networks in the face of the trauma. Or, it can be used to strengthen an existing positive belief (for example, "I am worthy"), building a superhighway of well-rehearsed thinking where there once was a washed-out dirt road.

These two Brainspots allow me to "titrate" (measure and adjust) the healing experience for my clients. For trauma survivors who are over-whelmed by painful memories, I can help their brain to access resources and build their resilience. For clients who have repressed or become completely dissociated from the trauma, I can use distress Brainspots to "thaw out" the memories and emotions that were locked up in the freeze response. The approach can be tailored very specifically to the client and can include great variation from session to session and issue to issue, so that steady headway can be made, while minimizing the chances of overwhelming the client.

Peak performance clients—those seeking to strengthen their sense of competence under stress—can be asked to imagine a positive or successful moment in their lives and then find a resource correlate in their field of vision that builds confidence and self-efficacy. Dr. Grand has famously used this approach, known as the *expansion model*, with stage actors, business executives, and world–class athletes.

Dr. David Grand is internationally recognized as a trauma therapist and peak performance coach. His book *Emotional Healing at Warp Speed: The Power of EMDR* received national attention, and he has appeared on several network television programs. I often recommend his work to new clients with trauma. For years, he taught his iteration of bi-lateral trauma therapy, known as "Natural Flow EMDR," all over the world.

Working with a competitive figure skater in 2003, David noticed that when he did EMDR eye movements by passing his fingers back and forth in front of his client, there was a reflexive response in her eyes consistently happening at the same point with each pass. She wanted to add a key element to her program, a triple loop, but had been unable to execute it, despite rigorous training. Although she had done a lot of work to release trauma that might unconsciously sabotage her performance, she felt blocked. David noticed the eye response and stopped his fingers directly over the spot within her visual frame of reference and told her to keep staring at that specific spot. Within minutes, a wealth of memory poured out of the young woman, along with a dramatic emotional release.

She went out the next day and nailed the triple.

"Where we look affects how we feel," is Dr. Grand's mantra. Combining aspects of EMDR with this new discovery, David called his new modality, *Brainspotting* (BSP). Many people have come to regard it as a kind of advanced or accelerated EMDR, although in some ways, it is its own critter, as we say in Texas.

Brainspotting relies on *fixed* eye positions to trigger specific neural networks in the client's brain. These networks can be activated to harness the brain's innate ability to heal itself. By activating networks that uncover and release buried trauma, the client becomes free from unhealthy, unconscious drives. By firing neural networks associated with the strongest and most healthy coping and healing mechanisms that the client already has established, they find it fortifies their existing resources, strengthening their ability to work through trauma and build resiliency in life. There are now more than 5,000 Brainspotting therapists around the world healing trauma and improving peak performance from the boardroom to the bedroom.

For some clients, the eye positions can be supplemented with *bio-lateral* audio. This is music or sound that is played through headphones that gently rocks back and forth, alternately getting louder in one ear and then the other, stimulating bilateral processing (similar to EMDR) while the client looks at a fixed point in space, indicated by the pointer, activating a Brainspot. For the record, this is a different technology from binaural beat frequencies (BBF), although they are often confused. It seems for this process to be optimal, there needs to be a profound attunement between the therapist and client.

So, we are back to the concept that, "It's the relationship that heals."

The range of applications for Brainspotting is staggering. It can be used to evaporate anxiety and panic attacks. It allows trauma to be resolved, in my estimation, with more speed and with less painful abreactions than EMDR. Phobias, those pesky irrational fears that keep some of us away from elevators, closets, airplanes, or our friend's pet snake, can usually be eradicated in just a few sessions. It can be used to break up depressive patterns of thought. Brainspotting allows deeply held negative beliefs to be erased and healthier positive cognitions to be "installed" and strengthened. I began to use Brainspotting immediately when I returned from Santa Fe, thrilled to see its phenomenal healing influence on my regular clients. Increasingly, I was stunned by the speed with which previously intransigent, lifelong issues could be cleared. Even on occasions when I had as little time as a single day.

* * *

GLORIA'S IRREVERSIBLE COMPULSION

As far back as she could remember, it was always peanut M&Ms—there would be a big bag on her dresser right by her bed. Sitting beside the candy was *The New York Times* crossword puzzle. Gloria would fluff the pillows, climb into bed, and set the covers just so. She had one of those laptop desks that you could use in bed. It looked like a TV tray shaped like an oversized kidney bean. Underneath the desktop, it was stuffed like a beanbag chair. Wrapping the covers around her, the comforter surrounding her with the warmth of a mother's hug, she snuggled into place. The desktop was painstakingly nestled into her lap.

And then . . . *only then* . . . would she reach over and open the bag of M&Ms. There would be a rush of rich chocolate aroma escaping from the bag. It was intoxicating, the scent beckoning, offering the promise, no, the *guarantee*, of pleasure: dependable, unwavering delight would be delivered. Then, there was the anticipation of the shiny, brightly colored orbs emerging in a row from the bag like ducklings. They would roll playfully in her hand before she would quickly herd the handful to their destination. Her head tipped ever so slightly upwards as her lips parted, her tongue extending, like an illicit lover rushing to meet her partner.

There would be the initial rush of sugar as her tongue hugged the cool smooth surface of the sweets to the roof of her mouth, sucking slightly so as not to break the surface but to begin to drain the pleasure they offered. Next was the brief anticipation as the candy remained motionless in her mouth for the shortest of unbearable instants, giving way to the crackle of the candy shell as her molars broke through with abandon to the sweet creamy chocolate, saliva flooding her mouth. This intense delight was followed by the happy crunch of peanuts exploding with every bite.

Her pencil worked furiously—three down, four across—and her mouth and her mind were busy. It was unthinkable to do anything else every night at bedtime, because to *not* put those peanut M&Ms into her mouth and to *not* solve the crossword puzzle would mean wave after wave of anxious thoughts filing her mind: a high-speed fast rewind, a review of the entire day. *What did she do? What did she say? What should she have said? Why did she say that? She was so stupid, so foolish, and so ignorant! Didn't she realize how insensitive she was? Didn't she? Didn't she realize how ugly she was? Didn't she see the looks on their faces? Why did she say and do things like that?* It was an avalanche of cruel taunts, falling like dominoes through her brain, relentless. No, it had to be the M&Ms, and it had to be the crossword puzzle; it was the only thing that could save her. But the thing that saved her was killing her; she was morbidly obese.

Gloria arrived in my office smiling and good-natured, bright and insightful. Although she could be cynical and sharp, I liked her instantly. She found a way to laugh at nearly everything. She explained that the M&M's strategy had gone back as far as she could remember.

She hadn't always been this overweight. She explained that some ten years ago, she had gone into recovery for her alcoholism. Like many people with addictions, her old behavior seemed to shift to a new target, and the longer she quit drinking the more she gained weight. However, she admitted the M&Ms habit had been going on "forever."

For years, when she was drinking, she ate so little that she didn't regard the M&Ms as a problem. They had little effect on her weight. But now it was different. She wanted to know if I could help her break the hold on this ritual and had flown in for a four-hour extended session. As always, I tried to explain what I thought we might accomplish, and what we might not, in that period of time. But she said she understood. We briefly discussed her history, going over her written intake form. She was already familiar with the Brainspotting process, having read about it on a number of websites, plus having heard about it from friends.

In addition, she had previously used EMDR to resolve some other trauma. All of this worked for us, as it meant she was more open and familiar with this kind of therapy. After about an hour, we were ready to begin Brainspotting.

"Imagine that you're sitting in bed. You have the crossword puzzle in front of you. Now let the compulsion come up for you."

Gloria closed her eyes and immediately began to fidget in the chair. She told me flatly that it was just impossible, unimaginable to think about going to bed without the M&Ms or the crossword puzzle for fear of being at the mercy of her cruel inner critic who would mercilessly tear her apart for any comment, any "sin,"—real or imagined—that she had committed during the day. She rated the cravings at a "ten."

I had her gaze at the tip of the pointer, and we gradually adjusted its position based on her responses. I asked her to focus on how the experience felt in her body. And then, the memories came.

Gloria grew up with a father who was an alcoholic, who was often on the road as a traveling salesman. Even though he drank, Gloria idolized and adored her father, who cut a dashing figure like a 1940s leading man with his double-breasted suits and slicked back hair. Her mother resented her father, his absence and his drinking, and hated the fact that Gloria liked him best.

"My mother played the victim role to a 'T'. Most of my memories of Mother consist of her wringing her hands and talking about Daddy and what he had done to piss her off. It was almost like she wanted me to agree with her about what an ogre he was. My sister, who was younger, was prone to this manipulation, and mother always sided with her. Somehow, the family got divided, and it was always me and Daddy versus Mother and my sister." She sighed. "But that didn't do me much good with Daddy gone most of the time. I was outnumbered."

As Gloria continued to process the compulsion, other memories came to mind. "It's Christmas, and Mother bought me and my sister some new clothes, but Daddy is really angry at Mother for spending too much on us."

"Does that make you angry at your father?' I asked.

"It's weird, but it doesn't," Gloria said flatly. "Actually, I remember feeling incredibly guilty, like I wanted what we got, but also I wished Mother hadn't done it. I wanted to scream at her for spending too much, and tell her all she did was make Daddy upset, and then my sister and I felt guilty."

Then another memory came. It was fascinating to watch the brain, stimulated by the process, making linkages.

"I'm seeing this one crystal clear," said Gloria intensely. "I'm probably about six or seven years old, and I am sneaking out of my bedroom into the kitchen. I know I'm not supposed to be here. I know this would upset my mother if she knew, and that is part of the excitement. I have a secret; I'm breaking the rules. I am very quietly pulling up a chair towards the cupboard. Now I can reach up and grab the white bread and peanut butter. I get it down, and I get the jelly from the refrigerator, and I make myself a big peanut butter and jelly sandwich. And I pour myself a glass of milk. And now I can take this back to my bedroom and eat it all by myself."

"What does that feel like?" I asked Gloria.

"*It's exciting*," she said with a youthful giddiness, her eyes widening. "My heart is pounding, but I feel like I have power, like Mother can't control me. And my reward is that peanut butter and jelly sandwich, and boy, is it ever good! I think all the carbohydrates help calm me down so I can sleep. I remember some nights listening to Mother and

Daddy fighting and not being able to sleep."

"Uh-huh. So now you have some comfort and relief . . . even a kind of power."

"Yes!" She said nodding vigorously. "I'm sure that's how I felt!" Suddenly, Gloria frowned, seeing something unfold.

"What's happening now?" I said.

"My sister hears me one night as I make my way to the kitchen. She tries to do what I do, but when she drags the chair up to the cupboard, it screeches and she makes all kinds of noise. I tell her to *be quiet*, but she is younger than I am and clumsy. Thanks to my sister, we both get busted, and Mother and Daddy are screaming at us and each other. I hate this! I hate this! I just want it all to stop, to all go away. I want to go to my room by myself where I can eat my sandwich and have my milk."

As Gloria continued to process the experience, other memories came: growing up in a Catholic school with nuns that thought everything was a sin. There were spankings on the hand with rulers and waiting for God's punishment for something she had done that surely was unforgivable. Now, she remembered. "So every night when I'm supposed to be praying, I must have gone over and over in my head what I was going to go to hell for! I hate them!"

I couldn't help but notice that as Gloria cried, she was wringing her hands. No doubt just like her mother. Then slowly, over a period of minutes, the tears subsided, and Gloria got very still.

"I feel really peaceful now," she said quietly. "This reminds me of how I feel after I had my peanut butter and jelly sandwiches when I was a kid." There was a gentle smile on Gloria's face. I paused for a moment before making an important connection.

"And yet you haven't had anything to eat," I said very gently and waited for it to sink in. Gloria frowned, as if wondering how that could even be possible. Then her eyes darted around off the pointer, and she heaved a heavy sigh.

"How did that feel?"

"Good," she replied automatically. I could see that she was second-guessing her immediate response. But then she thought about it for a moment and took another deep breath, her head gently nodding. "Good." This time it was like she was almost sure.

"What is happening now, Gloria?" I asked.

"Nothing really . . . I just feel good," she commented, sounding somewhat surprised. "Is that okay?"

"Is it?"

"Yeah . . . it's nice, actually."

"What do you notice in your body?" I queried.

"I don't know . . . maybe a kind of heaviness in my feet . . . my shoulders are relaxed. And there's like a warmth in my chest," she said softly.

"Do you ever remember feeling this as a child?"

"I don't know if I have *ever* felt like this . . . this still. There's no anxiety here."

Two and a half hours had gone by since we started the Brainspotting.

"Gloria, let's come back to the cravings. You're sitting in your bedroom. You have your laptop desk in front of you with a crossword puzzle on it, and you're looking toward the bag of M&Ms. On a scale from zero to ten, where ten is the strongest cravings you've ever had, and zero is none or neutral, where do you find yourself right now?"

"I'm at . . . a zero? Can that really be? I'm at a zero. I am. I'm really a zero." I could hear the excitement begin to build in her voice. "I don't know if I'm fooling myself, but it feels like the whole thing is no big deal. I don't need to eat the M&Ms. Is that really possible?" She asked me with no small amount of disbelief in her voice.

It was possible. Gloria's twenty-year M&M habit came to an end that day. Gloria went to bed that night with her crossword puzzle, but not her chocolate friends. The compulsion was gone. The habit was ended.

But then things got even better.

Gloria called me on the telephone, long-distance, some eight months later. Inspired by her victory over chocolate, Gloria joined Overeaters Anonymous.

"I figured a twelve-step program helped me get over alcohol, why not try it for my eating disorder? I thought it would be hard, and there are certain foods that I sure miss, but overall, the program has been easy! There is just something magical about twelve-step meetings."

She had lost fifty pounds and the M&M compulsion had not returned.

"I can't believe it," she said excitedly. "I feel like a whole new person. My clothes fit better, and I walk totally different. Gregg, have you ever picked up a ten-pound sack of potatoes? Imagine walking around carrying five of those. Now imagine dropping all those potatoes, and think about how relieved you would feel. That should give you some idea what this is like for me."

"That's wonderful!" I said. "If I may say so, I am so proud of you, Gloria."

"You may!" responded Gloria beaming. "But it's more than that, Gregg. Remember that inner critic? She's not gone completely, but it's much better. I just don't beat myself up as much as I used to. Now when I screw up, I give myself a pass most of the time. Honestly, a lot of the stuff I used to think was unforgiveable was really mundane, trivial stuff anyway! I figure I can learn from my mistakes, without beating the hell out of myself. It's nice. I still have more weight to lose, and honestly, I have been plateauing here lately," she admitted, "but it's a hell of a start."

*   *   *

BRAD'S BREAK-UP

Brad was a sandy-haired charmer in his late thirties. Good-looking and charismatic, he could have passed for a male model in his designer suits and expensive dress shirts. Brad always came to his appointments in suits, even in the heat of the Texas summer. Apparently, he had never heard of the concept of casual Fridays. He had a penchant for French cuffs with ornate cuff links.

"Some people say they are still in style and some don't, but everybody always looks at them and gives me compliments, so I keep wearing them," he said with a shy smile.

He liked to live a little on the edge. He was a financial advisor, but he did some day trading on the side. Sometimes he was lucky, and sometimes he was smart, he told me. But usually, if he wasn't one, he was the other, and when the market turned, he had always found a way to bounce back.

But Brad was having trouble bouncing back from a breakup with his long-time live-in girlfriend, Melissa.

"I'm just devastated. I feel empty inside. I feel like I will never, ever fall in love again, like it's all just hopeless," he said, his voice weary with emotion.

Admittedly, he should have seen the writing on the wall. She had gotten busier at work, and when he came home, he always played first-person shooter video games. Brad admitted he had spent less time with her. She was looking for a real commitment. What was holding him back? She gave him my telephone number, telling him he needed counseling, but he refused, saying everything was fine. She would argue that she wanted marriage and children. But he would ask her, "Can't we just let things unfold?" After ten years, she had seen just what had unfolded, and she was getting tired of waiting.

She'd been drinking more, and his pleas for restraint had gone unheard. Their sex life wasn't what it used to be, but hey, didn't that happen to everybody after a few years? And sure, she had talked about a co-worker, Nasim, a lot lately, but at the time, he hadn't given it much thought. Brad was too busy making money.

When Melissa finally told him to move out, he was blindsided and devastated. He couldn't focus on work, and he had caught himself withdrawing from life. For three weeks, he had been living in his new apartment, trading sporadically on his computer, but unable to "nest" in his new place.

"I've got boxes everywhere, but I just can't get motivated. I can't even find the energy to hang a picture on the wall. It's like . . . what for? I am never really going to feel at home anywhere. Why bother?"

He felt abandoned and hopeless, and alone, so alone—like he would never have anyone ever again.

After a couple of sessions going over his history and seeing that Brad was comfortable with me, we engaged in Brainspotting. I asked Brad what the most painful thought was about the breakup. He said he remembered driving by Melissa's house, "the house that was *my* house too, for ten years!" In the driveway was Nasim's car at three o'clock in the morning. It was a week after the breakup.

As Brad looked at the tip of the pointer, an initial wave of pain flowed through his body.

"She's with somebody else, now. I can't believe it," he said, his voice cracking. Ten years, and now she is with somebody else, overnight, just like that! And there is nothing I can do!" he moaned, the tears spilling over the edge of his lower lids. Brad immediately wiped them, often dabbing at this eyes with wadded up tissues as though he could will the pain to go back inside.

But after only a few minutes the memories shifted.

"Everybody leaves; they just all go away. When I was a kid, five years old, Dad left; he just disappeared, like he didn't have a family. I wasn't such a bad kid—I wasn't. How does anybody do something like that? I mean, how do they live with themselves?" he exclaimed, as though asking the universe. "And then poor Mom . . . " he tried to choke back more tears. "Poor Mom had to work all the time. She worked at a garment factory during the day and then got off and worked at a Denny's as a waitress, just so we could eat. Sometimes she would bring home leftovers from the restaurant."

"Where did that leave you after school?" I queried.

"Where do you think?" Brad said tersely, eyes blazing. "I was alone. Alone at home! I would come home, make myself a peanut-butter-and-jelly sandwich, and stare at the walls. Thursdays were good, because I could watch *Star Trek* reruns until she got home. Most days my sister came home, and she would look after me. Lynn was a godsend. She loved me, but I knew I got on her nerves. Lynn was six years older than I was, and she wasn't my mother, but she had to be, because Mom worked till almost eleven at night! Shit, life just wasn't fair—not to me, not to Mom, not to poor Lynn, looking after her kid brother."

He crumpled, overwhelmed, and buried his face in his hands. I decided we should close down the session, so I offered Brad some soothing imagery for the last few minutes of the session. He left feeling raw, but okay.

The next session started once again with the target image of Nasim's car in Melissa's driveway. But Brad's mind didn't stay there long.

"I am imagining Melissa getting in the car with this Nasim guy, and she is laughing and flirting with him, like she did with me when we first met. How can she do that?" he asked incredulously.

But then the scene changed, and Brad was about eight years old, and he was looking out of the front window of his childhood home, watching his then fourteen-year-old sister, Lynn, drive off with a high school senior. He could feel the cold pane as he pressed his hands against it, his face so close that his breath clouded the glass.

"She promised we were going to play a video game. She promised!" Brad anguished, reliving the experience. "And she said we would order pizza, and then this guy just drives up and honks, and she is gone! She promised! What is so wrong with me that everybody leaves?"

Lynn, as it turned out, had gone boy crazy at fourteen. Abandoned by her father, she craved male attention and learned that sex was the ticket to get that attention, at least for a while. Brad sat quietly, looking at the pointer for a long time and then released a deep sigh of resignation.

"So then *she* was gone, too. First Dad, then Mom, then even Lynn. It was so unfair. I guess I can't blame her. Who would want to stay at home with a dumb little kid?"

Brad sat in silence for a long time. Finally a look of grim determination came over his face. He began to breathe more quickly and a bit deeper.

"So you know what? I started getting into video games. When I played those games, I was always in control, you know? Anybody I didn't like, I could just shoot them. In that world, I was always in control. And with Lynn gone all the time, I could do what I wanted. Mom was working, so I would go ride bikes and skateboard with my friends and smoke dope back behind the greenbelt."

"Was your mother ever suspicious?" I asked.

"She was never there!" Brad blurted, with a strange mix of sadness and delight.

"So you learned not to count on others; you learned to take care of yourself."

"Goddamn right, daddies leave and mommies are busy, and big sister is out fucking the football team, so yeah, I'm looking out for me!" Brad said indignantly. "You can't count on anybody; they're all off like a bunch of selfish pricks, only thinking of themselves. What does that do to a kid?!"

"What about weekends? Was your mom ever off work?" I asked gently.

"She was in her room, depressed." He looked at the pictures in his mind's eye. "Yeah, depressed and exhausted from double shifts. She started drinking more and more. Dad screwed her over good, and she never forgave him, but that took all her energy—just hating Dad and working two jobs. I ran away at sixteen and never looked back."

At the end of the session, I asked Brad how distressed he was when he thought about seeing Nasim's car in the driveway.

"About an 'eight,' but you know, I'm not sad, I'm pissed! Who is this guy? And how come HE gets Melissa? And why does she get to leave, and I am stuck staying behind? It's like I have some kind of curse or something. Fuck her! I don't need this shit!"

Strangely, I knew Brad was making headway. There was still a lot of distress, but he was processing through the sadness and owning some of the anger at Melissa. These were very different emotions than the sadness and hopelessness that he had originally presented.

He was also making some very important connections that I knew would change his life forever, even if he had not yet put the pieces of the puzzle together.

At our next session, Brad came in the door irritated. I asked him how he had been, and he said, "Pissed off, all week long."

We started Brainspotting, and the anger blossomed.

"Honestly, I am mad at all of them. I was just a little boy, and they left me. I needed them, and they left me!"

"Why do you think they left you, Brad?"

"Shit, I don't know, I was a kid, I can't figure out what makes adults do what adults do."

"I am going to move the wand around. Let me know where you can feel a shift in your body—a shift into a more adult, mature, objective way of seeing."

I shifted the wand into a number of positions, and then suddenly Brad was very emphatic. "Right there!" He reached up and grabbed the wand to adjust the Brainspot. "I feel . . . solid, like I have my feet on the ground or something."

"Look again at your whole childhood, and see if you don't notice something different as you look at it from an adult's perspective."

Brad got very quiet. Minutes passed.

"You know, I don't know why Dad left. I don't guess I'll ever know." He said dispassionately. "But," he hesitated, anticipating the wave of emotion that was coming, "Mom was gone, because she loved us. She grew up poor and knew what it was like to go hungry, but *we never went hungry, because she worked two jobs.* And we never were homeless, because *she worked two jobs.* It wasn't about me . . . I mean it was *all* about me and Lynn. She would come home bone tired; they worked her to death."

Brad looked into the distance.

"I am remembering something. I am about six, and Mom has come home, and I was trying to bake her cake or cookies or something for her birthday and . . . " he smiled a sad, sweet smile, "I had made one hell of a mess in the kitchen. At first when she looked at me, I thought she was going to be angry, but instead she started crying. I thought I had hurt her somehow. She covered her mouth and said, 'Oh, Bradley, you deserve so much more . . . I'm so sorry!' And then she was overcome and ran to her room. She couldn't have been more than about thirty, trying to raise me and Lynn without Dad. I didn't understand it at the time, but I think I do now."

"What do you see?"

"That she loved me—she really loved me. She did her best and that meant most of her time was just spent keeping us alive. All I wanted was to have time with her, but she had to work. She could have been so much more, if she had any time, but she made sure we were safe and fed, and that took all she had."

He was quietly crying, sniffing back the tears.

"And Lynn?"

"Aw, she went boy crazy, she just wanted attention—anybody's attention—and she got it. Anything to get out of that house. She tried, she really did. Sometimes she even made her boyfriends take me along on dates with her and buy me dinner or a ticket to the movies." He paused. "I can only guess what she had to do later for that," he said with a laconic sadness. He thought for a moment.

"Aw, hell, if I could've gotten out of there, I would have." He frowned as something dawned on him. "In fact, you know what? That is *exactly* what I did. In my twenties, I dated a lot of women. Actually 'dated' isn't exactly the right word, if you know what I mean. I never let anyone get too close though. I learned my lesson about people leaving you all the time."

"So you got to 'win' by being the one who left," I said.

"Yeah, I guess so. Well, it beats being abandoned," he said sheepishly.

"So you got to 'win'; you got to be your father."

"Well, I never thought about it that way."

"I know," I said firmly.

"Well, what would you have done?" he said defensively, his voice rising.

"Not getting close became a way to protect yourself," I said coolly.

"But I *wanted* the love and attention of women!" Brad said in irritation.

"Of course, but not too much. Too much might tempt you to stay and then get your heart broken. So you took care of yourself by holding back."

"But I *stayed* with Melissa. *I stayed for ten years!*"

"Did you Brad? The guy that got stoned on the weekends and played video games? The one that worked all the time?"

"I am *not* my father!" Brad said tersely through gritted teeth.

"You were trying *not* to be. Staying with Melissa for ten years was a huge step for you, unprecedented, courageous. But, unconsciously, you pulled back."

Brad was fixed on the tip of the pointer. Minutes went by. He began to choke up.

"You're right. I did. I didn't mean to . . . I thought I was doing good, just being with one woman for ten years."

"It's more than your dad did," I said with genuine admiration. "But you couldn't quite take it to the next level, Brad. Melissa felt this. She tried to tell you in her own way. If you don't know after ten years whether you want to spend your life with someone, when *would* you know?"

There was a deep pause.

"I know." Brad took a slow breath. "I was just so scared, and I didn't even know I was scared."

"Dope will make a lot of pain go away for a day or two. So will work."

"But what did I do as a kid that made everybody leave?" he fired, his frustration rising again.

"You know the answer," I said, my voice just above a whisper. "Look deeply from your new perspective. Ask that part of you that knows the answer."

His eyes narrowed, looking at the pointer as though it could give him the answer. And strangely, suddenly, it seemed to do exactly that. *"Nothing!"* Brad blurted, perhaps louder than he intended. He blinked several times, transfixed with his answer. "Nothing," he said again, this time more softly. "Nothing. It was just the way it was," he reported dryly. "But I thought it was me, and as long as I think it's me, I am going to spend the rest of my life waiting to be left and not letting anyone get too close so I won't be left. Wow. *It's my fear of being left that got me left.* Shit. Who knew?"

Brad sat staring at the wand, ruminating, for a long time. Then suddenly he broke out laughing.

"Well, *that's* not gonna work, is it?" said Brad in a wildly animated voice, a crazy broad grin spreading across his face. He deliberately shifted his gaze off the end of the pointer and looked at me, shaking his head in disbelief and laughing.

One of the EMDR therapists I trained with was part of a humanitarian response team that went to Oklahoma City in the wake of the bombing of the Murrah Federal Building in 1995. Trained clinicians gave one or two weeks of their time, many traveling at their own expense, to help victims, first responders, and relatives of those who were killed. Laughter would be the last thing you would expect from such traumatized patients. But the therapist said he consistently saw this kind of response deep into the processing, when their clients turned a crucial corner. The counselors dubbed this moment, the "giggle response."

With my clients, it often comes when someone makes a sudden and deep cognitive shift, and they "get" the whole truth of the experience, almost like someone gets a joke. Research at Harvard, in which subjects were placed in an MRI while watching a *Seinfeld* episode, demonstrated that "getting" jokes, activated the prefrontal cortex, the part of the brain involved in complex problem solving. It is a genuine change in perspective in which the client sees the ridiculousness of the coping they have devised for themselves, and it just becomes goofy. As I said at a workshop at Omega at the Crossings years ago while discussing humor and creativity: Maybe you can't have an "Aha," without a "ha!"

So Brad sat there, smiling at himself, realizing that the very thing that he put in place to protect himself led to his abandonment. In a weird way, it *was* kind of funny, like trying to open a door labeled

PUSH by pulling on it repeatedly.

In our final session, I asked Brad to close his eyes and imagine Nasim's car in Melissa's driveway one last time. Brad discovered that the experience was all but completely desensitized.

"You know, it's just . . . it's just sad," he said in resigned tone, tinctured with tenderness. "Not overwhelmingly, not cratering me. It's just like, well, too bad that it played out that way. I don't blame Nasim, hell, I don't even know him. And Melissa was right; the guy I was? He was gun shy, waiting to be left. When I think about it, I don't know that Melissa was really right for me, either. She got to where she drank so much I worried about her—shades of my mom, right? And she is kind of an Earth Mother type and all into Renaissance literature, and I am a football and reality–TV guy who likes fast cars and nice suits." He laughed. "I went to a party with her co-workers at the university, and they looked at me like I was from another planet. What were we thinking? I mean, it was good for a while, but we probably should have split up a long time ago."

"As you think about going out and dating again, how do you feel?"

"Good. Confident . . . not in a cocksure kind of way, but like, hey, I am not a bad guy. And I think, when I'm ready, I could trust someone to love me." He paused and looked at me with an honest smile. "And *I am not ready yet*, Gregg," he said emphatically.

"That's okay," I said with an easy smile. "You'll know when."

"I stayed with Melissa for ten years, I just wasn't present; it's like I wasn't really fully there. And now I see that made it all harder, not easier for me. So, yeah, I'm okay. Strangely—and this is not anything against Melissa—I feel like I kind of dodged a bullet. I hope she and Nasim are happy drinking wine and reading Dante and Erasmus together. "

There were other issues that we might have explored more deeply—what sex meant to him, his relationship to marijuana, alcohol, and work—but Brad decided soon after to move to Denver to get a fresh start. In a telephone call some two years after his therapy was completed, he reported to me that he was filled with gratitude for the work we did and what he had learned. He was dating, enjoying his work, and his life was worth living. He said he was still astonished in what we covered in those four seminal Brainspotting sessions and how what might have been years of guilt and worthlessness was truncated into a few weeks. He had a new clarity on life and his own apartment that he called home—with pictures on the wall.

*   *   *

Brainspotting, to me, came to feel like a fast-track EMDR. After Brad, I had a number of other clients who came to me in pain from a break-up. Similarly, Brainspotting helped clear the worst of their pain in just a few extended sessions.

At first blush, it would seem that after a relationship ends, the over-whelming sadness of the loss is unavoidable. But the truth is that the pain is not rooted solely in the breakup. As with Brad, it goes much deeper than that. "I miss my ex-partner," is not going to go away over-night. But as it turns out, there are a lot of other deeply held beliefs that often come up when a relationship ends:

"I am a complete failure."

"I am unlovable."

"Everyone always leaves me."

"I can't trust anyone."

"I always pick the wrong kind of partner."

And the list goes on and on.

These *can* be resolved and worked through *independently* of the grief of the loss. As you can imagine, you can survive missing your ex-lover if you feel like you are still a decent human being who is loveable and did their best, even if you made some mistakes. You can go on with your life, if you still feel sure that you can learn from your errors and be trusted to find someone new who is a better partner, more suited to you.

For many of my clients, Brainspotting has been their ticket to free-dom when they felt "addicted" to their partners. "I know he is bad for me, but I just can't leave!" is a line I have heard from dozens of female clients. Sometimes these relationships are driven by the guilt that they are afraid they will feel if they break up, or a fear of living alone. It turns out, if these irrational beliefs are released, someone *can* leave an "addictive" relationship.

One client—a successful, charismatic lawyer who could've passed for Denzel Washington's kid brother—couldn't let go of a seven-year relationship in which he was shamed by his live-in girlfriend on a daily basis and spent literally tens of thousands of dollars trying to make her happy. He reached out to me when things had reached a crisis. Daily, she would shriek at him that he was the cause of all her problems, and she unjustly accused him of multiple affairs. My sense was that she was delusional, in the grips of a severe personality disorder.

"I can't leave her," he said in his first session, "she needs me. And the guilt would kill me. Who abandons someone who is in that much pain? Besides, I'm ugly. No one would want me." I bit my tongue, as my mind raced to any number of my female clients who would be thrilled to be with someone as generous, kind, successful, and attractive. He admitted to being miserable for years, but powerless to leave.

"I keep thinking about a chess game I once saw. When one of the players saw he couldn't win, he just took his pieces off the board. Some nights, I think that's the only solution."

"What do you mean?" I asked, my face puzzled and concerned.

"I put my gun on the bed some nights and think, *Maybe I will just quit playing the game. Maybe that would be better for everybody.*"

But after three extended two-hour sessions, he broke up with her, as he realized that his inability to leave her was not based on love, but a fear of abandoning her much the same way he was abandoned by his parents as a child. The enormity of the guilt, and the sure sadness he had so readily anticipated, all but evaporated in real life. Instead, he found himself enveloped by a transcendent freedom.

"It's as though I've been let out of a box, and I am running free across a green field. It's like a millstone has been taken from my neck!" he said excitedly.

As much as we think our grief is only about the loss in front of us, there are layers that are deeply connected to our past. If we can undo those layers, we may still miss our partners, but we will heal and love again.

We all have met people who have become bitter and isolated for years after a break-up, while others seemed to have grieved, learned from their experiences, and gone on to start over with someone new. Brainspotting seems to be able to untangle the Gordian knot of feelings so that a new beginning can happen sooner.

As amazing as Brainspotting was at resolving trauma and anxiety, halfway through Dr. Grand's workshop, it dawned on me there might be an even more profound use for this technology. If Brainspotting could be used to strengthen confidence and self-esteem and enhance peak performance, what would happen if the client focused on a *spiritual* experience? What if a memory could be replayed and enhanced, bringing a once-in-a-lifetime vision or transcendent experience into the here-and-now? What if we could take a life-changing moment and replay it over and over, reliving it with all its intensity, deep-soaking in its wisdom and power?

What if we could take that experience even deeper?

My heart was racing; my head, spinning.

8

Spiritual Activation: Hardwiring Your Brain to God

"For those people who are graced with a mystical experience
. . . the crucial question is what to do with it . . . the aim is to
extend a single peak experience . . . to change an altered state
into an altered trait, or as Huston Smith put it so eloquently,
to transform flashes of illumination into abiding light."

Roger Walsh, ND, Ph.D

I was holding a collapsible silver pointer in my hands, and it was fully extended.
These days, people use laser pointers, but this was an instrument used
by teachers from another era to gesture to countries on a roller–blind
Mercator projection map that pulls down from the ceiling or to point
to the dairy section on the chart of the four major food groups. Like an
old–fashioned car antenna, it could be extended outward to a full
length of thirty–six inches or collapsed down to six.

June, my client, was a social studies teacher who was depressed, but
very grounded in reality. She had been staring at the end of the pointer
for over thirty minutes. June's mother suffered from severe Alzheimer's
disease. After years of caring for her, June was struggling with whether
or not to institutionalize her. Suddenly the brainspotting session took
an unusual turn.

"I know you are not going to believe me," she said casually, as though she were about to dish on her favorite movie star, "but all the rainbow colors have stopped whooshing from your stick, and Jesus just stepped out of the end of the pointer."

It was another day at the office.

During my Brainspotting training in 2007, I had an epiphany in the middle of a workshop. I wondered: What if we took a spiritual experience and "looped" it in the brain, playing the neural networks of enlightenment over and over? What would happen? Could we relive the experience? Could we take it even deeper? If, in fact, meditation develops certain circuits in our brain to access our spirituality through repetition, might this be a shortcut, a way to hotwire our brains to God?

Or could we even *hardwire* our brains to God?

I couldn't wait to get back home to try it.

Several weeks later, we went to my training colleague Jack's house and set our chairs up in his backyard overlooking Austin. Surrounding us were mighty live oaks, verdant shrubs, and colorful flowers. Kinetic metal sculptures turned and creaked softly in a gentle spring wind. I was feeling closer to God already. *Maybe*, I thought to myself, *we need an office out in Jack's backyard.*

When I travel around the country and tell people I'm from Texas, folks that haven't been here always think of it like Road Runner cartoon country—flat with scrub and saguaro cactuses. But Austin and its surrounding area are a part of the state that is known as the Texas Hill country. While it's not the Rockies, it's hardly flat and dusty, with gentle peaks climbing to nearly a thousand feet. Creeks, lakes, and wildlife preserves flank the city. There's a reason why Stephen F. Austin built a colony here.

As we settled into our chairs, I asked Jack if he wanted to go first, but my motives were hardly generous. I explained that if the process went as I anticipated, then I might be in no shape to hold the pointer after I catalyzed my spiritual experience. Jack smiled and agreed.

I asked Jack to think of his most profound spiritual moment. He sat for a moment, pondering. "Let me go back to that place." He closed his eyes and took a deep breath, almost as though he was taking a drag on an imaginary cigarette. A moment or two went by as he offered a long exhalation and allowed himself to return to his epiphany.

"I have to go back many years to retrieve this. It was a powerful experience. I don't even remember exactly how it happened. I was just looking around one morning—the sky was this perfect blue, the grass was intensely green, the weather was just perfect. On that morning, in that moment, there was this dawning of awareness." He grasped for words, knowing how feeble they were. "I finally knew who I really was. It was a great day, a perfect day, a day I realized I didn't need alcohol or pot or whatever to be present, to be happy."

I smiled. In the many years I had known Jack, I had seen him drink the sum total of one margarita. He meant it.

"It was a moment in time in which I realized my real relationship to the Universe. There was this sense of being in one place at the center of my being as well as this overwhelming connection to all that I could ever imagine existed: a unique simultaneous experience of a very intimate connection to my deepest self and also the larger connection to everything. It was life changing."

"Okay," I said very quietly, trying not to break the spell. "Open your eyes and follow the pointer." Jack smiled, amused, even in his heightened awareness, that he was "playing" client, while I "played" therapist. As I positioned the pointer, Jack tapped into a requisite-felt response in his body. We established a resource Brainspot, and we knew we had fully activated the process.

Minutes went by. Occasionally, Jack would take a deep breath and exhale again, and his body would become even more relaxed. His breath became very, very slow, his eyes far away in another realm. It seemed to me as though his wrinkles disappeared, and I could see the face of a young man in his twenties.

Twenty minutes passed, not a word spoken, only the trees whispering as a gentle Texas breeze caressed our faces. I watched intently, deeply attuned to Jack. Was that the tiniest of tears in the corner of Jack's left eye? Jack was not given to intense emotions. It was rare that I saw him angry or even sad. But there was this glistening in his lower left eyelid. He was moved, deeply moved.

Suddenly, he took a deep breath. "I'm . . . uh . . . " He blinked rapidly and exhaled. "I'm done, I'm cooked," he remarked flatly. We had been on the Brainspot for more than thirty minutes. Jack rubbed his eyes, twisting his chin first left then right, stretching his neck. He took another breath. His eyes gazed a thousand miles away.

"Well?" I asked, unable to contain myself, but not wanting to be too pushy.

"*Well*," Jack said, chuckling and looking directly at me. He reached up and rubbed his neck, looking around the backyard. If I didn't know Jack, I would've guessed he was making me wait for it. But he wasn't. He was gathering his thoughts.

"I, uh, started out kind of reliving the experience. But I went beyond it." He paused. "It was kind of an out-of-body experience. In the original experience, I had a perspective of being in my body and what was around my body, but this was more like a perspective of being . . . body-less. I mean, I had a location for my body, but I wasn't attached to it." He blinked several times and took a breath.

"Was that frightening in any way?"

"No, it was this . . . blissful, amazing thing. I was connected to myself and everything. But then it became almost overwhelming. It was almost like eating a rich dessert—like it was too rich, too much. I couldn't stay there for an infinite amount of time . . . at least not at this point in my life. But I was expanded with a sense of deep connection to all that there is."

"So, you fully recaptured the experience?"

"No," he mused, glancing at the sky briefly. Then he returned his gaze to me, his expression sincere and intent. He leaned forward.

"Gregg, it wasn't just a recreation of the initial experience; *it was an expansion and deepening of the original experience.*" He paused again, looking for words. "It was humbling. Powerful. I am left with a stronger sense of self."

Reflecting on the experience later, Jack put it this way: "The power of my mystical awakening years ago was life-changing. It's like someone turning on a light switch, and you are just flooded. It just happens. You are somehow changed without knowing how. By themselves, these experiences become a light in the darkness. But Brainspotting takes this point of light and can give your mind a direction, a path. In Brainspotting, you can consciously process the experience. It told me *why* I had the experience. It helped me to *integrate* the experience, even years later."

Then it was my turn. Jack played counselor, asking me to focus on a spiritual memory. I chose an experience that, looking back, I now regard as the turning point for my decision to return to school to be-come a counselor, although I did not know it at the time.

I was attending a workshop with Dr. Frank Allen in Houston, Texas. Frank was amazing and talented. He has a reputation as a therapist's therapist, and he wasn't afraid to work on the common boundary between spirituality and psychology. I had discovered Frank in 1988, at an "A Course in Miracles" workshop in Austin, in which he simply (seemingly) asked people provocative and belligerent questions, only to watch them burst into tears and have their lives miraculously change. Here were the miracles I had read about in the *Course*, playing out in real time in front of me! Not an hour into the workshop, an inner voice told me: *Follow him. He has been where you are going.* (I was not a counselor at the time. I thought that meant I should pay attention for the weekend!)

The day after the workshop, I felt like someone had shaken my entire body and hung me out to dry. The whole world looked differ-ent: I had to find out why.

I began doing literally every workshop Dr. Allen offered, often mak-ing the three-and-a-half hour drive from Austin to the Houston Jung Center after getting off a late shift, in the middle of the night—sleeping in my car, because I couldn't afford a motel. I scraped together money, getting scholarships when I could, to participate in Frank's three-day, four-day, and sometimes week-long intensives around the country.

As I sat in Jack's backyard, my mind drifted back to a workshop in which there were probably fifteen or twenty participants. Frank had instructed us to close our eyes, relax, and just listen to a piece of music for twenty minutes. The composition was *Novus Magnificat: Through the Stargate* by Constance Demby, a powerful, if somewhat theatrical piece that was alternately light and dark, loud and soft, tearfully sad and then celestial and blissful.

I closed my eyes and watched as my unconscious spun a prophetic web of images. I was inside a beautiful beach house with a vaulted ceiling out on a point that overlooked the ocean. Initially the weather was beautiful as the setting sunlight danced orange-gold on the gentle waves. Although I did not see my family members, I had a sense that this was my ancestral home.

As I looked through the large plate glass windows overlooking the ocean, I could see in the distance a storm was coming—gray at first, then ominously brewing into a swirl of deep black and silver clouds. The thunder rolled and echoed; the lightning flashing, casting frightening shadows across the living room floor—evil incarnate reaching toward me. The window rattled; the floor trembled. I clung to the relative shelter of the house as long as I could, but I somehow intuitively knew I had to leave. I knew my family was still in the home, but I also knew they had made their choices.

I managed to make it some fifty yards distance from my house just as lightning struck the beleaguered structure. It exploded in a violent burst and then collapsed as though in slow motion. I stood transfixed, awestruck, and unable to turn away from the building that had been my home, my only safety. I saw the last smoking timber fall on the smoldering heap; there was no going back now, not ever.

I sought shelter in some boulders on the beach and survived the storm, but the weather had wrought lasting damage. I looked out onto the beach, and there were hundreds of dead seagulls scattered haphazardly across the shoreline. The unfortunate carnage was too much for me, and I began crying. I felt incredibly sad. Crying, weeping in desperation, I came out from the rocks and reached down and picked up one of the dead seagulls, cradling it in my cupped hands, petting its dead body, and feeling the softness of its downy plumes. The bird was cold and still. My tears and the rain fell on the feathered corpse.

Then the wind began to quell and a stillness fell over the landscape.

I looked out to see an image of a flying Christ, luminous arms spread to each side coming from the horizon. He carried a glowing radiant heart in his hands. He came closer and closer to me now, perhaps some thirty or forty feet above my head. I was looking straight up at him. As he approached, points of light emanated from his body and fell like snowflakes to the ground. It was almost as though he was *raining light*. Some of these pinpoints of light landed on the unfortunate creature in my cupped hands.

The bird glowed with the light, and then awakened. He shook his feathers like a Blue Jay drying himself after a birdbath. He looked up at me briefly, as if to say thanks, and then flew off. Spontaneously, I reached down and picked up another seagull, and once again lights fell on the bird's body, and she returned from death. I continued to work, picking up seagull after seagull, watching them all come to life. It was a profound and beautiful experience.

From somewhere far away, I heard Jack ask me how much in touch I felt with this spiritual experience, with "ten" being the most richly connected I'd ever been and "zero" being no spiritual connection at all. My eyes teared up, even as I thought about the experience, and rated it at about a "seven." I had touched my vision in my imagination, but it certainly was not as powerful as the original experience. At least . . . not yet.

Jack asked me to open my eyes as he slowly moved the pointer in order for me to pinpoint the area in the visual field where I felt most in touch with the experience. I could feel what Eugene Gendlin called a *felt sense*, a visceral internal response in my body. Jack finally landed on a position somewhat outward and upward towards the right in my field of vision, and held the pointer in place. Roger, Houston, we have a Brainspot.

We both waited.

Initially, there was a warmth around my heart that seemed to expand and get bigger and bigger. Then I noticed the lump in my throat. Both grew in size and became tighter. This eventually burst out through my throat, and I began to weep. This went on for about three minutes, and then I became very still and calm, feeling very present in the moment.

I was aware of Jack.

I was aware of the breeze on my face.

I was aware of the tip of the pointer.

I was aware of the feel of the chair underneath my body.

I was aware of my feet on the ground.

I was aware of the cry of birds in the distance.

I felt solid.

Present.

Real.

I remembered doing a guided imagery meditation on an audio CD led by Thich Nhat Hanh.[16] He said to breathe in, repeating to yourself, "Mountain," and then to exhale, saying "Solid." It was curious to simultaneously feel the spaciousness and comprehensive vision one has on a mountain and simultaneously feel very connected and grounded. I briefly flashed on the idea that this was similar to Jack's experience, although I did not feel "body-less" at all. To the contrary, it was as though I could feel the soles of my feet going down into the earth, becoming very rooted, and yet my head was high, high, high up somewhere in the clouds. Maybe this is what is meant by the expression "in the world, but not of the world."

Then, unbidden, the workshop returned.

Novus Magnificat ended on a very long, slow resonant note that faded to silence over what seemed to be minutes. I felt like it had been hours. Slowly, people raised their heads up from the floor where they had been lying. The room was thick with the blanket of silence and stillness as I looked into the eyes of the other workshop participants. I could see that they, too, had had an intense spiritual experience. Making eye contact around the room, I felt incredibly connected to them, even though I had met nearly all of them only the day before. *How was that possible?* I wondered.

Even as I marinated in the sweetness of my numinous experience, immediately my own inner critic began to pick it apart. I remembered my friend Layton had just told me about a dream that he had that included a flying Christ. *How trite!* I said to myself. *Jesus Christ, you couldn't come up with your own symbols; you had to steal someone else's experience! And what was all this business about healing seagulls and lights falling on them! The music had been sweeping and dramatic,* I told myself. *I am just making all this up!*

I told Frank and the group about the experience. I also told them about my self-doubt and how I thought I had fabricated the whole thing.

"Why are you crying?" he said.

"I don't know," I blurted, utterly confused.

"Something about this touched you. What is it?"

I held my breath and shook my head "No," embarrassed that everyone was looking at me and that I was using up everyone's time. I buried my face in my hands.

"Will you look around the room?" Frank asked firmly.

Something about his insistence broke through my shameful reverie. I slowly looked up at him. Though his expression seemed measured, his eyes were moist. The "why" of this completely eluded me.

"Will you look around the room, and tell me what you see?" he said emphatically.

With a great hesitance, I stared vacantly around at my fellow workshop participants, all of whom I had gotten to know and love. My gaze fell ever so slowly over each of them, languishing on each of the beings scattered on the floor. The first thing I noticed was that they were all looking at me with love.

Next, I saw that one person was lying on their side with their right elbow supporting themselves while their hand cradled their face. Others were lying flat on their backs with their knees drawn up and their feet flat on the floor. Still others sat upright cross-legged. Elbows akimbo; appendages seemed to be at all angles.

"What do you see?" Frank repeated.

Suddenly, my heart swelled and my breathing gradually accelerated. My mouth tried to form words, but it took me several attempts. I felt like a very young child, the last to comprehend a concept that everyone else understood.

"*Seagulls*," I said in a tiny voice, barely audible. "They look like . . . " I gasped, grasping at what it all might mean. "They look like seagulls on the beach with broken wings."

I burst into tears, weeping.

"Well," said Frank with all the sensitivity of a foreman addressing his day laborers, "you'd better get to work picking 'em up."

I could have killed Frank. My stomach pitted. The enormity of the responsibility hit me, and the argument rushed from my mouth, my voice cracking as I tried to sputter out a rebuttal.

"*But Frank, I don't know what I am doing! I am not some enlightened being, I'm not a counselor!* I wouldn't know where to *begin* to heal people!"

"If you're waiting around to be perfect, these people are going to have a long wait," Frank in a blasé tone, gesturing around the room.

"*But I don't have a clue how to do this!*" I said angrily.

"You don't have to," said Frank, completely nonplussed. "Just be willing."

Frank turned his attention to others, while I remained pie-eyed, wet-faced, no doubt white as a sheet and completely oblivious to the rest of the group. I am sure I remained in my world for at least an hour or more, while others shared.

Later in the workshop, someone was having a powerful emotional release lying on a mat weeping. Frank asked us all to place hands on the person who was crying and send them loving, supportive energy. The moment my hands made contact with her body, an inner voice—in a gentle, but flat tone—said simply this:

Be my hands.

I felt a radiant warmth streaming from my hands, as though they were two faucets flowing with an energetic light. Yet another wave of tears arrived, and I felt a gratitude that my concern might bring healing. I felt a layer of my unworthiness fall away.

Still later in the workshop, my friend Layton was grieving the loss of his father. Suddenly, I felt like his father was inside me, anxiously trying to give him a message. I babbled something and immediately three groups of hands shoved me in the center of the circle with Layton. I felt like I was barely there, but whatever message I brought offered healing to Layton that day, and I was glad to help, if still somewhat lost and overwhelmed. It was the beginning of an acceleration of "gifts of the Spirit" in my life.

My vision was perfect. It was not my job to fix or heal anybody. All I had to do was be the hands that picked up the seagulls and then let the Christ light fall upon them, and they would come "back to life."

"I, of myself, can do nothing," Jesus said. "It is the father in me that doeth the works." Maybe this is what is meant by the prayer in Edgar Cayce's *A Search for God*[17] material: "Here I am Father, send me, use me." All that is required is the "little willingness" that *A Course in Miracles* calls for, and miracles can be done.

"Imagine God couldn't come to Earth today," suggests multiple near-death experiencer Dannion Brinkley, "and he sent you. What did you do for Him today?" We are *all* the saviors of the world, as the *Course* points out, through the Light within us. We all have vital, important roles to play in the healing of the planet that needs us desperately. This is the core of Andrew Harvey's *spiritual activism*. This is Jesus' admonition to "feed my sheep." We *are* our brothers' keepers. It is time for spiritual boldness. The chief impediment to our participation is our own unworthiness.

In time, I better understood my initial panic. "Our deepest fear," says spiritual teacher Marianne Williamson, drawing on the wisdom of *A Course in Miracles* in a quote widely, but erroneously, attributed to Nelson Mandela, "is *not* that we are inadequate. Our deepest fear is that we are powerful beyond measure. It is our light, not our darkness that frightens us most."[18]

My vision was both immediately apropos and prophetic. As the years passed, it became apparent just how accurate my imagery was. A storm did brew up in my family of origin. My family, as I knew it, did crumble, and in many ways I had to leave the apparent "safety" of the structure of the family behind me as they could no longer protect me. I did come full circle to reunite and reconnect with a number of my family members, but the focus of my life became healing others and myself.

In addition, this revelation eventually led to my return to school to study counseling and oddly resulted in another prophecy being fulfilled. Eventually, after finishing my master's degree, I interned under Dr. Allen, who had conveniently moved from Houston to Austin to open a private practice. Just like the inner voice had told me to do the first time I met him, I was "following him." And he had indeed "been where I was going."

As the balance of the memory was activated, the initial stillness and peace gave way to deep earth vibrations coming up through my feet, past my ankles, and into my thighs. Simultaneously, I felt a larger energy wave coursing through my body. I also noticed an intense current behind my eyes, moving up into my forehead into the area of the third eye. This vibration was much, much faster. The best way I can describe it is as a crackling sensation.

It was as though my body could not contain it, and periodically it would shake violently. I have had this kind of experience before, and to put it very simply, I have come to regard these experiences as God "tuning" me up. Cayce talks about spiritual individuals as vibrating at a higher energy level. My model for the journey is that as we grow, our baseline increases. As we let go more and more of our identification with our bodies and our egoic self, we identify and allow more of the divine resonance to be present and expressed. But similar to Jack's experience, it was almost as though my physical body reached a point of overload. It was like someone running too much current through an electrical wire, and the insulation couldn't handle it.

I began to gasp, blinking back tears. I asked Jack to stop. I closed my eyes and pressed my face into my hands. The pressure felt good on my cheekbones. I rubbed my eyes. Jack asked me where I was at spiritually on the scale of one to ten.

"Seventeen?" I said. "Can I do that?"

Jack chuckled. "You can do it any way you like."

I smiled. I was glad to be with Jack and from this place of intense love. I was filled with gratitude for his friendship, wisdom, and support. There is a special bond with those individuals that are a part of your spiritual soul pod. Jack and I had both been there for each other in our most painful moments. It was glorious to share these transcendent ones with him, too. And I was, once again, reminded that this was more than just raw technique. It was Jack's attunement to my process that offered the safety that allowed me to go deeply into this amazing memory. It was a good fifteen or twenty minutes before I returned to earth, trailing clouds of glory.

Our success (and need to ground ourselves) could only mean one thing: It was time for Indian food. We celebrated over *sambar* and *dosas*. Nothing like some chutney to get you back in your body.

I called my technique *spiritual activation*. We are often told by others that our thinking is in a rut. Imagine a wagon going back and forth into moist earth, cutting deep ruts into the road. When the wagon approaches the road later, after it has dried, it becomes very easy to fall into those ruts and follow them as a guide. In some ways, that is a very apt analogy. Familiar ways of thinking are strong neural networks, long fired, and well-rehearsed. That's how some older individuals can tell you a childhood memory, many times recounted from forty years ago, but they can't remember what happened yesterday.

My theory is if we can take a profound spiritual experience and replay the neural networks associated with that moment, then we are literally grinding it into our consciousness more deeply and expanding our spirituality within us. The enhanced memory of this virtual experience, well-rehearsed by the brain, can become a spiritual touchstone that we can use in daily meditation to make deeper meditations as familiar and unforgettable as riding a bike.

What if we could get ruts in our thinking that would help us stay connected to God?

*   *   *

In June of 2009, Kevin Reger and a team of volunteers for the Association for Research and Enlightenment (A.R.E.) welcomed me like family to lead a three-day retreat with record-breaking attendance at the University of Wisconsin-Whitewater. The weather was a pleasant change from the blistering Texas heat. Just months from my training in Brainspotting with David Grand, I was anxious to see what Spiritual Activation could do.

It was going to be a long day with an IADC demonstration in the morning and Spiritual Activation demonstration in the afternoon. It was a rare IADC that day in which there was very little traumatic release and the volunteer leapt almost immediately into beatific tearful contact with her daughter who had passed just a year earlier. It was moving and beautiful and probably a lot more pleasant for the audience than many other IADCs in which the first hour is spent in anguish.

Later in the day, after a cursory explanation of Brainspotting, I screened volunteers from the audience for a spiritual activation. I settled on Tessa, a short middle-aged woman, dressed casually in jeans and a T-shirt. She told a story of "hitting bottom" and coming to terms with the alcoholism that had ruined her life. Some eight years had passed since the day her denial had been ripped from her awareness, and she found herself sitting alone in her living room, fully cognizant that she would have to stop drinking, but utterly clueless as to how she would do that. How could she face the world sober? It seemed impossible. She went through bouts of weeping and hopelessness. She fell to her knees in prayer to a God she didn't really believe in only, to her astonishment, to have a sense of peace wash over her as a radiant white light entered the room, and she was flooded with joy.

After plugging her into some headphones that played bio-lateral sound, I asked Tessa to focus on the experience, and gently moving the pointer in front of her, we found the resource Brainspot, the eye position that expanded the felt sense of the white light experience.

"I'm going higher and higher!" she exclaimed.

Within minutes as she gazed at the pointer, the energy grew inside her. "It's like I'm flying with angels!" she squealed with delight.

Suddenly, she was breathing faster and faster, a broad grin spreading over her face. "Oh, my God!" she said, obviously filled with utter delight. Then, unable to contain the vibration within her, she began to alternately stomp her feet back and forth, faster and faster, like she was running in place as she sat in the chair.

"Ooooooooooo!" she said, her pitch rising. And then, in front of nearly 200 people in the teaching amphitheater at the University of Wisconsin, Tessa screamed these words at the top of her lungs:

"OH MY GOD! THIS IS BETTER THAN SEX!"

The audience was stone silent for a moment.

"I'll have what she's having," I said dryly, without missing a beat.

The entire auditorium burst into laughter for a good three minutes. Tessa eyes fell from the tip of the pointer. We grinned at each other as I thought to myself, *hey, maybe there are a lot more interesting applications of this therapy than I thought!* Later, I jokingly asked Tessa if she wanted a cigarette. She laughed, completely unashamed. After the experience leveled out and settled in, Tessa told the audience, just as Jack had told me after his experience, that she not only recaptured the experience, but somehow *went beyond it.*

Have you ever read the stories about near-death experiences in which participants are declared medically dead but find themselves floating above their body, seeing Beings of Light, feeling Divine Love and being greeted by their loved ones from the Other Side? Wouldn't it be wonderful to be able to hear a "play by play," of an NDE, live, as it happened, narrated back to Planet Earth through some kind of Cosmic Radio?

In June of 2010, more than a hundred people sat spellbound in Memphis, Tennessee, as a woman, fully conscious, not under hypnosis, with her eyes open, "crossed over" and described her near-death experience in *real time*—even though she had never had one before in her life. All thanks to Spiritual Activation.

I was leading a one-day workshop at the Unity Church in Memphis and had planned to demonstrate Spiritual Activation in the late afternoon. As part of the presentation, earlier in the day, I offered a guided imagery called *Discover Your Destiny* that helps people intuitively look ahead at what is next on their spiritual journey. In that exercise, under hypnosis, I ask people to symbolically imagine their sojourn and, at one point, I tell them that they are carrying three tools in a knapsack with them and to look and see what these tools are. Afterwards, while in small groups, they discuss what tools they "saw" in their experience and what they might symbolize.

Norma, a pleasant woman in her early 50s, raised her hand to ask a question. "I have a tool, but I just don't have a clue what it is for or how to use it?"

"What did you get?" I queried.

"Well, this is weird," she said tentatively, with a thick Southern accent, "but in my knapsack in the imagery was this silver stick that could telescope outward and extend, kind of like a car antennae."

"Did it look like this?" I asked, reaching into my breast pocket of my coat and removing my Brainspotting pointer, snapping it out to its full length. The audience gasped, audibly.

"Yes," said Norma, her eyes widening.

"I think I just found my volunteer for the Spiritual Activation demonstration," I said to the audience with utter conviction.

Norma, as fate, or perhaps God, would have it, was the perfect subject. She had a powerful experience a few years earlier in which she was riding a lawnmower in her front yard and heard voices singing *Amazing Grace*. Not angelic voices, but more like the mix of the melodious and the tone deaf that you get in a small town church in East Texas on a Sunday morning. Norma shut down the engine of the mower to listen, only to discover that she was the only person who could hear the voices. It dawned on her that this was a heavenly choir of spirit beings who were welcoming in her mother to heaven, who was, as far as Norma knew, still alive.

She rushed in to tell her husband about the vision. She was convinced that it meant her mother had crossed and within five minutes the phone rang: It was Norma's sister with bad news. Their mother had died just minutes before.

It was a remarkable and moving story in and of itself. But as Norma stepped onstage to join me for the Spiritual Activation demonstration, neither Norma nor I could have possibly anticipated how astonishing the next half hour would be.

For about the first ten minutes, we adjusted the pointer to maximize Norma's emotional and physical experience of the memory. She initially rated herself at about a "six" or a "seven" on a spiritual connection scale, where "ten" would be the most connected to the Divine she had ever experienced and "zero" would be not at all connected.

As she stared at the pointer, her breathing changed as she remembered the experience of that day. "I keep hearing 'the Face of God' . . . but it's not a face at all," she remarked curiously. Then she found herself suddenly physically hotter and hotter. "It's them . . . " she said her voice quivering, "they are here! It's all of them!"

In her mind's eye, an intense internal vision appeared, completely unprompted by me. Norma saw impressions of all her family members and friends who had crossed, all expressing themselves as radiant beings of light. She saw all the pets and animals she had ever owned, surrounding her and loving her more deeply than she had ever imagined. It was clearly ecstasy. The love was more than overwhelming—it looked like Norma could barely contain the experience.

"I feel like I am being watched over," she said, and felt the enormous reassurance that not only did they love her now, but they would be there when her time came to cross. We watched, awestruck, as Norma stumbled for words, desperately trying to express the glory of the Other Side.

Norma left the stage, barely thirty minutes later, after seeing her mother and her relatives, reuniting with her animals, and touching the "Face of God." As you can imagine, I forlornly wished that there had been some kind of record of her experience, so others could share—if only vicariously—through her story, her words and the sound of her voice, the power and majesty of that moment.

And then, I remembered that earlier that morning, the woman who was handling the sound in the church, apropos of nothing, casually asked if I wanted the presentation recorded.

And I had said yes.

Sometimes, all you can do is step back from the mystery and let your jaw drop.

Norma's amazing experience was captured that day on digital audio, along with a typical smart-ass presentation by a somewhat irreverent counselor from Texas. It's available on Amazon as a three- hour, 2-CD set known as *Exploring the Mysteries of Your Mind* by Gregg Unterberger. (Member FDIC. Offer void where prohibited. Does not include tax, title, license, or dealer prep. No one under 17 admitted without parent or fake ID.)

Sorry for the unsolicited plug. But it really is worth owning. Even better than an Electric Dog Polisher.

*   *   *

ANGELA AND THE FIFTY-FOOT ANGEL

Angela came to me for a single three-hour session. She was a slight woman in her seventies with a kind smile, a gentle bearing, and a penchant for brightly colored scarves. Angela came to see me because she had given birth to her eldest son in the 1960s and had barely lived to tell about it. After we reviewed her general history, I encouraged her to tell the story in detail.

"This was years ago, Gregg. Hospital care wasn't exactly kind and compassionate back then. As a woman, I wasn't given much credence as a patient. I was more like a job to be completed," she said, her thin lips pursing tightly over her teeth.

"How so?" I asked curiously.

"Well, I told the doctor the baby was coming, and he didn't believe me. He waved his hand as though to dismiss me and said he was going to dinner. I felt frightened and so alone. But then I shrieked in pain as I felt the baby suddenly move in my body. Again, the doctor said I was overreacting, but as he bent over to take a look, I literally exploded, splattering blood all over his face. I have never known such pain in my life. I thought I really might die."

I am sure the look on my face was a mix of concern, amazement, and incredulity. *How could a doctor be so insensitive?* It was another era. And yet, I had heard those kinds of stories from other clients, even now. One of my father's friends, who happens to be a doctor, used to joke: "You know surgeons, never in doubt, occasionally wrong."

"There's more," she paused, looking tentatively at her feet. "I hope you don't think I'm crazy," she added timidly. (By now, you should know I hear that a lot from my clients.) I waited a moment for her to look up and smiled gently and reassuringly. She continued.

"Well, just before I passed out completely, I had the strangest sense of peace in the face of the pain. And . . . I swear to God, I am not making this up . . . I saw what appeared to be the robe of a giant angel. As I looked up over my feet in the stirrups, immediately behind the doctor, I saw this radiant white robe that filled the floor of the entire room behind him. I mean, just as I am giving birth to my son, there was this figure . . . I don't know, maybe fifty feet tall or something. An angel, I guess." She took a deep breath, obviously moved by the memory. "But I passed out before I could even look upwards to see who it was."

Angela paused and then leaned forward with the smallest of grins on her weathered face and a bit of mischief in her eyes.

"You know what, Gregg? I've always wanted to know what that was. And when you talked in the lecture about spiritual activation, I felt compelled to work with you. I want to go back and find out what happened."

I smiled at Angela, admiring her courage and curiosity in coming to me. But I did feel a twinge in my stomach, and I knew I needed to give voice to it.

"We can do this," I said earnestly. "But I need to remind you that we aren't just going back to the angel experience. The setting in which this happened was a very traumatic one. As we turn your awareness toward this moment, the horror of that pain may become real again. It could get messy."

Angela nodded understandingly with a determined look. "That's okay."

"On balance," I said, "if it's still encoded as trauma, we will likely desensitize it—a good thing—and there is still the possibility of transcending the pain and going deeper into the spiritual realm."

"I trust you, Gregg."

"Thank you, Angela. I just want to make sure you go into this with your eyes open."

I was astonished what happened next.

I had Angela imagine the moment, the blood spattering the doctor, the feelings of assuredness alongside of terror and sharp pain. I steeled myself for the possibility of a flashback that we would have to unravel. As Angela gazed at the pointer, we moved it around to find the Brainspot that took her closest to the feelings of peace and safety. Within a few seconds, the hospital room disappeared from her mind, leaving the trauma behind. And although her eyes were open, staring at the pointer, her consciousness entered another dimension.

I had an intuitive feeling that this session might be important. So, I balanced the pointer at a forty-five degree angle, wedging it between my legs and the arm of the chair, to maintain the Brainspot. This allowed my hands to be free to make notes on my clipboard. What follows is not a recreation from my memory, but an actual word-for-word transcript of what happened to Angela as she explored the realms of light.

"I don't know where I am. Everything around me is a big pink fog. I can't hear the baby crying anymore. [It's like I am in] nothingness . . . it's very, very pleasant."

She paused, breathing easily, apparently drawing in the energy.

"I am in the top of what I saw [the giant angel]; I am IN that. I don't have any cares, no worries. I am at one with this energy." Angela began breathing faster, a beatific smile blossoming over her wrinkled face. Tears slipped over her lower lids.

"Oh, I am so loved, I am SO loved. I had no idea that anybody cared this much." She started to weep uncontrollably. The convulsions lasted for several minutes. She was overwhelmed. Then she got very quiet for a minute or two.

"I can see a pinpoint of light." Her eyes widened as a look of wonder came over her. Moments passed.

"I'm in a really white light now." She frowned as though studying something. "There's movement around me. I see these, like, orbs of light. They are very familiar. I see a lot of golden light and movement." Her smile blossomed again.

"I am supposed to be here." She nodded resolutely. "I know them. I'm looking to see if my son is here, but I can't make out any faces." She paused.

"I feel like I am in a vast place and out beyond this light it's totally black." Her head tilted. "There is someone close to me. Who *are* you? Wow . . . a very bright gold light. It's grabbing me up in its gold. I'm being embraced. Oh. OH!" Angela began to breathe faster, rhythmically.

"I am being filled up inside me . . . pumped full of this light. It feels so wonderful." She beamed. Then suddenly her expression changed to one of longing.

"The gold is backing away . . . 'Wait . . . don't go!'" She paused, being drawn to someplace new. "I can't see all the people. It feels like I am far off in outer space. Way off, there are needle pricks of light. I am not afraid . . . it is so infinite . . . so big." There was a sudden intake of breath, a reaction to the enormity of the experience. As I heard it, I remembered taking a breath like that when I first saw the Grand Canyon. I was overwhelmed by the huge chasm, very literally taken aback. Then, as I watched, she settled down again.

"I am back in the pink . . . purple now," she reported. "Light and dark purple. It's close around me like I am part of it. I am . . . I am a part of this, a part of all of this. I see these orbs floating around . . . now they are circling me." She smiled broadly, amused. "They are playing with me! I feel this little showering of all these lights all over me," she squealed with delight in the voice of a four year old.

"Yellow, now. The gold orb is back; it's right in my face. It's huge, it encompasses all my vision. There's a form inside. A face? Or what? I can't see what it is." There was a long pause.

"It's not like a body. It's someone. I'm being pulled into it. Yes. YES." She was smiling, laughing uncontrollably. After a minute or so she caught her breath, able to find words, able to reflect. "This is SO familiar, so comforting." Her voice drew down to almost a whisper. Her tone reflected a reverence and surety.

"I have been here before. This is where I belong."

We sat in a deep silence for several minutes. The look of wonder on her face was that of a very young child seeing a Christmas tree for the first time. Her expression radiated love.

"I feel like I am being pulled back," she commented with a slight sadness. "There is a dark hole. I was there. I was right back to where I belonged."

Her tone implied an acceptance of her true home in some other spiritual realm and also of the unalterable truth that she still lived in the material world. Angela took several deep easy breaths, her eyes falling off the pointer. She looked around the room for several minutes as though returning to this reality. I remained in silence, honoring the moment, unwilling to break the stillness. Finally she spoke, somehow looking at me, but also through me.

"It's like always knowing that there is something else," she said in a faraway voice. "I think I've always known there was more to life than the material world. But today, I felt what it was. *It's real.*"

So what happened to Angela? Maybe she used her memory as a conduit to "tune in" to another dimension. Maybe the entire experience was an actual memory of something that happened at her son's birth that she had blocked or forgotten. And I couldn't rule out that this was all a figment of her imagination, although I wondered where such imagery would come from. If she was going to make it up, why not see Jesus or God or at least the face of the fifty-foot angel? If she was creating a happy fantasy, why not see her son, whom she was looking for so adamantly? If this was all wish fulfillment, why not "see" who was inside the golden bubble? It didn't make sense to me.

Of course, no one can be sure. But you *can* be sure that Angela was completely convinced of a Higher Power that was there at her son's birth and is with her now. She believes that heaven is a real place and is her real home. Not only did she experience it, she *remembered* it. It was familiar; it felt familiar. For Angela, what you or I think doesn't matter. Her life will be forever changed.

So, I know what you're thinking. (See? All that psychic development stuff I've been talking about is really paying off for me.) You're thinking . . . okay, wait. Before I tell you what you're thinking, let me grab my forehead and frown slightly so it will look impressive. Is that it? Or, does it look like I'm about to pass some gas?

Whatever . . . it'll do.

You're thinking, "Geez, Gregg, that all sounds swell, but what are the odds that I will stumble way down Texas way and win the grand prize of a nifty spiritual activation session to put me in touch with *my* fifty-foot angel?" Well, like they say on the TV quiz shows, "Thank you for playing! And, for being our guest on the program, we have a special parting gift for you: *Brainspotting: The Home Game.*"

Yup, it'll be more fun than Parcheesi with Aunt Agnes.

Brainspotting for Spiritual Activation

Brainspotting, at first blush, seems like an amazingly simple technique. But there is a reason why most ethical practitioners have extensive mental health training and experience with trauma counseling even before they become certified as Brainspotting professionals. Under no circumstances should you try to treat trauma, depression, or anxiety in yourself or anyone else based on what you read in this chapter, any more than you would break out a butter knife to remove a tumor by following a medical drama on TV.

Having said that, there is room for the average Joe (and Jane) to take advantage of this technology—using it judiciously and with good common sense—to experiment with Spiritual Activation. This cardinal rule, however, must be followed:

If the process induces ANY painful memories or uncomfortable emotional reactions, stop using the modality immediately. *Period.*

I often pair people off in my workshops to work with each other to hold pens or pointers in specific positions to spiritually activate an experience. Even with amateurs "playing therapists," it is amazing the kinds of results we get: people often moved to tears as they re-experience their most precious memories—feeling expansive, peaceful, and connected. I warn them, as I have warned you, NOT to continue if they feel the slightest bit uncomfortable, and to-date there have never been any issues. Except one.

The woman approached me on a fifteen-minute break, anxious and in tears.

"What did you do to me?" she demanded angrily.

I knew it wasn't really a question. As it turned out, she completely ignored my advice, and when a traumatic memory intruded on her spiritual activation, she thought she would try to "push through it." But she couldn't, and she didn't, and I spent the next twenty minutes grounding her somewhere back behind the podium in the Hilton ballroom. She was considerably better when we finished, but she was so uncomfortable that she had to go home, leaving the workshop before it was over. I had "ruined her day," she said.

So there it is, kids, my cautionary tale.

It's okay to take an aspirin, but even aspirin can kill you if you take too many. Please use your common sense.

Instructions for Self-Brainspotting for Spiritual Activation

The following are some instructions for how to play with this at home. You may want to have a friend read them to you, or you can record them and play them back to yourself. Yes, you can pick up and put down the book several times as you learn the technique, but it's a bit intrusive.

- Get seated comfortably, and relax.
- Turn off the radio or television. Soft, slow music without vocals or silence may enhance the experience. (I don't recommend Polish polkas or blues songs sung by artists whose nicknames are infirmities.)
- Dim the lights a bit if possible, but you will need some light to see, as your eyes will be open after the first few minutes of internal focusing.
- Make sure you have at least thirty minutes to explore this experience.
- Do this in a place of privacy or with a safe and supportive friend in the room and with time to allow for your complete and utter focus.

Okay Bozos, obviously NOT in the car, while skateboarding, or driving heavy machinery . . . or light machinery for that matter, what does weight have to do with it? You shouldn't even be operating your Veg-O-Matic or electric dog polisher while you do this.

Start by picking a memory of your deepest or most profound spiritual experience: maybe it was a transcendent meditation, a moment in nature, a visceral feeling of being connected to the Divine. Please pick one that is untainted by any other trauma or negative experience. Some people in dark moments have had moments of Great Light, but these are *not* good targets for self-Brainspotting. Stick with something pure and untouched by any physical or emotional pain.

Close your eyes and remember as much about the experience as you can. Visualize the place, the people you were with, the clothes you were wearing—all of it. Engage not only your mind with imagining the visual elements, but use all of your senses. What did that experience feel like? What did it sound like? What emotions did the experience touch? What was the temperature that day?

Take your time. Let the experience become as real as possible. Notice what is happening in your body. Is there warmth somewhere? Chills? A deep sense of energy, peace, or release? Is there a lump in your throat? Do you feel energy in your heart or other chakras? What does this memory feel like to you RIGHT NOW as you look back on it?

Imagine a scale of "one" to "ten" in your mind. For some people, it's helpful to imagine a meter or the entire scale of numbers in their mind, almost like a speedometer or thermometer. As you experience this RIGHT NOW, how does it feel to you? "Ten" would be the most intensely connected to the Divine you have ever felt. "One" would be disconnected or neutral. Remember this rating scale is only for what it feels like to look back on that particular experience from the NOW. In the moment, when it happened, you may have felt it to be a "nine" or a "ten," but right NOW you can only experience it as a "six." That's okay. The numbers back then are fixed and will never change. How you feel about it NOW can change . . . and we are hopeful that it WILL change!

So at this point, you have picked an experience and focused on it. You have checked in with your emotions to see how it feels and ex-plored how it feels physically in your body. You have allowed the memory to become as present as possible.

Now, open your eyes and stare straight ahead. Find an object or point directly ahead of you at eye level that you can focus on. Check in with your body. How does this feel? Look for changes in your body as you look out directly ahead at eye level. What, if anything, feels different? Make sure to keep your breathing easy and regular.

Next, keeping your chin still and exactly where it is, let your eyes shift to the far left at the same level. It's as though you were looking at a completely flat horizon, like when you are looking at the ocean and you cut your eyes (but not move your chin) to the far left of the field of vision, but still stay on the line of the horizon. Find an object on the far left to focus on. Now breathe and check in with your body. Does it feel any different looking in this direction as you think about your memory? Look for changes in your body—see if you feel more expan-sive, or closer to those kinds of happy tears we have when we are moved by beauty. Then come back to the center point of your field of vision. In which direction is your connection to your experience the strongest?

Now, keeping your chin in place, let your eyes move along the ho-rizon to the far right and see how that feels. You may compare these three points: 1) straight ahead, 2) far left, and 3) far right, to see which one offers the most pronounced positive response or deepening of the experience. For some people it is dramatic, for others, more subtle. If they all seem pretty much the same, you might ask yourself, *Which one do I like the best?* Or, *Which one feels the easiest?*

If you are not sure, pick one anyway. Remember, this is a very subjective process. There are no absolute right or wrong answers here. Feel free to "fine tune" the experience. It may be that your Brainspot is just slightly off center, or not all the way to the right or left, but just slightly to one side. That's fine.

Now that you have picked a direction—left, straight, or right—to focus on, allow your eyes to move upwards toward the ceiling—again, keep your chin level. As you look around, your eyeballs should be moving, but not your head. Now, how does it feel to look up? Again, does the connection to the memory increase? Does this enhance your positive feelings or emotions? Look for how it feels in your body. Now, come back down to eye level. See which one you like best or which offers the most spiritual resonance.

Finally, allow your eyes to move downward, keeping your chin level. Pick an object or mark to focus on. See how your body reacts or if the positive emotions increase.

To review, at this point you should have picked an optimal direction to gaze at on the horizontal plane—more right, left, or straight ahead. Then from that spot, you should have allowed your eyes (only) to move upwards and downwards to pick a spot on the vertical axis as well. You have paid attention to your reactions in your body and emotions to find a spot where you feel most responsive to the original spiritual memory.

Now, simply gaze at that spot. Trust your experience. Let it evolve or change. As long as it keeps deepening, changing, and morphing, stay with it. For many people, it is hard to stay with the expansiveness. It may feel like you will explode or "top out" if you allow it to keep getting bigger. It may bring forth emotions—tears of joy, playfulness, or giddiness. As long as they are positive, allow them. Stay with it if you can. If you want to close your eyes, feel free to do so, but only if it enhances the experience. Oddly, it can be a way to turn away from it. If you do close your eyes, imagine that your eyeballs are continuing to gaze in the exact same direction. Eyes opened or closed, give yourself some time on the Brainspot. A minute or two is typically not enough. Be patient. Trust your mind and emotions, wherever they take you. Set aside your judgment. Let it unfold.

For additional ideas on self-Brainspotting and for more on the technique in general, check out *Brainspotting: The Revolutionary New Therapy for Rapid and Effective Change*[19] by Dr. David Grand, the developer and the Obi-Wan Kenobi of Brainspotting.

Over time, you can try this exercise with different images or memories. Focus your thoughts on a Divine figure. Think about a teacher or guru. Remember an experience with someone you love (not deceased and not your ex), and see what happens and what information flows. Experiment. Enjoy!

Of course, not everyone has such a touchstone experience that can be catalyzed through Brainspotting. While it was exciting to see people touch into their deepest spiritual experiences and relive them, many of my clients, even those who had spent years on the spiritual path, have been seemingly denied so much as one such moment.

It was my pleasure and honor to introduce them to states of consciousness that might allow for these transformative moments—without hypnosis, years of meditation, or psychedelics. Simply using music and harnessing the power of their breath, I have seen hundreds of ordinary people have these numinous spiritual experiences, filled with powerful energies in the body, reunions with loved ones who have passed, visions of celestial lights, past-life memories, even direct contact with angels, Jesus, and the Divine; all through a powerful technique called *Transpersonal Breathwork*.

9

Exploring the Cosmic
Realms of Breathwork

"[The] opening of the centers or the raising of the life force
may be brought about by certain characteristics of breathing—for, as indicated, the breath is power in itself . . . "

Edgar Cayce reading 2475-1

Brenda's eyes were wide with terror, a gale force wind at her face. Her hair was
flying wildly behind her—like some kind of horrific Medusa. Sheer
panic coursed through her body—a never-ending electric shock.

There was paper flying everywhere.

For more than twenty years, Brenda had been afraid of paper. Yes,
paper. She felt silly. *Who was afraid of paper? Heights, maybe; snakes, sure. But
paper?* Now, a successful executive in her thirties, she could handle
paperwork on her desk without fear, as long as the sheets were se-
cured by binders or paperweights. But if it was loose on a desk, it
somehow became a threat in her mind. In particular, she found papers
tacked to a bulletin board terrifying. There was something about how
a gentle breeze in the building would pick up the bottom two corners
of a sheet, causing it to lift as though by some unseen force, apparently threatening to come at her. *And do what?* She would ask herself.
The fact that others found the bulletin board a place of friendly curiosity didn't stop its presence from striking terror in her, cutting off her

breath and causing her heart to pound.

Brenda, hair perfectly styled, dressed in heels and her power suit, would find herself clinging to the wall of the hallway opposite of the bulletin board, like a scared child. *What's wrong with me?* It was embarrassing. Sometimes her friends would tease her. They would hold a blank sheet of paper at arm's length, just inches from her face, and rattle it. Brenda would shriek and cover her face as though scalding water had been thrown in her direction. They would laugh, but it wasn't funny to her. She felt frightened and ridiculous. For some strange reason, paper had always seemed dangerous.

Now, here she was in a wind tunnel with thousands of sheets being blown at her. It was her worst nightmare, but this was no dream: Brenda was not asleep. She covered her face, screaming, begging it to stop. It was as though someone had turned a giant fan towards a giant desktop and reams and reams of paper came fluttering at her, rattling like angry snakes. Petrified, she found herself going fetal, hugging her knees as though they could offer some comfort. She buried her face into the crook of her arm, desperately praying it would all end soon. But the storm did not abate. The moment seemed to go on for eternity; she was frozen with fear. Something about the idea of a corner of one of the sheets ripping at her body permeated her.

But then suddenly, emboldened by some unseen spiritual force, she managed to lift her face out of the crook of her elbow. *I will not live this way any longer!* She was angry now. She stood up, screaming into the windstorm of sheets overhead, her wailing unheard by anyone, blowing backward into her agape mouth. The sheets were colliding with her now, smacking flat and hard against her stomach and breasts, all but feeding on her, then crawling, lizard–like, toward her ribs, seemingly digging in their claws, hanging on till the last moment, shredding her skin, before being ripped from her body by the hurricane–force winds. Brenda immediately got back down. *If I could just grab them out of the air*, she thought. She found herself alternately looking up, furtively squinting, and then ducking as papers helicoptered toward her. Somehow, she found the courage to extend her right arm fully, though paper slashed mercilessly at the outstretched appendage. Quickly standing and simultaneously bringing her hand down in an overhead swing, she snatched a paper out of the sky! To her astonishment, the moment she touched it, it turned to a heavy stone. Rotating her wrist upwards, she looked down in disbelief at the rock in her outstretched hand. A rock! Awestruck, she dropped it. *Thunk!*

It dawned on her: Stones are heavy; they cannot be blown into your face. Suddenly, the solution was clear. Frantically, Brenda began grabbing papers out of the air. She snatched one sheet after another and another and another. *Thunk!* They fell to the floor, now faster and faster. *Thunk!* Soon, there was less and less paper in the air and more and more rocks on the ground. *Thunk!* Now, it was different. It was almost as though she was consciously slowing down the paper in her mind, the way a professional baseball player can see the ball leaving the pitcher's hand in slow motion. No, more than that, she felt like some kind of cosmic outfielder, making catch after catch with ease and, with each rock, feeling more mastery.

One after another, Brenda the Alchemist turned paper into stone, and they fell to the ground, harmless. In time, the wind died down to a dull roar. The sheets no longer rushed at her in droves, but were more like a scatter of leaves blown about by a gentle October wind. They were easy pickings now. Brenda felt her long brown hair, which had been blowing wildly behind her, gently settle on her shoulders. Everything softened. Everything became safe. Everything was still.

And now a memory—subtle at first, but increasingly real—came into focus. She was in second grade, and someone had come to school with a paper cut, but not on their finger or their hand. Somehow, a young boy had caught the stiff, sharp corner of a piece of paper . . . in his eye.

It had sliced his pupil!

There he was, in front of young Brenda, his eye covered in white gauze and bandages. She remembered her horror. Worse, Brenda suddenly recalled that this happened not only to one of her classmates, but in a bizarre twist of fate, two of her fellow students in the same year! Of course she had been afraid of paper. It could blind you! She tearfully saw herself embrace this younger Brenda and reassure her, hugging her tight. She was safe now. The nightmare was over. It was over!

In that singular moment, Brenda knew that her twenty-year panic over paper, a clinical phobia, had vanished in an hour. Victoriously standing on the rubble of rocks that once struck unrelenting fear in her gentle heart, Brenda experienced a mix of bliss, relief, and accomplishment.

Kneeling, I leaned over Brenda as she lay on the yoga mat in the workshop space. I had watched her hands frantically grabbing the air earlier, but now she was peaceful, smiling beatifically. As her psychotherapist, I knew Brenda was not on drugs or delusional, but in a mystical, visionary state of consciousness, intentionally induced through yogic breathing techniques; evocative, sweeping music; and a roomful of supportive therapists and participants. Her Higher Mind had directed her toward this powerful symbolic representation of her fear to bring healing. And healing had been done.

The unique therapeutic modality I developed is called Transpersonal Breathwork. Based in the work of Dr. Stanislav Grof, one of the founding fathers of Transpersonal Psychology, it takes workshop participants into mystical states where they report healing childhood emotional wounds, remembering past lives, contacting loved ones who have crossed over, even "touching the face of God." Over the past thirty-five years, thousands have participated in various forms of Breathwork. Their experiences, whether they are real or imagined, often bring profound healing and spiritual growth.

There is more to Brenda's story. This is just what she accomplished in the first hour of her three-hour Breathwork experience. But before I share that with you, maybe you should know a little more about Breathwork and from "whence it came."

Hmm, sounds a bit ominous, doesn't it? Maybe somebody should hum the Twilight Zone theme.

*   *   *

You have experimented with drugs.

Really.

Not like most people have "experimented with drugs" when what they really mean is that they did lines of coke or dropped acid along with shots of tequila in hot tubs with a half-clad member of the opposite sex. No, you have an M.D. and a Ph.D. You have worn the white lab coat and given measured doses of hallucinogens to schizophrenics, patients with severe depression, bi-polar disorder, even murderers. And you have seen phenomenal healing take place.

It all started when you were a young psychiatric resident at the University of Prague. A strict Freudian, you were among the first individuals to use diethylamide of lysergic acid (LSD), in a clinical setting in a sanctioned experiment. To your surprise, you had an indescribable vision of cosmic consciousness: an intense white–light experience. You came to regard that vision as the single most influential and important moment of your life. Then, for more than twenty years, you conducted therapy with hallucinogens, first at the Psychiatric Research Institute in Prague and then in Baltimore at the Maryland Psychiatric Research Center as assistant professor of psychiatry at Johns Hopkins University. You came to believe that there was much more to the self than the ego and the physical body.

But now, here it is, 1975, and standing on the brink of America's Bicentennial, the government has pulled the plug on your research. Now, the visionary healing modality that you developed, *psycholytic therapy*, cannot be used. Frustrated, you decide there must be another way to access these altered or mystical experiences, which you call *non-ordinary states of consciousness*. You look to tribal cultures around the world and discover that for thousands of years, there have been culturally sanctioned ways to enter into these states of consciousness; sometimes using substances, but often using music, rhythm, ritual, and unique breathing techniques.

Part "accident," part luck, and partly through intention, you develop what you call *Holotropic Breathwork™*, an astonishing healing modality that makes these profound mystical non–ordinary states of consciousness available to virtually anyone, without the aid of drugs of any kind.

You are Dr. Stanislav Grof, one of the founding fathers of Transpersonal Psychology, the so–called "Third Wave" in the field, and in the eyes of many, the most sophisticated and advanced theory of the Self ever advanced. Developing this work with your wife Christina Grof, you maintain that the desire to transcend ordinary consciousness is inherent, appropriate, even necessary, so that the individual may embrace a larger reality. Over the next twenty–five years, you will observe your work and its permutations, spreading healing around the world, touching tens of thousands of participants. You come to regard your work not so much as your creation, but a task the Universe assigned to you.

*   *   *

ME: Even after pretending that you were Stan Grof, you probably have a few questions.

YOU: As, a matter of fact, I do. Thanks for making this a dialog and not just a monologue. What exactly is Breathwork?

ME: Okay, but you are going to make me go into lecture mode. Ahem. Breathwork is a drug-free, intentional way to enter into a non-ordinary state of consciousness. In our day-to-day lives, we are "tuned in" to our normal everyday reality: plain-old ordinary consciousness. You know where you have to go to the cleaners, you need to walk the dog and wash behind your ears (like your Mama always told you), but mystics throughout the ages have tuned into other states and gained profound insights into what their lives are about: cool experiences with visions, emotional and physical healing, a sense of having lunch with The Big Guy upstairs. It's kind of like changing the channel on your TV. When you change the channel of your TV, your TV itself doesn't change; you are just receiving information on a different channel. People have taken hallucinogens, fasted for days, or prayed and meditated extensively to "change channels" and reach these mystical states. Think of Jesus in the desert for forty days and forty nights, or Buddha in contemplation under the Bodhi tree. Breathwork is simply a contemporary way of catalyzing these states that non-industrial cultures have been accessing for thousands of years. I say, why should the tribal types have all the fun?

YOU: Thousands of years? Really?

ME: Really.

YOU: How did people in ancient cultures get to these non-ordinary states?

ME: Through a variety of means. Contemporary and ancient non-industrial cultures have used chanting, drumming, and dancing to access non-ordinary states. And, uh, oh yes, peyote. They still use peyote, a hallucinogen in the Native American Church, but as I understand it, you have to prove your Native lineage to participate in peyote ceremonies, so that probably rules out Yours Truly, Mister White Guy.

In *The Vedas*, Hinduism's Holy Scriptures written at least 1,400 years before Christ, there is much praise for Soma, which refers to a Deva: a god who is made manifest in a plant. Ah, not just any plant, but one that many scholars believe is some kind of hallucinogenic mushroom. The Hindu scriptures say:

> "This Soma is a god,
> The soul from earth to heaven he lifts,
> So great and wondrous are his gifts,
> Men feel the god within their veins,
> And cry loud in exulting strains,
> We've quaffed the Soma bright,
> And are immortal grown,
> We've entered into light,
> And all the gods have known."[20]

So, all those yogis who lived high in the Himalayas, maybe they really were living *high* in the Himalayas.

In Mexico, there is a mushroom known as the "Flesh of the Gods," that was used by tribal shamans for years. In contemporary Brazil, there is a Christian church that uses hallucinogenic potion known as Ayahuaska. Yes, you heard me right. They take it in a ritual fashion as a group and then they share their visions and dreams as part of a sacred ceremony, once a month. And for the record, drug addiction and alcohol abuse is significantly down in their communities. It has not led to an explosion of addicts. For more than 2,000 years, the Greeks conducted the Eleusinian Mysteries that included drama, a ritual setting with lighting effects, and music, along with a drink called Kykeon, which was very likely a psychedelic. If you are of a certain age, think of the Eleusinian Mysteries as an early attempt at a Pink Floyd concert—only done as a religious ritual.

YOU: Let's call a spade, a spade. Call them "sacred herbs" or entheogens or whatever, these are all drug-induced states, aren't they?

ME: I can see you are getting in touch with your inner Republican. Not all cultures used hallucinogens to achieve these states. In Australia, they use the didgeridoo—the low-droning sort of instrument you hear in a lot of spa music (and Quantas commercials) to enter what the aboriginals call, "The Dreamtime." Or they fast in the wilderness to get a vision on a "walkabout." Native Americans call this a *vision quest*. The Sufis—the mystic sect of Islam—dance and whirl in circles to achieve a non-ordinary state, getting dizzy for God. Ever hear of Rumi?

YOU: Yeah, I think I would like to do some "roomys" about now.

ME: Not mush-roomys. R-U-M-I. He was a mystic poet. He wrote some incredible stuff, some of which I don't understand. Maybe I haven't whirled around enough. Stuff like: "This is the way you slip through into your inner most home. Close your eyes and surrender." Hmm. Sounds like Breathwork, come to think of it. Anyway, he whirled in circles and got as messed up as a can of worms, and then yelled out the poems as he spun, and his students wrote them down. Pretty wild, huh? Kriya Yoga includes a "breath of fire" technique, similar to hyperventilating like a Chihuahua in heat, to alter consciousness. Other cultures used repetitive prayers or mantras to introduce the non-ordinary state. Yes sir, I am talking 'bout the Catholics and their prayer beads and their twenty "Hail Mary's." It turns out that there is some new research that suggests that focusing consciousness on a single idea over time encourages the production of anandamine, the so-called "bliss" neurotransmitter that is stimulated by the use of marijuana. I think it is interesting to note that most psychedelics simply stimulate the release of substances *that are already in our body*.

YOU: So, you are saying that if I focus my thoughts on one thing long enough, I could get high?

ME: Yes, you could get "high" to a greater or lesser degree simply by focusing. Have you ever just sat and stared at something for a while, and felt peaceful? And time goes by, but you don't know how much? Have you ever been "enveloped" by a piece of art or music, and lost sight of what was happening? You were in a non-ordinary state. Hindus call this *single-pointed consciousness*. That is why the Buddhists are so focused on "being in the present moment." That's the whole notion of, "Be still and know that I am God." Of course, Breathwork will take you far, far, deeper than those momentary highs. But you get the idea.

YOU: Sounds like this stuff cuts across all cultures, right?

ME: Yeah, it looks like everybody wants to catch a little buzz. William James, one of the very first real psychologists, wrote the grand-daddy of books about all this titled, *The Varieties of Religious Experience*, and he liked to mess around with laughing gas—you know, that stuff you suck up like soda pop at the dentist office? And do you have a guess as to why they called the Quakers, the Quakers? And the Shakers, the Shakers?

YOU: The guy on the oatmeal box? Let me guess. They entered an altered state where they "shake and bake?"

ME: That's right. They entered non-ordinary states and "shook" or "quaked" with the power of the Holy Ghost.

YOU: No wonder he's got that goofy little smile on his face.

ME: Yeah, it turns out, if you are blissed out enough from quaking, you don't mind wearing a funny looking hat.

YOU: Kind of figured it wasn't the oatmeal. But people don't really do that stuff anymore, do they?

ME: Actually, yes. In contemporary America, we have the Charismatic Christian Movement, which uses music and preaching in rhythmic, feverish cadence to induce non-ordinary states. Ever heard of "Holy Rollers?" You can bet the "Holy Rollers" were neither a Catholic roller-blading team nor religious dope smokers. They entered a spiritual state and commenced to . . .

YOU: . . . roll around on the ground? Really?

ME: Yup. They report feeling like they are in a state of rapture and don't exactly feel like standing when they get a download from the Holy Spirit. This kind of physical activity happens all the time in Breathwork.

YOU: Wow. So I guess this stuff looks pretty weird when it actually happens.

ME: It does. Taken out of context, it can look very strange. There are some videos on the Internet that make Breathwork look all creepy and woo-woo. But if you looked at a video of doctors, out of context, doing cancer surgery, that wouldn't look pretty either. "Wait a minute, they drugged her, and they are cutting her open *to make her better? What the . . . ?*" But it wouldn't mean that it couldn't be ultimately healing. Hell, if you came down from another planet and didn't know what a football game was, you would think we had a pretty weird culture with grown men in funny outfits paid millions of dollars to run around with an inflated dead pig under their arms, while audience members dressed in the same colored outfits all chanted stuff and screamed as guys dressed like zebras blew little whistles. And most of them aren't even under the influence of anything, unless you count the NFL. So . . . yeah, people in Breathwork blissing out and laughing their heads off, because they get the cosmic joke without a hit of acid or a bottle of Jack in sight . . . it does look, well, different. But what counts is the healing.

YOU: Speaking of being under the influence: Let's say I go out and do about a half–dozen shots of Jose Cuervo tequila. Wouldn't I be in a non–ordinary state?

ME: Sure, just not a very interesting one, especially when *you're* drunk. The difference is that in Breathwork, you are not intellectually impaired; you always maintain "one foot" in a normal level of reality. In psychotic states, where there is amnesia or confusion, you lose that footing. But there is no question that in the midst of a group Breathwork session, it looks like something out of the loony bin. The difference is that you will be completely in control of being out of control. You can pop out of the non–ordinary state anytime you want, by simply returning to a normal breathing pattern. Try *that* with LSD. Once a "wave" comes on an acid trip, you are pretty much along for the ride. But not so with Breathwork; you can take back control at any time.

YOU: This is blowing my mind. You mean all great religions and tribal traditions include this same drive to alter consciousness?

ME: Absolutely. In non–industrial cultures, the shamans or priests were people who had experienced the non–ordinary state and brought back wisdom. Sometimes it was spiritual wisdom, other times it was more like survival information, such as which way the herd was moving or what crop to plant and when and where the rain would come. Think of it as a mystical version of Doppler radar. In fact, when you think about it, the source of all great religions is this non–ordinary state. Somebody goes up into the Ethers . . . shakes God's hand . . . and suddenly, they know what's up. Revelation. Then they come down from the mountain and try to find words to explain it for all the blue-collar types. Of course, the bitch of it was, how do you explain the Infinite to the masses? You have to use ideas that they can understand like, "Heaven is filled with streets paved with gold": Symbolic expressions for what is ultimately a non–symbolic experience. But the Infi-nite is beyond explanation and lots of people couldn't, or didn't want to, enter these mystical states. So, all religions made up rules and dogma, complete with all the politics and power plays. *These rules took the place of direct experience of the Divine.* More enlightened teachers intended rules only as an *interim* understanding of the Infinite, sort of like this: Hang on to these ideas until *you* get to hear it directly from the horse's mouth, The Mighty Equine in the Sky. But the rules were never meant to replace direct experience of the Infinite!

Unfortunately, people clung to the rules and forgot that they were merely a reflection of the Wisdom of the Infinite designed to point toward Truth. And so organized religion was born—THE RULES—and things have pretty much sucked ever since. Welcome to a world filled with killing in the name of Christ and Allah. But even with THE RULES, there have always been people who were curious or who were unwilling to swallow religious dogma, hook, line, and sinker. Parts of ourselves and our culture keep yearning for these non-ordinary experiences. We crave more than just THE RULES. We want to know spiritual Truth directly.

YOU: Okay. So when teenagers used to go to a rave, dance all night, and start "rolling," that is to say, they take the street drug Ecstasy, you mean they were really enacting a contemporary version of an ancient ritual to reach an altered state?

ME: Yes . . . basically, although, I am not condoning the use of illegal drugs. Now, what is missing for most of those people is the spiritual intention. In other words, they are not using the experience to consciously further their healing. They are choosing to escape the agonies or boredom of ordinary consciousness, sure. Although they may have a transcendent experience, most of the "rave crowd" would not know how to integrate it and make it healing or useful in their lives. That is why we have therapists in our workshops. In addition, our participants' intention is different. They come for spiritual healing; they want to "leap ahead" on their spiritual journey. Pardon the plug. And besides, street drugs are not only illegal, they are dangerous. Geez, you just don't know what you are getting, do you?

YOU: So, who came up with this "no-drug" approach to non-ordinary states again?

ME: Dr. Stanislav Grof.

YOU: What–is–loff who?

ME: Stanislav Grof studied non-ordinary states of consciousness induced by various psychedelic substances in clinical settings for more than twenty years: He supervised virtually thousands of hours of hallucinogenic trips. Didn't you read that part? I thought the second person voice might really get your attention. Anyway, initially, Grof did research in Prague at several research facilities and eventually served as Chief of Psychiatric Research at the Maryland Research Center and as Assistant Professor of Psychiatry at Johns Hopkins University School of Medicine. Grof has concluded—and I quote: "Psychedelics, if used properly and judiciously under expert guidance, represent extraordinary tools for psychiatry and psychology."

YOU: I'm forgetting all about my inner Republican now. I wanna party with that dude. And this guy sounds like a wheel with major credentials. So he messed around with acid, huh?

ME: Please. He did years of research with hallucinogens in controlled settings. More than that, he is seen as one of the founding fathers of Transpersonal Psychology, along with Dr. Abraham Maslow. Add the work of Carl Jung and Carl Rogers, and you have what is perhaps the highest evolution of psychological thought. You may remember Maslow from Psych 101; he was the guy who came up with the idea of "peak experiences." Does this stuff all come together or what? Anyway, to make it short, Transpersonal Psychology suggests that there is a higher dimension or aspect of the self, beyond the personality and even beyond the unconscious. Some people see this as a spiritual aspect of the self. So, *transpersonal* from "trans," meaning beyond and "personal" meaning—duh, having to do with one's person. So, *beyond one's person.* That is where Breathwork can take you, beyond your physical body and the personal egoic sense of yourself. Grof has called this work the Psychology of the Future.

YOU: Let me guess what happened. The government shut down his psychedelic research?

ME: Very good, Grasshopper, you know our government well. Eventually Uncle Sam pulled the plug on all psychedelic research, and Grof's grant was actually the last one to go in 1975. So he had found this profound healing modality, the use of hallucinogens combined with counseling called "psycholytic therapy"—but he couldn't use it anymore! Over a period of years, as Scholar-in-Residence at the Esalen

Institute, he developed an alternative approach to catalyze non-ordinary states of consciousness without drugs he called Holotropic (Hoe-low-troh-pick) Breathwork. From the Greek *Holos*, meaning wholeness, and *trapein*, meaning toward, in short—a kind of breathing that can move you "toward wholeness." Sorry about all the definitions. I hope you are taking notes. There will be a pop quiz at the end of the book. (Ha! Made you look!)

YOU: Quit that! I will forgive you, but only if you satisfy my curiosity. How in the heck did Grof find a way to have psychedelic, mystical experiences without drugs?

ME: He combined several ideas. First, a kind of rhythmic deep breathing that actually induces biochemical changes in your body. Often people in psychedelic therapy—people who were tripping—would spontaneously breathe in this accelerated manner when they encountered an emotional or energetic block. Now, maybe you have seen one of those old black-and-white movies from the 1940s where a doctor in a spiffy white lab coat with a giant reflector on his head, grabs the hysterical patient, slaps the shit out of them, and says, "For God's sake Ethel, snap out of it!" Turns out, this is not such a good idea. And not just for Ethel's complexion or the doctor's liability insurance. Grof discovered the accelerated breathing *actually helps to facilitate moving through the energetic emotional block*. So, not only does the yogic breathing induce the non-ordinary state, it moves clients through psychological roadblocks that would normally stop them cold in traditional therapy. Think about it. The moment that you freak out about something, or are faced with trauma, what do you do?

YOU: Drink heavily? Light up?

ME: No, before that.

YOU: Let me see . . . I hold my breath?

ME: That's right; we hold our breaths to try to repress our emotions. When we are in danger, we often freeze like the proverbial deer in the headlights. It's an old response from a part of the brain that's designed to help us survive. If we are motionless, prey can't see us as well. But what do you think happens to all that energy?

YOU: I dunno, I guess it gets held in the body or psyche somewhere? Maybe it's like a chronic tension or the mind somehow turns it into pain?

ME: Roughly speaking, that's what trauma experts like Dr. Robert Scaer, Dr. Francine Shapiro, and Dr. David Grand and mind–body doctors like Dr. John Sarno think. Breathing through an experience, like Brenda did in her wind tunnel, allows one to move through and resolve that fear.

YOU: Okay, so Grof had people do the magic breathing both to induce the state and help people move through energetic blocks. What else?

ME: He played evocative music, like native drumming or powerful symphonic scores, which he cranked up really loud.

YOU: What, no rock 'n' roll?

ME: Truth?

YOU: Truth.

ME: When Grof first started experimenting with this work he played . . . The Grateful Dead . . . sometimes.

YOU: *You're kidding me.*

ME: Nope. But he figured out that having lyrics only tied up the conscious mind with language and words and wound up distracting or even preventing the mind from entering the non–ordinary state.

YOU: Bummer. What else?

ME: Finally, Grof created a unique set and ritual setting for the work, where, as we discussed, healing was the intention and personal and emotional safety was paramount. When I lead Transpersonal Breathwork, we spend a Friday night just going over all the stuff you and I are discussing: the nuts and bolts, logistics, how to breathe, what to expect, the works. Then we start early on Saturday.

YOU: Sorry, but I don't get up until the crack of noon.

ME: You'll have to make an exception. Saturday morning you will pair off with a partner. It might be a friend who came with you–if you can find one—or it can be someone you meet at the workshop. In the morning, one of you will be the "breather," and the other will be the "sitter." The breather has the experience, and the sitter's sole job is to support the breather in any way that they are needed: an extra blanket, getting them water, handing them a tissue, even giving them a hug if they ask for one. The experience is three hours long, and then we break for lunch. After lunch the breather and sitter switch places; the person who was the sitter in the morning is now the breather and has the experience. We still have several hours at the end of the work-shop to share our experiences, ground ourselves, and integrate the work we have done. Tens of thousands of people have participated in various forms of Breathwork all over the world.

YOU: Hey, what's all this Holotropic stuff, anyway? I thought this was called Transpersonal Breathwork.

ME: I have a profound respect for Dr. Grof and his protégé, Tav Sparks, and have trained with both of them. Holotropic Breathwork is trademarked by Grof Transpersonal Training. I have also experienced Integrative Breathwork, pioneered by Jacquelyn Small, who worked with Grof for many years before developing her own model though Jackie is retiring. Her work is being perpetuated by Karen Finley Breeding. If you participate in a Holotropic or Integrative Breathwork session with any of them, you would be very likely to have a powerful experience. Having said that, in my estimation, there are some limits to their models. My approach to the music is somewhat different, and I also have unique techniques to integrate and ground people's experience in a way I believe is more complete.

YOU: This guy, Edgar Cayce, the famous psychic—did he have any-thing to say about Breathwork?

ME: I do presentations around the country for Edgar Cayce's Asso-ciation for Research and Enlightenment (A.R.E.), and I call this the W.W.E.S. question: *What would Edgar say?* Well, when Edgar Cayce was alive, there was no such thing as Holotropic or Transpersonal Breathwork, but there were Kundalini–type breathing exercises, dat-ing back centuries, which are very similar to what we do in Breathwork. I like to say that what we are doing is an ancient ritual in a contemporary setting! One woman queried Cayce about this tech-nique and here is what he said, "[F]or in the body there is that center in which the soul is expressive, creative in its nature . . . By this breath-ing, this may be made to expand . . . and opens the seven [spiritual] centers of the body . . . Thus, an [individual] puts itself [in touch] with all it has *ever* been or may be. For, it loosens the physical consciousness to the universal consciousness." (2475–1)

YOU: Whoa. Back up the bus. This kind of breathing opens up the spiritual energies to move up through the chakras, loosens my identi-fication with myself as a physical body, and *puts me in touch with all that has ever been . . . or may be?*

ME: Yep, sorry but that's about all it does. But the reading also goes on to caution the person that preparation and readiness is necessary to do this breathing safely. I take that admonition from Cayce very seriously, and we do all we can to establish trust, set intentionality, and align our participants spiritually so that this work can be done safely. We always begin our sessions with White Light imagery to guide and protect us. Our outcomes have been uniformly positive, so we believe that we are doing this appropriately and reverently. We also take extra steps to make sure that people's experiences are well integrated, so when they leave, it's not just that they took the magical mystery tour, but they can apply the wisdom of their visions to their everyday life. But as it turns out, there is an even stronger Cayce connection to what we do.

YOU: Try me.

ME: Cayce gave more than 14,000 trance readings, and he went through a very specific ritual to get into the non-ordinary state. In researching Breathwork, I discovered that Cayce himself, just prior to taking questions, *spontaneously breathed quickly and rhythmically from his diaphragm for several minutes.* So it may be that the very technique that Cayce used to induce his trance—at least in part—is what we're using in Breathwork to access the same state!

YOU: It sounds amazing (sighs). But I could never do this stuff; I'd blow it. What if I breathe wrong? What if I don't like the music? Will it still work?

ME: If you follow the instructions, you will find it extremely hard to stay out of the non-ordinary state. The breathing technique is very simple. As to the music, I typically spend somewhere in the neighborhood of forty to fifty hours selecting, programming, and digitally mastering three-hour custom tracks, especially for these experiences. (Yeah, my friends are a little worried about my obsessive tendencies there.) Plus, I have been known to switch music around during workshops to tailor things to the participants. At a Breathwork Experience, you would likely hear a wide variety of musical influences from all over the world—Celtic, Native American, African, Indian, and American— much of it from the sacred tradition—along with cool spatial effects and natural recordings to create lush soundscapes. Tracks feature lots of native ritual instruments—including some you've probably never heard before. Songs are sung in everything from Senegalese to Lakota Sioux. As I said, I don't want you to get distracted by the lyrics, so most of it is in foreign languages or are instrumentals. To top it off, the experience is so intense, most people don't remember much of the music after the session. For certain people, the kind of music is everything, for others, it's nothing. It's odd; it somehow matters very much and doesn't matter at all—more spiritual paradox, I guess.

For the record, the first time I did a workshop as a participant, I hated the music—and twenty minutes into it, I was in a non-ordinary state and had a mind-blowing trip. But in my estimation, I have gone much deeper and had more profound experiences with different music. The bottom line is that everybody is afraid nothing will happen, but after over a decade of this work, I can only think of maybe one or two people who didn't catalyze the state . . . and frankly, there was probably another unconscious agenda going on there.

YOU: Okay, but breathing for three hours? I'm gonna be bored out of my skull, right?

ME: Yeah, I get that a lot, but only from people who haven't done Breathwork. Actually, people are totally engaged with their own internal visionary, kinesthetic, and emotional experience and often report when we are done that it felt like only ten or fifteen minutes had passed. I have had people get pissed off at me for bringing them out of the state after three or three and a half hours, because they wanted to stay longer!

YOU: Yeah, but I can't even meditate for ten minutes!

ME: What's great is you don't have to make your mind blank or focus on a mantra during Breathwork. You would be missing the point if you did! All you have to do is keep doing the breathing. You don't even have to *remember* to do the breathing! *It is your partner's job* to watch your respiration and keep you on task by giving you a nonverbal signal—perhaps a tap on the shoulder—if your partner finds you losing focus. People never believe me when I tell them this, but although the breathing takes some effort, in the big picture, it's actually much, much easier than meditating.

YOU: I have heard some forms of Breathwork will allow people *without* a background in counseling to be certified as Breathwork facilitators. Are you sure that this is okay?

ME: I read somewhere that a psychiatrist with Breathwork experience blogged that allowing someone without a psychology degree to facilitate Breathwork is like handing a 357 Magnum to a two year old. To be sure, this is intense deep work. It may well be that there are those empathic, intuitive facilitators that can be every bit as effective as those with years of training and experience in counseling. But, if it were me? I would want to make sure that whoever was supervising my Breathwork session had at least a master's in counseling, all things being equal. I have done a lot of this work, and it can get pretty wild.

YOU: You mean, I can't do this alone?

ME: Well, I'm not the breath police, but this is where Stan Grof, Jackie Small, Edgar Cayce, and Yours Truly all agree. This is powerful stuff. *Never* do this without the supervision of someone trained in Breathwork. Truth is, it is a much more loving and transformative experience done in a group setting, anyway.

YOU: Well, you blew me away with that story about Brenda getting over a lifelong phobia in a single session. I'll bet you have seen some other amazing things happen in Breathwork.

ME: Did I tell you about Lola?

*   *   *

LOLA: GROWING UP AND GETTING FREE

Lola was a quiet blonde in her late thirties, a victim of physical and sexual abuse. Beginning in childhood, she had become accustomed to men hurting her, and she continued this unconscious pattern in her romantic relationships. Though I could see she carried a weariness in her eyes, she still maintained much of the beauty, grace, and glamour of the career that had served her for many years, that of a professional model. In particular, her face lit up when she smiled. I sensed the youth and optimism could still be kindled, but it had often been smothered under years of pain. When she came to see me in individual therapy, she told me she had "grown beyond" violent men. But, by her own admission, her current boyfriend was very controlling, telling her what to wear and who she could have as friends. He constantly criticized her about how to raise her little girl, although he himself was childless. "I know I need to leave him, but I can't bring myself to go." He was older, fit, very attractive, and quite wealthy, "a diamond in the rough," she said. But the more I heard about him, the more I recognized just how "rough" he was—often judgmental, stoic, and cold. Although, she lacked for little financially (a far cry from her destitute childhood), he was emotionally unavailable. After six sessions, Lola was sensing a shift—she saw how even though he was a less violent version of her father (and her two ex-husbands), there were still enormous similarities. Yet she still found it unthinkable to leave him. "He *needs* me," she said pleadingly, offering the oft-repeated mantra of emotionally abused women.

In Breathwork, Lola struggled to attain a trance state, opening her eyes periodically, calling me over for help. "I'm just not doing this right, am I?" I assured her that she was, that she had only been breathing for fifteen minutes, and that it often took up to an hour or more to catalyze the non-ordinary state. But I knew that this was simply Lola looking to a male figure for validation or approval. So when she asked a second time, a few minutes later, I simply turned the question on her. "How do *you* think you are doing?" I asked quietly. She responded, "Well, I am doing the breathing just like you told me . . . and I do feel a little lightheaded." I smiled gently and said, "Then I think you can trust that. Trust yourself, Lola. It's time to begin to trust yourself more." She nodded knowingly and offered a cursory smile that told me she was not completely convinced. But within another fifteen minutes, it was clear things were happening for Lola. She began to moan in discomfort and gently rock on the ground. Periodically, she flinched, her eyes scrunching tightly. This began to build progressively, and the groans became louder as she began to thrash. The sounds became shrieks, and she began to thrash her hands and feet. Her sitter, Linda, a kindly older woman, quickly grabbed the extra pillows she brought and put them under Lola's hands and arms to keep Lola safe. Finally, the shrieks became full-fledged screams that continued for some time. Her energy finally reached a crescendo as she repeatedly slammed her fists into two overstuffed pillows by her sides. Then her body slumped, and for probably two minutes her face and posture were frozen, resolute. Then she relaxed, as though her body, once ice, was melting, and began to sob. Linda, her sitter, softly took her hand, and Lola responded immediately, pulling Linda into a hug, clutching her close to her chest as she wept. Linda stayed with her, intuitively letting her gentle and stable touch offer what words cannot: a tactile sense of presence, comfort, and safety.

When I looked in on Lola a bit later in the workshop, she had broken her embrace with Linda and was lying apparently very peacefully with a soft smile on her face. Of course, neither Linda nor I had any idea what the content of Lola's vision was, but it was obvious she had reached some level of resolution.

It was only later in the workshop that we began to understand just how both painful and beatific Lola's vision had been.

After some frustration in catalyzing the trance state, Lola said that she relived a common occurrence from her childhood: her father beating her with a wide black leather belt with a heavy silver buckle. Towering over her, he repeatedly whipped her, telling her that she was worthless and "a bad girl." Lola felt herself going fetal, and while she didn't feel the pain of the strap, she did sense the impact, panic, and fear that she had experienced as a child. She started crying, something she didn't do as a child, because this would have resulted in her father telling her to, "Shut up, or I'll give you something to cry about!" As Lola allowed her tears, she had the very unique experience of both feeling alone and sad as a child and simultaneously being comforted in the now by her Breathwork partner, Linda. This dual focus is not uncommon in Breathwork, or in non–ordinary states, for that matter. It is almost as though consciousness can process or reprocess the experience from multiple levels. In fact, this may be a key component of how Breathwork heals. Somehow, by revisiting the experience in the context of love (Linda's care and support), a new experience is encoded in Lola's memory in which the assigned meaning is different. Instead of being alone in her pain, she is comforted: her pain is seen and matters. In therapy, this is known as a *corrective emotional experience.*

Then, as Lola both watched from a third person perspective and experienced herself as a child, she found herself growing up, getting bigger, and bigger. In addition, her rage and anger, always hidden from her father and barely acknowledged by Lola, grew bigger as well. Finally, she found herself as an adult, looking slightly down at her father, never a tall man. "Nooooooo!" she shrieked like a wild animal in pain and angrily wrested the belt from him, rearing backward, holding it high in the air and coming down hard on his back with every muscle in her body. *Thwack!*

Her father fell to his knees, groaning in pain, a look of incredulous shock on his face. Frozen, she towered over him, stone-like, immoveable, breathing fire, her teeth clinched, eyes wide with fury. "How do you like that Daddy?" she blurted, eyes wet, her hands shaking. "It HURTS doesn't it?! DOESN'T IT?" Her father hung his head in shame. "NO!" she scolded him. "No, Daddy, NO! NEVER AGAIN, DADDY! Do you understand me? NEVER again!"

For a few moments, she stood over him, her chest heaving, her hand and arm carved in stone above her head, clinching the belt, the buckle slowly swaying like some kind of grotesque pendulum, counting the moments that had taken an eternity. He didn't dare look up. Finally, the buckle was still. Although her arm remained resolute like the Statue of Liberty, somehow, slowly, the tightness in her fingers relinquished, and she felt the belt slither through her fingers, her father no longer a threat.

She heard the thick leather and heavy buckle hit the floor with a clank and a thud.

The silence was eerie; the tableau, spectral.

"Never again," she said flatly, under her breath. Her arm fell suddenly to her side. She stared at him for a final extended moment. Then, slowly turning, Lola left her father crumpled on the ground and walked away. The rage was gone.

There was only sadness: a recognition that her father was never going to be who she wanted him to be. And now, there were just tears. They came slowly, haltingly at first, and then gut-wrenching sobs. Tears for every man who had hurt her. Tears for every person who had touched her without her permission. Tears for all the times that she herself had willingly surrendered to an angry man, attempting some kind of cosmic "do-over" where her dedication would somehow transform their insensitivity into kindness, and she would "win" the game she lost in childhood.

And then quiet. Stillness. And . . . what was this?

Peace.

Then, slowly, she felt better. Revitalized. "Never again," she had told her father. And she had heard herself. And she now knew that her pain was worthy to be noticed and attended to: the workshop leaders, Linda, and the group demonstrated that with their tears and hugs that came as she shared her story. There might be other men in her life, but she knew beyond a doubt that she would never let herself be abused physically or emotionally like that again. She was absolutely certain she would—and could—stand up for herself from now on.

And she felt safe, *really safe*, for the first time in her life.

The next week, Lola informed her boyfriend that, although she was very grateful for his generosity, she needed and deserved more from a man, and the relationship was at an end.

*   *   *

NORRIS: A PICNIC IN HEAVEN

Norris, a good-looking, muscular young man in his late twenties, came to Breathwork carrying the kind of horrible childhood that most folks only think of as happening in a Dickens novel. Norris had long-ish, curly dark hair, deep-set brown eyes and a little boy smile tinged with hope. Some tattoos on his arms made him look a bit more edgy than he really was.

I had worked with Norris in individual therapy for about six months, and he had made considerable headway. He had grown up without a father, but with an alcoholic mother who had an uncanny knack for picking angry, violent men for boyfriends. She was often absent, inebriated, or emotionally vacant when Norris was a child. Typically, the focus of her attention would be on the latest alcoholic she was dating. His grandmother, also a drunk, was a more stable figure in his life in terms of her physical presence. But she, too, hated men and repeatedly told Norris that they were evil and manipulative. They only wanted one thing, she said, and that was sex. Periodically, she would storm into Norris' room in the middle of the night, apropos of nothing. Her anxious breath filling the room with the smell of cheap wine; she'd beat Norris with a yardstick, screaming and shrieking, "You are no better than the rest of them!"

As a therapist, I recognize that there are degrees of abuse. Many of my clients grew up in homes where physical punishment was commonplace, administered by well-meaning parents who were very much products of their own time and culture. But research has demonstrated repeatedly that this approach is not only abusive, but ineffective. Physical punishment breeds bullies. Perhaps the best that can be said is that in some households, at least there is a clear cause–and–effect: You did not clean your room, so you will be spanked. While less than ideal, at least the pain is not random or haphazard.

But Norris was regularly hit by his grandmother in a violent drunken rage in the wee hours of the morning for no reason. The message Norris was left with? He had done something wrong, but he didn't know what. Or maybe, it was that he himself was defective. The beatings continued well into his teens, because, he explained, as much as he hated her, she was increasingly frail, and he was afraid if he did fight back, he might actually kill her.

Norris entered his prime, deeply conflicted about his masculinity. He believed that because he was a man, he was inherently flawed. He liked sex, but was afraid that if he had sex with a woman, then he had somehow "perpetrated it" upon them. His days were filled with a sense of generalized anxiety; years of "training" had convinced him that punishment might come at any hour of the day or night. His central nervous system was amped up, always on guard, waiting for the inevitable pain and betrayal. Not surprisingly, he found himself dating a series of women that had been sexually abused as children. Initially they appreciated his reticence to initiate sex and idealized him. "Oh, Norris, you are so different than those other guys who just want to get into my pants," they would coo romantically. Those were the sweetest words that Norris could hear from a woman, so different from the messages of his childhood. But these moments of respite were short-lived. Typically, when he finally did make a move, they castigated him. When his advances triggered their own unresolved memories, they cast him in the role of sex maniac, sometimes shrieking at him or even hitting him. He would show up in my office after one of these evenings, looking exhausted and hopeless, staring vacantly at his shoes. "Maybe," he would say wearily wringing his hands, "Grandmother was right about me."

In the few months that we had worked together, we made considerable headway, and he felt increasingly less anxious, if not altogether happy. He began to see how each of the women he dated brought their own preconceptions to their relationship, and he began to at least consider the concept that he was not evil "like all the men that hurt my mother and grandmother."

Norris was torn. Although he had "experimented" sexually as a teenager, he felt he was heterosexual and was strongly attracted to women. But there was so much shame in his family around being a man, that he denied himself of healthy masculine energy and told me, "If there is a man's club, nobody gave me a membership card."

Norris had been reticent to approach working in therapy with regard to the nightly beatings he received from his grandmother. I honored that reluctance, knowing that if I push abused clients to work too quickly on these issues, I will be seen by them as an abuser, not a healer. While I know that I cannot and should not prolong this work indefinitely, simply because it is painful for clients to face, I try to go out of my way to be sensitive to their own organic timing.

And now, he would be attending my upcoming Transpersonal Breathwork Experience. Unlike some methods of shamanic journeying, that set out a specific intent for the ritual, Breathwork operates on the assumption that some part of the individual—their unconscious, the Higher Mind, or perhaps God—will take the Breather towards the experience and healing that is in their best interest in their personal journey. I couldn't imagine that Norris would go anywhere but toward the violent experiences with his grandmother so that he could face them head-on and reach a resolution.

But I was wrong.

As Norris began to breathe deeply and listen to the music, he felt himself becoming pleasantly numb, a kind of quiet joy settling into his chest and around his heart. It was in sharp contrast to the ever-present gnaw of anxiety that he always felt when awake. Then, he felt himself being "lifted up" as though he was moving through layers and layers of clouds. The journey upwards was filled with contrasts of light and shadow, subtle pastels, and brilliant primary colors. Then the clouds cleared, and he found himself in a city park that was near his childhood home. On the picnic tables were fried chicken, potato salad, deviled eggs, and celery stuffed with peanut butter—all of Norris' favorites. It was warm and sunny with a delicious breeze. He felt a refreshing coolness in his right hand and looked down to discover an open Mason jar filled with Southern "sweet tea," almost black and loaded with real sugar, a forgotten thrill from childhood. He sipped the tea, the intense icy sweet bitterness flooding his mouth; it was like tasting it for the first time. He swallowed, savoring the aftertaste.

Exhaling, he looked around to find himself surrounded by loving faces. His Uncle Billy was there, balding with a round belly, a big grin plastered on his face. "How are ya, boy!" he said, in a voice too loud by twice, pulling Norris toward him and engulfing him in a clumsy polar bear hug, clapping Norris' back hard enough to wind him. Norris smiled and teared up as he smelled the stale Aqua Velva on Billy's neck and the safe and familiar touch of a man he respected and loved. And looking over Billy's shoulder, he could see his Aunt Nadine's slender frame in her velour jogging suit, wearing too much mascara, her lipstick almost on target today, despite her Parkinson's. She was smiling adoringly, thrilled by his presence.

Then there were his cousins Nicky and Toby. The fair-haired Toby was quiet and quite shy but always seemingly honored to play with Norris, who was several years his senior. And Cousin Nicky! There was only one Nicky, a year older than Norris, always up for adventure, larger than life, looking for trouble, always finding it, and only too happy to drag Norris in behind him. And who was that in the distance? It was Mrs. Crosby, his art teacher from Bertram High, grey hair piled high, carrying a plate full of brownies with walnuts, shooing flies away with her free hand. Stocky and full-breasted, she toddled toward him on high heels, ever the fashion plate. "Noooooooorrrrriiiiis!" she sang, his name performed as an entire symphony as only Mrs. Crosby could. She was always so kind, so loving and supportive. She believed in him, his masculinity never a threat, his sensitivity never a detriment in Mrs. Crosby's eyes. Norris owed his career as a graphic designer to her. It was "Missus C," who saw his spark of genius, not his mother and grandmother, who laughed at his crude drawings of superheroes.

As the afternoon wore on, there were heaping plates of food, garnished with ebullient laughter and sentimental stories of times gone by. Aunt Nadine regaled the reunion with familiar family myths of Norris and Toby, led astray by Nicky, the Artful Dodger of the bunch. In her gravelly voice, she told the tamest of the tales so as not to embarrass Norris, but concluded by admitting there *were* other adventures: "some legal, some illegal, mostly harmless, all hysterical." This well-worn pronouncement brought shrieks of laughter, Uncle Billy nearly choking on a deviled egg. "I'll tell what really happened!" eagerly offered the avuncular Nicky, to which Norris countered with mock menace, "Nooooooo, I don't think you will!" and there was another round of guffaws.

There were memories of staying with Uncle Billy and Aunt Nadine one Christmas, where no one got drunk, everyone sang carols, and there were Tonka trucks under the tree for Norris. Uncle Billy even watched *A Charlie Brown Christmas* with Norris and laughed at Snoopy's antics. This same TV special had been dismissed year after year as "stupid and childish" by Norris' grandmother, with a wave of her hand, despite Norris' pleas to her to watch it with him. But Uncle Billy sat in the big, plaid, threadbare Barcalounger, watching Linus and Lucy on an ancient rabbit-eared TV set, his pudgy right palm on the boy's left shoulder as Norris sat cross-legged on the floor. It had been a simple enough act for Uncle Billy, just watching a show with a child. But it was everything to Norris.

They were all there—the most caring of his family, his favorite teachers, neighbors and cousins, too loud, too crass, gravy on their shirts. There were chubby wrists bedazzled with garish costume jewelry from Wal-Mart frantically waving over brimming paper plates, blue-hairs casting spells over the fried chicken, emphatically punctuating with their hands yet another endearing childhood anecdote about Norris. They all loved him, however imperfectly, and they were all perfect in their imperfection.

Norris had a picnic in Heaven. And it *was* Heaven, too. He could tell, because he was loved and cherished and admired and adored. He was a man, and it was okay. He was creative and sensitive, and it was okay. He belonged.

And every one of those people he saw had died.

Uncle Billy had been taken by a massive stroke while mowing his impeccable lawn one hot summer's day, and his beloved Nadine followed soon after. Nicky and Toby had been hit by a drunk driver while still in their teens, and Missus C had passed peacefully at home, the day after Christmas, just last year. But they all had reached across the gulf of time and space to have one last lunch with Norris.

Some hours later, toward the end of the workshop, Norris shared his experience with the group. He looked around at the others, his eyes moist. "I feel so bad," he said, his voice choking. Then suddenly, he giggled through the tears. "I mean . . . " Norris looked perplexed for a moment. "I mean . . . I feel good . . . so wonderful. So wonderful!" He breathed rapidly, in and out, almost unable to bear his good fortune, intermittently crying, yet smiling. "You know, I really was loved, *really loved*, by a lot of people growing up. It's just that for so many years, when I think of my childhood, I think about Mom passed out on the sofa or Grandma coming into my room in the middle of the night with the most awful look on her face . . . " He broke off, weeping, burying his head in his hands. I looked around at the group. They, too, were crying, visibly moved by Norris' plight. "That look . . . " he whimpered, "that look was worse than the beatings. It seemed to say that I was somehow inherently bad, that I was a mistake." He gulped at the air, frantic to admit what was coming next. "I didn't even want to be alive." He wept quietly in his hands, desperately trying not to make any noise. Three hands, male and female, filled with compassion, emerged from the group; gently falling on his shoulders and back.

"But today," he swallowed hard, "today, I saw something different. I saw all the people who loved me." He paused, grasping the enormity of what he was about to say. "I saw all the people who *love* me, even now. When I said I felt bad earlier? It's because I forgot that so many people love me." Something about Norris' story touched me, and I could see it had touched the group. They were wiping away tears. Norris' story reminded all of us how easy it is to focus on the few people that judge us or who are unkind while completely ignoring those who cherish and support us. In those moments, we can't see ourselves clearly, and we may actively reject the love of those who are dearest to us. What a tragedy!

Norris drew a long slow breath. He pondered for a long moment, his brow furrowing as though asking himself, *how could I have forgotten?* Then clarity arrived, his face glowing, the dawn breaking. Norris became visibly calmer. "It's like I couldn't see them, because my mother and my grandmother were standing in the way. Their memories were so big, so angry. But you know what I saw in those heavenly faces? I saw that I am all right. I deserve to be happy. I am creative. I am a man, and it's okay to be a man." He sighed deeply and settled into the thought as a big smile lit as gently as a butterfly on his face.

"And what do you see on the faces here in the room?" I asked, offering to ground Norris even more deeply in his new reality. For the briefest of moments he hesitated, retreating, glancing towards the floor, fearful he might somehow see his grandmother's gaze in someone across from him. But then his head starting nodding spontaneously as though his body answered my question before his brain could convince him otherwise. He looked up and around the room at a circle of nine people, awestruck, touched, and moved by his experience, his courage, his ability to survive, and the unmistakable innate radiance that blazed from his eyes. "You guys love me, too," he whispered, his voice breaking ever so slightly. Everyone smiled and nodded gently. "I think you do," he said grinning. He kept scanning the circle, drinking in the love and the warmth so freely and joyously offered by the group. "I really think you do." He looked down briefly, offering a deep sigh. Then he looked up and paused briefly for impact. "Maybe," he said coyly, his grin taking on a mischievous twist, "maybe heaven is here, too."

I think he was right.

Norris sporadically continued for several years with me in individual therapy after his Transpersonal Breathwork Experience. He increasingly found himself less anxious, less likely to take on the projections of women that he dated, and in general, he grew more comfortable in his own skin. Breathwork, while in my experience a powerful healing modality, does not automatically obliterate the need for ongoing therapy, especially in cases where there is extensive, repetitive trauma. But Norris' childhood memories would never again focus solely on the abuse of his mother and grandmother. The pantheon of influential figures in his mind had been revised to include the smiling, loving faces of Uncle Billy and Aunt Nadine, cousins Nicky and Toby, the gentle Mrs. Crosby, and so many others . . . all thanks to a special picnic in heaven.

*   *   *

EVAN AND NADIA: SOULMATES REUNITED

Nadia was in her early forties. She had been a long-time client of mine. I often work with people who have very little sense of who they are, but initially, Nadia was completely confused about her identity in a way I had never seen in a client, before or since. She constantly wanted to know what I thought about her and about her choices and I constantly would redirect her and ask, "What do you think about your life?" Her parents and her society had made so many demands on her, some spoken and some unspoken, that it seemed she had no center, no inner compass. She lacked what Carl Rogers called an "internal locus of evaluation." In her individual work with me, she slowly made headway, working her way through issues of sexual abuse with her grandfather, parents who hadn't a clue about being parents, and a volatile ten-year marriage that had ended in a painful divorce. She worked through her issues with her boss—a former boyfriend who still had interest in her—and found ways to say no to him. She negotiated a well-deserved raise as well as emotionally separated herself from his business and personal life. Synchronistically, as she released her boss emotionally, he found the love of his life and got married. Increasingly, she had a sense of what she liked, what she didn't, who she was, and where she was going. Nadia, for the first time in her life, felt relatively comfortable in her own skin.

It was then that she met Evan. He was older, tall, silver-haired, and worldly. He was a professional pilot and was nearing retirement. Although he was clearly a strong individual, he was a staunch pacifist, the kind of man who would walk away from a fight, even if he was in the right. Soon, they started to see me for couples counseling, as Nadia was still yearning to explore what a healthy romantic relationship might look like. I could see Evan cared for Nadia and was typically very patient with her, drawn to her beauty, her child-like wonder, and her dark sense of humor. On balance, she was drawn to his quiet nature, his sincere devotion to her, and his willingness to help. Still, her history had taught her not to trust men, and it became clear she had a knack for testing his limits

If Evan was clearly smitten, Nadia was more reticent. Evan's work took him out of town regularly. While he did his best to stay in touch with Nadia when he was away, Nadia was furious when he didn't contact her, unreasonably saying he obviously didn't care for her and wondering whether he was having affairs. I am not so naïve to think that Evan wouldn't lie to me. But there was certainly no hard evidence of adultery that Nadia could muster, outside of some days where Evan called less than two or three times a day. As best as I could tell, Nadia's complaints were more likely due to Evan's grueling flight schedule and poor cell phone coverage combined with Nadia's abandonment issues. Sure enough, as we dug deeper into Nadia's past, she had good reasons for those fears. Her father had been a traveling salesman who had been away for weeks at a time. Her mother had admitted that she had ample evidence to suggest that Nadia's father had stepped outside the marriage a number of times.

In a particularly poignant session, Nadia tearfully remembered her family moving to another city and intentionally leaving her pet dog on the porch. She was only seven. As they drove away, her heart broke as she looked through the rear window at her shrinking pet terrier, Murphy. "Oh, he'll be fine, Nadia, quit blubbering," her father had told her.

As she sat in my office, Nadia's eyes were wide and rimmed with tears, as she stared blankly into the distance, lost in the memory. "What did that experience seem to tell you?" I asked. "I thought . . . " she gasped, trying to find her voice through the pain, "I thought that if they could leave Murphy behind . . . what about me? Murphy was my dog, he was my best friend, a part of the family, and they just left him. I thought if they could do that, maybe they might leave me that way."

It was a breakthrough session. Her father's constant travel, his infidelity, and leaving Murphy behind had all coalesced in Nadia's unconscious as a deeply held negative belief: *I will be abandoned.* And now she had made that unconscious material conscious. I felt sure that Nadia could now make a clear distinction between Evan's inability to contact her at times and her childhood fears of abandonment.

Yet Nadia continue to attack Evan for going away on business. "You say you love me," Nadia said with a cold intensity, "but you are always gone, and you never call!" She was clearly ignoring his regular daily contact by text and phone.

"Nadia, how can you say that, honey?" he begged, almost apologetically. "I'm trying to get a satellite phone, but they are really expensive. And I have arranged with my boss to be home more frequently, but I have to keep my job!"

"Those are just excuses!" cried Nadia, crossing her arms and turning away from him."

Evan, unable to control himself, now turned to the offensive. "Jesus, what do you want from me?" he said to Nadia sharply. "You know that I love you, and I call you every time I can. But this is intolerable. You are my judge and jury; I can't win, no matter what!"

Interestingly, poor Evan had grown up with a hypercritical father who attacked him for every mistake. "You couldn't pour piss from a boot," his dad used to mutter to a wide-eyed seven-year-old Evan when he dropped the baseball his father had thrown to him. Dad wanted an athlete; young Evan favored books and model airplanes.

We were entering dangerous territory. If I couldn't find some way to help each of them soon, this couple, who adored each other, would soon break up. They were both on the verge of a self-fulfilling prophecy. Evan would feel like he was with his overly punitive father again and leave. Nadia would get what she both dreaded and expected: abandonment. It was a tragedy waiting to happen.

Still, both Evan and Nadia were spiritual seekers. They appreciated the idea that life was an earth school and that they had lessons to learn. So when I suggested that they come to my upcoming Transpersonal Breathwork Experience, they jumped at the chance.

"C'mon, honey," said Evan good-naturedly to Nadia.

"It all sounds pretty wild, but maybe we can figure out what all this shit is about." Nadia could not help but smile.

*　　*　　*

The vision in Evan's head was crystal clear. He had promised her that they would marry. One last flight, and he would quit flying forever. He loved her, and he wanted only her. The look on her face was unmistakably a contradiction of feelings: wistful admiration, an ache of sorrow, and yet filled with hope and anticipation. He kissed her tenderly, climbed up the stairs to the cockpit of his plane, and took off. She watched spellbound as his plane soared heroically upward, a bright bird in the sky getting smaller and smaller until the colorful speck finally disappeared.

It would be the last time she would ever see him alive.

But even as Evan watched—or more accurately, re-lived the vision—he knew it was not a glimpse forward, but backward. It was a grim look at his past. Yes, he was the aviator, but this was 1916, and he was a German pilot, a World War I ace. His name was Karl, and his precious fiancée was Gertrude. Evan and Nadia had been in love before in another life, and despite promising he would come back for her, his final flight had taken him not back to his beloved, but "home to heaven." He had been shot down by a British ace. Gertrude, crushed by the loss of her Karl, became depressed and broken-hearted, fell ill, and died a few years later. The loss was simply too much for her.

As the music in the workshop space slowed to a pastoral piece, Evan stirred, wiping dampness from his eyes. Suddenly, so much had become clear: his love of flying, his fascination with World War I, his commitment to pacifism . . . but most importantly, his heart filled with compassion as he thought of his beloved Nadia having been with him before. He also recognized how much pain and disappointment she must still carry from the experience. Of course she was distrustful! But not because of anything he had done, at least not in this lifetime.

At the end of Breathwork group sessions, I always give participants the chance to share their experiences. Evan told the group that he would share his story, but that he wanted to share it directly with Nadia. I positioned them on the floor, sitting cross-legged knee to knee. He tenderly took both her hands in his and slowly told her the whole story. Nadia listened spellbound, a powerful energy rising in her. As Evan completed the story, she exploded, filled with the pain of the memory. "You left me," she said sobbing, "you left me, and you never came back! After you had promised! YOU PROMISED!" It was as though some deep chord had been struck in Nadia. She was talking to Evan as though he was Karl! Hysterically, Nadia fell over into Evan's chest, sobbing, seemingly inconsolable. "You left me! You got in the stupid plane, and you left me!" Her face was buried in his shoulder, his arms wrapped tightly around her. Evan's mouth opened to respond, but I managed to hold up a finger over my mouth, unseen by Nadia. Evan caught himself, and instead of rising to his defense, he simply held his heartbroken girlfriend. Two, three, five minutes went by as her body slowly convulsed less frequently. Evan somehow understood what I could not tell him in that moment: that every second he held her as she grieved proved to Nadia—through an immediate experi-ence—*that he would not abandon her.* And yet, when Nadia's head finally rose up from Evan's embrace, there was both fierceness and great vul-nerability in her eyes. "You left me," she said almost imperceptibly.

Then her head bowed, unable to look at him, as she said it again. "You left me."

Evan reached over to Nadia and with two fingers lifted her chin. As he did so, she looked up, and a single tear spilled over her lower eyelid and rolled down her left cheek. "But I came back for you," Evan said in the softest of voices. "Trudy, I came back for you across time and space. I came back to make good my promise. I love you and want to marry you. I found you again in this lifetime, and I will never let you go." Nadia began weeping again, but these were very different tears. "I will never let you go," repeated Evan, with steely conviction, his eyes glazed with tears. Suiting action to words, he pulled her legs up, circling an arm behind her back and reaching under her knees, and pulled her into his lap, cradling her. Nadia softly whimpered like a lost child finally reunited with her mother as Evan gently rocked her, crying silent tears of regret and redemption.

And in that moment, Karl and Gertrude reconstituted their timeless vow, to spend their lives together, forever.

In the end, Nadia and Evan found ways to "split the difference," as they worked through their painful karmic patterns. Evan understood that the lack of contact triggered painful past-life traumas for Nadia and went out of his way to stay in touch with her when he was out of town. He also began to understand that part of what he loved about aviation was that it allowed him to "fly away" when things were difficult. Evan recognized that sometimes he needed to stay and work things out.

Nadia discovered that she couldn't trust that her emotional reactions were always honest reflections of what was happening with Evan. Her reactivity was based on not only Karls' abandonment in another life, but also the echoes of her parent's absence. "Easy, Nadia," she would say gently to herself when she found herself feeling "mistreated" by Evan's absence. "He loves you, he is different from your dad and granddad. Don't panic, this is just fear from the past. He is not likely to be shot down flying a commercial flight over Birmingham."

Evan made good on his promise to wed Nadia. Last I heard, they had been happily married for several years, but not before Nadia had shrewdly made sure that she would be taken care of financially if Evan died prematurely!

THE STORIES CONTINUE

Powerful, healing stories continue to come out of Transpersonal Breathwork Experiences. A woman with chronic asthma was healed when she breathed her way through a panic attack in the middle of Breathwork. At a two-year follow up, she was symptom free. One young lady experienced her energy merging with Jesus, and she became Christ and was crucified. "I experienced no pain as Jesus, only compassion for my disciples and family and forgiveness for my enemies. I knew, really knew, that they didn't know what they were doing." At the end of the workshop, I asked her to breathe and listen to the music that was playing when she had had the experience, to catalyze the state. She apparently moved into the Christ Consciousness again, and I asked her to energetically bless each of the participants as they knelt in front of her. People in the workshop said the heat and vibrations that came from her hands was palpable, and as we completed the exercise, everyone in the room, including the facilitators, stood awestruck, our eyes welling with tears.

And then there was Terrence, a recovering addict who used to shoot dope, whose Breathwork experience took him to the gateway of heaven and left him flooded with bliss and compelled to write poetry about his experience. "If addicts found out about this shit," he said, with a grin on his face, "they would never shoot up again!"

Interestingly, both Holotropic and Integrative Breathwork have increasingly found their way into in-patient treatment for addiction. It was the spiritual awakening of Bill Wilson that ignited the creation of the twelve-step program of A.A. I believe Breathwork has an enormous potential to catalyze such experiences and greatly accelerate healing the scourge of addiction.

One woman, Beth, popped out of the non-ordinary state in the middle of her session with such a stark intensity that I was initially alarmed. She pinned herself against the wall, staring at me with the look of a caged wild animal.

"Beth, are you alright?" I asked quietly.

"*I am not me,*" she said with a look of horror, trying to somehow merge with the wall behind her. "*I don't even exist.*" Her every muscle was tense. The more she spoke to me, the more I knew that she was in a tenuous place. "But everything that has happened to me *didn't really happen.* I mean, *not to me."* The longer she talked to me, the clearer I became that she had shifted her identification completely away from her ego. Her physical embodiment was not who she truly was . . . and she was terrified. Panic gripped her, an existential fear of her own "nothingness." "If that isn't me . . . then *who am I?"* she blurted, her voice quivering.

"That," I said very calmly, "is a great question. Can you go back in, breathe some more and explore that?"

She looked at me like I might as well have told her to jump into shark-infested waters. "The anxiety engendered by confronting the abyss of nothingness" warned psychologist Erich Fromm, "is more terrifying that the tortures of hell . . . I am driven to the border of madness—because I cannot say 'I' anymore."

"Beth, I am serious; go back in," I said firmly, knowing that if she quit now the terror might not abate. "Not around, but through" I said, echoing Jacquelyn Small, the developer of Integrative Breathwork. "Go back in, keep breathing, and ask that question 'Who am I, really?' to the deepest part of you, and see what happens." I spent more than a few minutes reminding Beth that she could come out of the state again, if anything was too much for her. Additionally, I assured her that I would stay nearby if she needed me.

In fact, Beth did go back in, only to discover her answer. She experienced herself as pure energy, waves of shimmering light, filled with bliss, casting rainbows in all directions. At the end of the workshop she expressed her gratitude. "I am not the little girl who grew up on the street with a homeless mother. That is my experience, and I can learn from it, but that is not really me," she said with tears of gratitude. "And *that* is very good news!" she exclaimed, a smile breaking across her face. "But just because I am not my history, it doesn't mean I am 'the nothing' either!" she said, the shimmering light flooding her brown eyes. She smiled. "It's more like," she paused, almost afraid to put a name on it, unworthy of the title. "It's like I am 'the everything.'" Then, taking a long moment, she looked deeply at each of the participants around the room and addressed them. "And so are you."

And then there was Lacy, who was facing an ugly divorce from an adulterous husband. She knew it was time to go, but she also knew he would try and wring her out for more money, because she was a successful businesswoman. Pulling her long dark hair out of her face, she tearfully told me in her last session before Breathwork that she had finally settled with him, paying him thousands more than he would have gotten in a court settlement. But, on balance, she said that she could tell herself that she didn't have to go to court, pay all the legal fees, and she felt she had given him more than enough. She would go on.

Breathwork brought her a clarity that made the pain of the divorce more survivable. She left the workshop exhausted and went to bed early. The next morning, half-awake, a series of numbers went through her head. They meant nothing to her: they weren't her birthday or social security or anything familiar. She rolled over and went back to sleep, only to awaken again with the numbers and the odd feeling that they weren't in the right order. *Order for what?* She thought. She exchanged the order of the last two numbers. *That feels right. But, right for what?*

Then, the obvious came to mind, like something out of a B-grade made-for-TV movie. Could they be lottery numbers?

Lacy had never been a gambler and had never played the lottery in her life. But she had learned through pain the cost of ignoring her inner promptings. So, against all rationality, Lacy, all but laughing at herself, went to the local 7-11 and bought the Pick Five numbers.

She nailed it. ˋ

Every last one in the exact order.

And won $14,021.00.

Upon hearing this, a new line for my new Breathwork brochure suddenly lit up in my mind!

DO TRANSPERSONAL BREATHWORK
WIN THE LOTTERY!*
*Outcome not typical. Individual results may vary.

All kidding aside, the story was much more remarkable than that. Remember, Lacy had settled with her husband for an additional amount that was well beyond what she anticipated he would get in court? Two weeks before winning the lottery, she had agreed on a lump sum: $14,021.00, the exact amount, to the dollar, that she would later win in the lottery.

I guess the Universe has its own sense of justice.

Remember Brenda from the beginning of the chapter, the alchemist who could turn paper into stone? I said there was more of her story to tell. Brenda's experience in the wind tunnel in which she conquered her fear of paper only took the first hour of her Breathwork experience. In the second hour, she found herself thinking about her great aunt Emily. When Brenda was a child, her relatives used to say, "Oh, I wish you had known your great aunt Emily," their faces beaming. "She was such a character, what a pistol! She was so much like you. She always cared so much for others. You two would've gotten along famously." Unfortunately, her great aunt had passed well before Brenda was born.

After Brenda concluded her experience in the tunnel, she felt very peaceful, and in her mind's eye a soft fog began to form. Indistinct at first, but progressively clearer, she saw her great aunt Emily through the mist. Brenda could not help but smile, noting the magical light in her eyes. "Oh, Aunt Emily," gushed Brenda, "it is so nice to finally see you! I have always wanted to meet you." Brenda was amazed at the feelings of familiarity she had for someone she had never met. Emily's luminous gaze radiated a kindness she had never known. "Everyone always said that we were so much alike," Brenda gushed. Emily smiled, and with a twinkle of mischief in her eyes placed both of her hands gently on Brenda's cheeks and pulled her closer, just inches from her eyes.

"Oh, my Dear," said Emily with a subtle smile. Brenda's heart leapt up into her throat. Somehow, she knew what Emily was about to say. "There's a reason why people say I am so much like you, Brenda." Aunt Emily paused. "I *am* you." Brenda's jaw dropped slowly in astonishment. A feeling of wonder warmly coursed through her entire body. Emily's smile broadened, and she gently nodded at Brenda ever so slowly, as if to allow her both reassurance and time to sink in.

"*I am you*," said Emily again, driving the point home.

It was in that moment that Brenda realized that she was the reincarnation of her great aunt Emily.

At the end of Breathwork workshops, people are often blown away:

astonished, excited, reinvigorated. Their lives have changed, and this can cause them to be very, very thankful (which is often uncomfortable for me). Although I cannot prove it, I do believe that there is something about the Transpersonal Breathwork model—whether it is our music, the lengths we go to in order to build a safe and supportive setting, or the techniques we use to integrate and ground the experiences in our clients so that they are useful and pragmatic—that may offer a more transformative experience than other forms of Breathwork. And, as a clinician, I am delighted that they are getting the growth they want, or at least, need. But I am reticent to accept too much credit. Referring to my co-leaders, I often find myself smiling and reminding grateful participants, "Remember, we just set the table. God serves the banquet."

10

Coming Full Circle: Return to the Edge

"For, all must be quickened—there must be the quickening of the spirit."   Edgar Cayce reading 2067-2

You may recall that I started this book with a dream that I had that ended with my new car, driven by my longtime girlfriend, going off the end of a bridge into clear waters. Simultaneously, within weeks of the dream, one of my best friends was admitted to the hospital with a life-threatening cancer, another close friend of mine lost her mother, my dad had a break with reality, and I got a "pack-your-bags" email from the woman I thought I would spend the rest of my life with. I was, as the dream foretold, driven over the edge.

A classic Hitchcock film begins with a foot chase over the roofs of city buildings with Jimmy Stewart playing a private detective. The bad guy leads the way, followed by a policeman and Jimmy in hot pursuit. Giving chase, the policeman leaps from rooftop to rooftop. Stewart tries to keep up, jumping from one building to the next, only to slide down a steep roof and clutch a rain gutter by his fingertips, his legs flailing thin air, the street hundreds of feet below. Seeing Jimmy's predicament, the policeman abandons his chase. Scaling down a slippery angled roof, the cop holds out his hand, imploring Jimmy to take it, but Jimmy is literally petrified. Suddenly, the policeman loses his footing and falls screaming to the pavement below. Jimmy watches in horror, eyes wide, dangling, the gutter creaking as though it might give way at any moment and send our hapless hero plummeting to his death.

Fade to black.

In the movie, we never do find out how Stewart gets down from the rooftop. Hitchcock simply fades into another scene where Stewart is safe and sound on the ground. Of course, we realize that the rooftop terror is the source of his fear of heights, convenient enough for a film entitled *Vertigo*. Hitchcock leaves Jimmy and the audience hanging. Thanks a lot. So much for the American Film Institute's number-one rated film of all time.

I, too, left you hanging. So, uh, thanks for hanging with me. I will be more compassionate and finish the story. You've got questions; I've got answers. Who's your buddy? Who's your pal? Who's your friend, huh? Me? Or Hitch?

We have now explored, at length, different approaches to accelerate our spiritual journey. I said in the second chapter that an in-depth exploration of so-called "organic quickenings" was not the focus of the book. But we will touch briefly on them before we conclude and perhaps offer the reader some small satisfaction in knowing the resolution of my own organic quickening.

The Tibetan Book of the Dead speaks of the *bardo* or *bardos*—the realms between our reincarnated, embodied lives. Buddhist meditation master Chogyam Trumpa Rinpoche reminds us, in his commentary, that *bardo* literally means *gap*. *The Tibetan Book of the Dead* can be seen as not only a pathway to a successful transition to the afterlife, but a guide to living life successfully. There are those times in our lives, where—through no conscious choice of our own—we are hanging in the gap. We are neither single nor divorced, we are neither healed nor ill, and we are no longer young but not yet old. We have no ground under our feet, our ego identities are in transition. Like Schrodinger's hypothetical cat, we are suspended in a quantum limbo, not dead or alive, but somehow both.

In fact, we are often in the gap. I have heard this experience expressed by clients and friends in different ways. "It's like I have let go of one trapeze, and I am flying towards the next—if there even is one—

and I'm unsure if I have a net underneath me." Dave, an introspective engineer in his fifties was floundering in the middle of one of my more intense workshops. With all the innocence of a child, in the middle of a group process, he looked at me with utter bewilderment, ran his hand through his thinning hair, and said, "Gregg, it's like you took my alphabet soup and threw it up in the air and the letters came down all funny."

It's like that sometimes.

For me, the dream represented a suspension between two realities. My car was going in slow motion off the bridge, headed toward the spiritual clarity of the crystal waters, but also toward sure destruction. The Hindu tradition tells us of the God Shiva, the destroyer. This idea is anathema in metaphysical circles in the West—a God who would destroy us? This harkens back to an Old Testament God who would send a flood to end the world. But how could a loving God, or God-dess, be a destroyer?

And yet, in a quickening, who or what we thought we were *is* being destroyed, but hopefully to be replaced by something better than the Beta version. Gregg 2.1 will be more compassionate, patient, and resilient than the original—a more accurate reflection, by increments, of his deepest identity—a radiant child of God.

When we leave high school, we have to say goodbye to the prom queen, football star, skateboard dude, or purpled-hair Goth we once were and say hello to the college student, breadwinner, or parent we are becoming. Rapid spiritual advancement calls upon us to sift through the ruins of our reality, piecing together what, if anything, needs to be saved from the Old World while we acquire and integrate new ideals and beliefs from the present moment for the New Normal. All growth depends upon this. If we are true mystics, we may have to say goodbye to the beliefs of narrow religion and hello to the wisdom of our new experiences. As the French essayist Charles Du Bos wrote, "The important thing is this: to be able at any moment to sacrifice what we are for what we could become."

Come Lord Shiva, you are welcome here.

In A.A.'s twelve-step recovery program, the individual says goodbye to the self that was an active alcoholic and embraces an identity of recovery, including making new friends, practicing new behaviors, and embracing new environments—"different playgrounds and different playmates." Similarly, if we live long enough, someone we love dies, and then we have to die from being a friend, child, parent, or spouse. The late meditation teacher Eknath Easwaran suggests a refinement of St. Francis' famous prayer: "It is in dying to [the egoic] self that we are born again."

In some ways, the choice is before us every minute. Will we continue to conduct business the old way, based on unforgiveness and judgment, reinforcing the sense of ourselves as limited physical beings? Or, will we stretch and grow and try to let go of our ego identities and identify more with ourselves as radiant transcendent beings? The spiritual teacher Ram Dass puts it this way. "Everything must change except the soul. Your preparation for dying is done by identifying with your soul, not your ego. Identify with your soul, *now*."[21] Of course, that is much easier said than done. Although the case can be made (and I'm gonna make it) that through the process of transcendent experiences in which we *repeatedly* see that our temporal egoic self is *not* our identity, then we can begin to step back from the ego and rest in spirit. The more direct experiences we have of ourselves as Divine, and the more we see that our temporal egoic identities are so transient, the easier it is to shift our awareness of our identity to spirit. We'll no longer see worth in putting a whole lot of emphasis on our ego, because it is so flimsy and fleeting.

This book is full of ideas to create conscious, intentional quickenings to forward your journey. But they can also be used when an organic quickening is overwhelming you, to accelerate through the quicksand of intense emotion. When my dream awakened me to the ending of what I had assumed for years would be a lifelong relationship, I cratered. I felt like life as I knew it was crumbling before me . . . because it was.

But I also dug into my toolkit.

Binaural Beat Frequency (BBF) technology became an everyday practice again. Usually in the afternoons, I made time to drop down into Alpha, where I would be less defended against my feelings and would allow for some emotional release. At bedtime, I used Delta audio to entrain long, slow brainwaves to get to sleep.

Breathwork offered clarity about how to move through the agony and logistics of the breakup. In a powerful Integrative Breathwork workshop with Jacquelyn Small, I remembered a lifetime in the Civil War in which my regiment was sent to fight a hopeless battle. We bravely refused to surrender, only to suffer dozens of needless deaths. We were outnumbered and outgunned from the start. It was an exercise in futility. I recognized that all wars ultimately ended with either one side being destroyed or, strangely, someone surrendering. The past life memory reminded me that there could be power in surrendering to what was true, accepting the things I could not change, as the Serenity Prayer urges. The reality was my relationship was over, and the sooner that I could embrace that fully, surrendering to the truth, the more quickly I would experience peace.

Sifting through the memories immediately after the breakup, I noticed that there were three salient excruciating experiences that my mind returned to again and again. I knew these had become traumatically encoded in my brain. In a series of three very intense three-hour long EMDR sessions, I targeted these moments in the breakup. On the other side of this powerful therapy my anxiety was lessened by about half. I could breathe again.

I also did more commonplace things to speed up my journey. I minimized my client load as a gift to myself and also to my clients, recognizing—however imperfectly—my limitations. Journaling was helpful, especially when it was late at night, and I found my restless mind recycling the painful details of the breakup. I reached out to my friends in ways that I thought were beyond my capacity, rehashing my drama, sometimes talking for hours to my close spiritual comrades. Paradoxically, I also needed more time to myself and *by* myself, and I consciously tried to strike a balance between over-isolating myself and constantly emotionally vomiting all over my friends. (Okay, a bit graphic there, kids, but that's what it felt like.) Sometimes, I disappeared into my room for hours at a time, a surprising turn for an extrovert like me. A housemate during this period called me "the invisible roommate."

Consciously being grateful for what I *did* have in my life has become central. How many times had I heard clients going through a divorce say, "Nobody loves me anymore!" Truly, I understand that when you lose the person you love most in your life that it is easy to forget about everyone else. But what I wanted to say to those clients is this: *Really?* Nobody *loves you anymore? Did you forget your mom and dad, your buddies, your family, your twelve-step group, your co-workers, your dog?*

Now, I had to ask that same question of myself. Some days it really sucks knowing the good questions. Yes, I had lost perhaps the most important romantic relationship of my life, but I had parents, friends, and pets who genuinely loved me! (I managed to get custody of the cats: Midnight, June Bug, and His Excellency Don Frito Lay.) But it took consciously focusing my mind to remember and affirm to myself that I was loved. More importantly, when I could quiet my mind long enough, I knew God still loved me.

Although, it was not my client's place to know the details, I could still see that—professionally—I was appreciated by them and by thousands of workshop participants across the country. In my worst moments, I found some comfort in the knowledge that I was still cared for and appreciated by many, if I would only look to see!

I walked several times a day, got massages—sometimes two or three a week. Often the gentle touch of a caring massage therapist was the only moment I looked forward to in the day. I joined a recovery group led by a local therapist. The When Your Relationship Ends (WYRE) group, led by Dr. Larry Miller, helped folks going through divorce or the end of a romantic relationship. New friends like Glenn, Angie, Selim, Buddy, and Jana were lifelines in troubled times.

I was determined not to be a bitter and rage-filled man five or ten years after the romance ended. And I was convinced that this could be accomplished by moving *through* the emotions in an accelerated fashion and not denying them.

Anne Lamott has pointed out that every prayer begins with two words: *Help me.* (I'm sorry, but I can't help but think of the movie, *The Fly*—either version—when I hear that.) But my singular prayer of asking for help was an odd one: *Father, burn away all that is not me. Help me to let go of all that I was that no longer serves me so that I may become yours.* Honestly, sometimes the pain was so great that it felt like my flesh was on fire. Be careful what you pray for, as they say.

But I was changing, transmuting.

Soon, I was sleeping better at night, my appetite returned, and somebody turned off the Coleman stove in my stomach.

Synchronistically, my life circumstances began to resolve as well. My dear friend survived the cancer that racked her body. We managed to get most of the marbles back in my father's head—he started to re-member who he was, who I was, and who my mother was, and with physical therapy he was back on his feet and getting around again within a few weeks. I walked my friend through her mother's death; my friend walked me through the end of my relationship. Some days we took turns crying. And then it was Christmas! Ho, ho, ho!

Ah, there's no place like hell for the holidays.

But we survived.

Well-researched assessment tools can gauge how well an individual is adjusting to loss after a divorce or breakup. About ten weeks after my dream Prius hit the water, my test scores were somewhere in the basement. But about five months out from the breakup, I was scoring in the ninetieth percentile across every axis.

Not only can conscious quickenings be utilized to induce spiritual awakening, they can be used to accelerate through the pain of the most difficult chapters of our lives. Perhaps this is what the Buddhists mean when they say that pain is mandatory, but suffering is optional.

Let me be very clear: Our feelings, our journey, cannot be ignored, it must be attended. As they say in Zen training, "Attention must be paid." We cannot deny or avoid the work.

My own internal teacher once offered a starkly clear picture of the spiritual journey. Imagine a cold muddy river that must be forged. Many people simply stand on the side and mutter, "I ain't going in that, and ya can't make me." Still others stand ready to go into the waters and say to themselves, "I'm gonna jump, I'm gonna jump!" but never do, and then they wonder why their lives never progress. Some people begin to forge it and stop knee-deep or waist-high. The mud and the cold continue to swirl around them. "Oh, it's so cold! When will it ever end?" And, of course, as long as they stay there, it doesn't. Their suffering is very, very real—they are not making it up; it can go on forever.

Isn't it interesting that often when someone accepts less than they want they say they "settled" for something? In the Old West, settlers were people who were on a journey, and when they stopped somewhere, they settled. *That* they settled wasn't in and of itself a bad thing; *where* they settled made all the difference. Likewise, right now, there are people who have "settled" in the middle of the cold, muddy stream. They are miserable—depressed, anxious, addicted, and traumatized. They are in genuinely horrible emotional pain. As long as they stay where they are, *they will suffer*, without question. They have settled midstream. Some have stopped from a lapse of courage or faith, some from a lack of hope or support, some from sheer exhaustion. Some have decided the benefits of victimhood are the best card they have in their hand, and they will play it eternally. But they have settled.

This need not be.

Optimally, we move as quickly as we can . . . and honestly, sometimes that isn't very fast. That's okay. Yes, it's cold and muddy and very messy. And yes, you get to complain as you go. Really! Gripe your ass off if you want to. It may not make you all that popular at dinner parties, but really, that's okay. Honoring that the journey is painful in ourselves and others is called . . . wait for it . . . *compassion*. Strangely, for many of us on the spiritual path, having some mercy for ourselves, well, that's a novel idea.

Dammit, we say to ourselves, *I know I need to meditate more, what's the matter with me?*

Or how about this one, *If there is one thing I am so angry about in myself, it's my anger!*

Oh, yeah! That's the ticket, *I will be angrier at myself for being angry at others and then I will be less angry!*

Huh?

I will be less forgiving of myself for being so unforgiving towards others and that is how I will learn forgiveness!

WTF?

Somehow, I just don't think that approach is gonna work. But maybe, some compassion for yourself, just the tiniest bit (hey, it's all you will give yourself right now, anyway), might be in order. It's a necessary skill. Honor the pain in the journey, just don't stop. When we reach the deepest part of the river, and we are up to our necks in mud, we want to give up, but we don't. Winston Churchill said, "If you are going through hell, keep going."

And finally, we start to emerge! Life improves as you come out of the cold and the mud. Oh, there's still plenty of clean up to do, but life gets better. Depending on your karmic path, maybe the next leg of your journey is nice and flat for a while, sunny and cool with lots of big trees and no mosquitoes. Hopefully, you get a break . . . and then you hit the next leg of the trip.

That you are going to get hit with another difficult leg *isn't up for grabs.* The spiritual teaching of *A Course in Miracles* tells us that the spiritual journey is "a required course. Only the time you take it is voluntary. Free will does not mean that you can establish the curriculum. It only means that *you can elect what you want to take at a given time.*" (Italics mine.) In other words, you *have* to take the class, *and* you don't have to take it *now.* But your lessons are inevitable.

What we really want to do is learn to navigate through the rough patches faster and with less suffering, don't we? "You can't stop the waves," meditation teacher Jack Kornfield observes, "but you can learn to surf." I once studied with a spiritual teacher named Coyote, who said, "the idea of 'following your bliss' is bullshit. *Follow your pain,* let it transform you. Bliss is the reward of lessons learned."

So, do we really want to dig our heels into the muddy river, settle into the silt, and then shriek at the heavens, pointing out to virtually everyone around us (and God) just how cold and miserable we are? I sure wanted to. But what I hated even worse was standing around in the river freezing my ass off!

So I moved. You can too.

Maybe I am out of my mind (it has occurred to me before), but I genuinely believe that in completing this lesson, I leapt ahead into what my soul had heretofore karmically "planned" *for my next lifetime.*

If you are like me, you would rather be a survivor than a victim. You want to sow the seeds of grace, not incur more karma. Cayce said that our lessons were right in front of us. To put it bluntly, as he saw it, our primary lesson was to come face to face with our ego (what he calls "self"), undo it, and then come face to face with whom we really are: radiant Children of God. It's really the only game in town, when you think about it. You don't want to spend another 200 lifetimes at Earth School. Even if *A Course in Miracles* is right and it's an illusion, it's a painful one. So saddle up and ride hard, Partner. Use the tools in this book to power through the tough times and hit the passing lane to more peace, more clarity, and more connection to God and the God in everyone. There is a faster way to get where you are going. Leaping ahead is a rush, and with every level up the mountain, the view gets better, even if we aren't at the summit.

On the Horizon

Are these the only paths to accelerate our journey? Of course not. There is a lot of exciting new work being done on the spiritual horizon. Dr. David Grand continues to pioneer work in BSP for peak performance and trauma resolution. Alecia Masood, RMT, is currently combining Brainspotting with massage and Jin Shin Do acupressure techniques in Virginia Beach, Va., to bring marked relief to individuals with chronic pain. Similarly, Jane Murray, a licensed massage therapist at GreenLeaf Massage and Bodywork in College Station, Texas, is combining progressive techniques like CranioSacral therapy, Zero Balancing, and deep massage with her keen sense of intuition to bring relief to many who suffer with ongoing physical pain. In addition, most report leaving her sessions with a sense of transcendent peace. Not surprisingly, a 2009 pilot study—conducted by clinician and researcher Dr. Lisa M. Chavez—studied veterans with PTSD, including many who were victims of torture. The research demonstrated clinically significant relief in both the physical pain and anxiety of veterans after treatment with CranioSacral therapy when compared to the group who did not get treatment—and in that latter group, symptoms actually worsened! According to Dr. Chavez, "this therapy works so well for body-mind conditions because it induces the parasympathetic branch of the nervous system, or as it is commonly called the 'rest and digest' state. This allows the entire body to enter a state of restoration, unlike psychoactive drugs that just dampen the sympathetic response."[22]

Breakthrough research is being done using EMDR to successfully treat Traumatic Brain Injury (TBI) that plagues survivors of falls, car crashes, and bomb blasts. Dr. Robert Scaer and Dr. John Sarno, among others, believe that a lot of chronic physical pain may be emotional trauma held by the body. EMDR, Brainspotting, and other cognitive interventions may be adapted to release this chronic tension and pain. My work using BSP for Spiritual Activation is developing rapidly, but

I feel I am just scratching the surface of what is possible. And there is no doubt in my mind that Spiritual Activation and Breathwork may be utilized to accelerate psychic development.

Dr. Eben Alexander, neurosurgeon, near-death experiencer, and author of the best-selling *Proof of Heaven*, has remarked that Binaural Beat Frequency (BBF) technology, while useful, has not really improved in over a decade. He is working with a company called Sacred Sounds to use guided imagery, BBFs, and the wisdom garnered in his near-death experience to bring back the "spinning melody" of heaven that he heard while on the other side in order to catalyze heightened states of awareness.

In Santa Fe, N.M., Jeff Strong believes he has extracted the healing elements from shamanic drumming traditions from around the world. His research suggests some symptoms of Attention Deficit Disorder and Autism may be reduced just by listening to these rhythms. He calls his work Rhythmic Entrainment Integration (REI).

Millions of people around the world—those suffering from addiction and their loved ones—have benefitted from The Twelve Steps and the recovery movement. Their ultimate goal is a spiritual awakening, and countless individuals have experienced quickenings taking this time-honored approach.

For nearly thirty years, *A Course in Miracles* has been a central teaching in my spiritual life. Its wisdom is bubbling beneath the teachings of some of the most popular metaphysical teachers of our era. There is a reason why wisdom teachers like Wayne Dyer, Deepak Chopra, Eckhart Tolle, Marianne Williamson, Kevin Todeschi, Neale Donald Walsch, Gerald Jampolsky, Jon Mundy, Gary Renard, and even Oprah Winfrey have all studied and referenced *A Course in Miracles*. While harder to quantify or explain than many other modalities, I can only attest that it has been a profound influence in my life and in the lives of many others I have known. The seeds of this book may well have germinated from three words from the text: "Miracles collapse time."

As an extension of my work with the *Course*, for fifteen years I have offered an annual four-day retreat, *The Heart of Forgiveness*, in a spectacular and sacred setting known as Zion Canyon National Park in Springdale, Utah. I have seen some memorable "leaping" there. I have witnessed miracles. Many have said the workshop saved their lives. More than one of these workshops has resulted in phenomenal shifts for the workshop leader himself. If you have ever doubted the power of love and compassion, come. Let us show you.

Some consciousness researchers say it may only be a matter of time before we can fully identify so-called "enlightened beings," analyze their brain states, and then magnetically or electrically "pulse" your noggin to think like the Buddha. This doesn't seem unreasonable. Using deep brain stimulation, the army has accelerated certain kinds of learning, truncating training times from months to weeks.[23] Similar kinds of magnetic stimulation seem to be capable of jolting the brain out of deep depression for a significant segment of the population. But for now, I humbly offer the aforementioned modalities to speed your journey.

How would you benefit from the approaches in this book? Your own inner knowing or inner teacher would be the best judge of which, if any, are pathways you will want to pursue. If you aren't sure what I mean by this, look back through the chapters and remember where your heart leapt, your throat choked, or a chill ran down your spine and that is probably an area you should explore. For my money, that's your inner knowing, goosing your goose bumps, plugging your spine into the wall socket, and turning on the sprinklers in your eyeballs.

Some Cautions

The contemporary psychologist Abraham Maslow reminds us of the importance of getting beyond dichotomous thinking, that nasty either/or, black-or-white thinking that plagues our society (and some political movements). In organized, entrenched religious systems, the direct experience of the prophets or teachers is often forgotten, and the emphasis focuses solely on the teachings. Religious students are encouraged to study the dogma and accumulate more and more intellectual understanding. In fact, in some religious traditions, spiritual experience is not only deemphasized but seen as inherently untrustworthy and potentially dangerous. Instead, studying the religious texts and arguing about them, *ad nauseam*, seems to go with this line of thinking. The idea seems to be to shove more and more facts about the Bible, Edgar Cayce, *The Power of Now*, *A Course in Miracles* and/or the

One True Way (OTW) into your head until its coming out your ears, and you can't hear anyone. Then the person's head is so full, it has to come out of their mouth, whether you want to hear it or not. Then they stuff in some more. This can result in a well-trained, very knowledgeable religious scholar or guru who rigidly follows his or her religion's rules of behavior, but wouldn't know God's love if it bit him in the ass.

On the other hand, the pendulum can swing in the other direction. Maslow warns of the dangers of obsessively seeking out spiritual experiences. We can become selfishly pre-occupied with simply looking for the next "spiritual high," becoming some kind of bliss junkie. These kinds of people almost float above their bodies, self-absorbed with another reality, and then wonder why their rent doesn't get paid. The lights and the feelings are so dazzling, the gilt of the lettering so glittering, they forget to read the text and take home the message. Yes, the goal is to be "in the world and not of the world," but we have to be *in the world* first. We can become so enamored of the quickening itself that we fail to integrate the lesson.

What do I mean by that? When my clients talk about their deepest spiritual awakenings in hushed tones and wide-eyed wonder, I always ask them, "What did you learn from this experience? Why do you suppose this happened to you right now at this juncture in your life?" The glories of these experiences are not enough. As thrilling as mystical fireworks can be, we need to integrate the experiences into our lives so that they shape and change our way of being. If we utilize these experiences to become more loving, more forgiving, and peaceful individuals, then and only then are we making real spiritual progress.

Maslow also warns of "the possibility that the inner voices and the revelations may be mistaken." If we are unwilling to honestly examine our experience then a "lesson from history that should come through loud and clear is denied and then there is no way of finding out whether the voices within are the voices of good or evil . . . Spontaneity (the impulses from our best self) gets confused with impulsivity and acting out (the impulses of our sick self) and then there is no way to tell the difference."[24]

Maslow sees the answer as a holistic approach to spirituality that includes both peak experiences (what might be called quickenings) and also spiritual study. We might call this an integration of the academic and the experiential ways of knowing. We can read and discuss the works of great spiritual teachers and also explore transpersonal Breathwork. We may do Bible study by day and listen to binaural beat frequency (BBF) audio at night. We can both honor our most profound spiritual experiences and also place them, with an open mind, under the scrutiny of our best critical thinking skills to better gauge their validity.

One of my clients, who was very ill, had a visionary glimpse of the other side. Her mother was waiting for her in a place of bright light, but when she moved toward her, her mother shook her head emphatically "no," indicating that it wasn't time for her to cross over. I was ready to explore this with my client and remind her that she could take comfort in her mother, waiting for her on the other side. But my client, coming from her own unworthiness announced, "See? Even my own MOTHER doesn't want me!" and collapsed into a pool of tears. It took me a while to help her see another perspective.

Another woman I'll call Abigail, had a profound workshop experience and heard an inner voice tell her that "the Light of the Christ is within you." It was so authoritative and real that she was convinced that it was true . . . and she came to believe that the unborn child growing within her was the rebirth of Jesus!

I probably don't have to tell you that well before her son became a teenager, Abigail became utterly convinced that her son *wasn't* the Second Coming. (As it turns out, only Italian mothers are completely sure about their first-borns. Ask their daughters-in-law.)

So while we shouldn't deny the potential truth of these experiences, we should bring our common sense to bear.

Again, if these quickenings are valid and legitimate, we should see a certain level of transformation in our day-to-day lives. "These are but lights," said Edgar Cayce, "but signs in thine experience, they are as but a candle [such] that one stumbles not in the dark." (707-2) After a quickening, we may stumble less, moving more quickly and with more direction on our spiritual path. My best guess is that as we "return" from these experiences and integrate them into our day-to-day lives, people will see positive changes in us. Then, we are on the right track.

The gifts of spirit are bearing fruit in the world.

Perhaps, in living in the deeper knowledge of a quickening or mystical awakening, we discover an underlying sense of peace, which, while not as profound as the original moment allows us a connection to our Higher Mind or an awareness of the Divine that we can *rest in*. Maslow coined the expression *plateau experience* to characterize an ongoing calm and feeling of well-being, regardless of circumstances, that he saw in some of his subjects. In other circles this might be called *the peace that passeth all understanding*.

How Will You Use This Book?

Maybe, you will dismiss it out of hand without doing any further introspection or research. I wouldn't blame you. A lot of this stuff still sounds pretty far out to me, and I was there when it happened! If this is you, thank you, sincerely, for taking the time to read this book. There are many paths to God or Truth, and I believe that all of them, faithfully followed, will take you where you need to go, even if you go by way of Tampa. Godspeed.

Some of you will simply read this book and make a mental note that, yes, these kinds of things *are* possible. Perhaps all that you have read will begin to work on you from the inside, rattle you a bit, and help you to remember that wherever you are on your journey, you don't have to be stuck there. No matter what your current pace is, you can go faster, you can leap ahead. And, because this book is such a riveting read, you will pass it on to others and/or buy it for your friends.

See, you thought of some people, just now, who would love this book, didn't you? Call me psychic.

In giving them this wee tome, you will delight them, the publisher, and Yours Truly. Thanks for passing on the torch. Mother Teresa inspired the lepers. You handle the leapers.

But I hope you don't stop there.

My deepest wish is that you find some small way to begin to explore some of these techniques. Many of these modalities require neither a lot of time, nor a lot of money. Be bold; get out of the bleachers and onto the field! Start now, *right now!* Get a BBF CD or audio download. Read more online or in a book about a modality that interests you. Pick an awakened moment from your past, and start using the instructions in this book; try some spiritual activation in the privacy of your own home. Join a twelve-step group, wan A.R.E. "A Search for God" study group or *A Course in Miracles* group. Grab an audio past-life regression and see what happens. Better yet, plunge into one of these pathways with a qualified therapist or workshop leader and see just how far and how fast you can go. Enough of being on the sidelines. Stop reading about someone else's spiritual experience and start having one of your own. Consciously quicken your life, and you'll leap ahead on your spiritual journey. Your life will be forever changed.

I'll see you on the other side of the river.

Endnotes

[1]Foundation for Inner Peace, *A Course in Miracles* (Foundation for Inner Peace, 3rd Edition, 2007).

[2]Brendan I. Koerner, *U.S. News & World Report* (March, 1997), Vol. 122, No. 12, 68–61.

[3]Bill Guggenheim and Judy Guggenheim, *Hello from Heaven: A New Field of Research-After-Death Communication Confirms that Life and Love Are Eternal* (Bantam, 1997).

[4]Michael Hutchison, *Megabrain: New Tools and Techniques for Brain Growth and Mind Expansion* (William Morrow & Co., 1986).

[5]D.K. Nauriyal (Editor), Michael S. Drummond (Editor), Y.B. Lal (Editor), *Buddhist Thought and Applied Psychological Research: Transcending the Boundaries* (Routledge, 2006), 163.

[6]David H. Ehl, *You Are Gods* (CreateSpace, 2011).

[7]Yaakov Astor, Soul Searching: Seeking Scientific Ground for the Jewish Tradition of an Afterlife (Targum Press, 2003).

[8]P.M.H. Atwater, *I Died Three Times in 1977* (Cinema of the Mind, 2010).

[9]The National Center for PTSD, *Understanding PTSD* (2013), www.ptsd.va.gov/public/understanding-ptsd/booklet.pdf
P.M.H. Atwater, *I Died Three Times in 1977* (Cinema of the Mind, 2010).

[10]Allan L. Botkin, PsyD, *Induced After Death Communication: A New Therapy for Healing Grief and Trauma* (Hampton Roads Publishing, 2005).

[11]Mary L. Smith and Gene V. Glass, "Meta-Analysis of Psychotherapy Outcome Studies," *American Psychologist* (1977), 752–760.

[12]Robert Stickgold, PhD, "What Is EMDR?" (EMDR Humanitarian Assistance Programs, 2014), http://www.emdrhap.org/content/what-is-emdr/.

[13]Stanislav Grof, *The Adventure of Self-Discovery: Dimensions of Consciousness and New Perspectives in Psychotherapy and Inner Exploration,* (Suny, 1988).

[14]Department of the Army (U.S.A.), *Army 2020: Generating Health and Discipline in the Force Ahead of the Strategic Reset* (2012), http://www.armyg1.army.mil/.

[15]David Grand, PhD, *Emotional Healing at Warp Speed: The Power of EMDR* (Harmony, 2001).

[16]Thich Nhat Hanh, *The Art of Mindful Living: How to Bring Love, Compassion, and Inner Peace Into Your Daily Life* (Sounds True, 2000).

[17]Edgar Cayce, *A Search for God, Books 1 and 2* (A.R.E. Press, 1992).

[18]Marianne Williamson, *A Return to Love: Reflections on the Principles of "A Course in Miracles,"* (HarperOne, 1996).

[19]David Grand, PhD, *Brainspotting: The Revolutionary New Therapy for Rapid and Effective Change* (Sounds True, 2013).

[20]W.J. Wilkins, *Hindu Mythology, Vedic and Puranic* (1900), www.sacred-texts.com.

[21]Ram Dass, et al, *Graceful Passages: A Companion for Living and Dying* (New World Library, 2006).

[22]Jenna Huntsberger, "Innovative Research Featuring Effective Treatment for PTSD (The American Association of Naturopathic Physicians), http://www.naturopathic.org/content.asp?contentid=228.

[23]R. Douglas Fields, "Amping Up Brain Function: Transcranial Stimulation Shows Promise in Speeding Up Learning," *Scientific American* (November, 2011).

[24]Abraham H. Maslow, *Religions, Values, and Peak Experiences* (Important Books, 2014).

Recommended Reading

Alexander, Eben. *Proof of Heaven*

Backman, Linda. *Bringing Your Soul to Light*

Botkin, Allan. *Induced After Death Communication*

Brinkley, Dannion. *Saved by the Light*

Ehl, David H. *You Are Gods*

Foundation for Inner Peace. *A Course in Miracles*

Frankhauser, Jerry. *From a Chicken to an Eagle*

Frankhauser, Jerry. *The Way of the Eagle*

Grand, David. *Brainspotting*

Grand, David. *Emotional Healing at Warp Speed: The Power of EMDR*

Grof, Stanislav. *The Adventure of Self-Discovery*

Grof, Stanislav. *Holotropic Breathwork*

Grof, Stanislav. *The Psychology of the Future*

Guggenheim, Bill & Judy. *Hello from Heaven*

Kirkpatrick, Sidney. *Edgar Cayce: An American Prophet*

Leeds, Joshua. *The Power of Sound*

Mundy, Jon. *Living A Course in Miracles*

Newton, Michael. *Journey of Souls*

Newton, Michael. *Destiny of Souls*

Newton, Michael. *Life between Lives*

Shapiro, Francine. *EMDR: The Breakthrough "Eye Movement" Therapy for Overcoming Anxiety, Stress, and Trauma*

Strong, Jeff. *Different Drummer: One Man's Music and Its Impact on ADD, Anxiety and Autism*

Taylor, Kylea. *The Breathwork Experience*

Unterberger, Gregg. *Exploring the Mysteries of Your Mind: Live in Memphis (CD)*

Upledger, John. *Your Inner Physician and You: Craniosacral Therapy and Somatoemotional Release*

Van Lommel, Pim. *Consciousness Beyond Life*

Wambach, Helen. *Reliving Past Lives: The Evidence Under Hypnosis*

Wapnick, Ken. *Forgiveness and Jesus*

Williamson, Marianne. *A Return to Love*

Weiss, Brian. *Many Lives, Many Masters*

Weiss, Brian. *Miracles Happen*

Weiss, Brian. *Same Soul, Many Bodies*

Weiss, Brian. *Through Time into Healing*

4TH DIMENSION PRESS

An Imprint of A.R.E. Press

4th Dimension Press is an imprint of A.R.E. Press, the publishing division of Edgar Cayce's Association for Research and Enlightenment (A.R.E.).

We publish books, DVDs, and CDs in the fields of intuition, psychic abilities, ancient mysteries, philosophy, comparative religious studies, personal and spiritual development, and holistic health.

For more information, or to receive a catalog, contact us by mail, phone, or online at:

4th Dimension Press
215 67th Street
Virginia Beach, VA 23451-2061
800-333-4499

4THDIMENSIONPRESS.COM

Who Was Edgar Cayce?
Twentieth Century Psychic and Medical Clairvoyant

Edgar Cayce (pronounced Kay-Cee, 1877-1945) has been called the "sleeping prophet," the "father of holistic medicine," and the most-documented psychic of the 20th century. For more than 40 years of his adult life, Cayce gave psychic "readings" to thousands of seekers while in an unconscious state, diagnosing illnesses and revealing lives lived in the past and prophecies yet to come. But who, exactly, was Edgar Cayce?

Cayce was born on a farm in Hopkinsville, Kentucky, in 1877, and his psychic abilities began to appear as early as his childhood. He was able to see and talk to his late grandfather's spirit, and often played with "imaginary friends" whom he said were spirits on the other side. He also displayed an uncanny ability to memorize the pages of a book simply by sleeping on it. These gifts labeled the young Cayce as strange, but all Cayce really wanted was to help others, especially children.

Later in life, Cayce would find that he had the ability to put himself into a sleep-like state by lying down on a couch, closing his eyes, and folding his hands over his stomach. In this state of relaxation and meditation, he was able to place his mind in contact with all time and space—the universal consciousness, also known as the super-conscious mind. From there, he could respond to questions as broad as, "What are the secrets of the universe?" and "What is my purpose in life?" to as specific as, "What can I do to help my arthritis?" and "How were the pyramids of Egypt built?" His responses to these questions came to be called "readings," and their insights offer practical help and advice to individuals even today.

The majority of Edgar Cayce's readings deal with holistic health and the treatment of illness. Yet, although best known for this material, the sleeping Cayce did not seem to be limited to concerns about the physical body. In fact, in their entirety, the readings discuss an astonishing 10,000 different topics. This vast array of subject matter can be narrowed down into a smaller group of topics that, when compiled together, deal with the following five categories: (1) Health-Related Information; (2) Philosophy and Reincarnation; (3) Dreams and Dream Interpretation; (4) ESP and Psychic Phenomena; and (5) Spiritual Growth, Meditation, and Prayer.

Learn more at EdgarCayce.org.

What Is A.R.E.?

Edgar Cayce founded the non-profit Association for Research and Enlightenment (A.R.E.) in 1931, to explore spirituality, holistic health, intuition, dream interpretation, psychic development, reincarnation, and ancient mysteries—all subjects that frequently came up in the more than 14,000 documented psychic readings given by Cayce.

The Mission of the A.R.E. is to help people transform their lives for the better, through research, education, and application of core concepts found in the Edgar Cayce readings and kindred materials that seek to manifest the love of God and all people and promote the purposefulness of life, the oneness of God, the spiritual nature of humankind, and the connection of body, mind, and spirit.

With an international headquarters in Virginia Beach, Va., a regional headquarters in Houston, regional representatives throughout the U.S., Edgar Cayce Centers in more than thirty countries, and individual members in more than seventy countries, the A.R.E. community is a global network of individuals.

A.R.E. conferences, international tours, camps for children and adults, regional activities, and study groups allow like-minded people to gather for educational and fellowship opportunities worldwide.

A.R.E. offers membership benefits and services that include a quarterly body-mind-spirit member magazine, *Venture Inward*, a member newsletter covering the major topics of the readings, and access to the entire set of readings in an exclusive online database.

Learn more at EdgarCayce.org.

EDGARCAYCE.ORG